THE
SELECTED LETT[...]
WILLIAM JAMES

THE SELECTED LETTERS OF

WILLIAM JAMES

EDITED WITH AN INTRODUCTION BY
ELIZABETH HARDWICK

ANCHOR BOOKS
DOUBLEDAY
New York   London   Toronto   Sydney   Auckland

AN ANCHOR BOOK
PUBLISHED BY DOUBLEDAY
a division of Bantam Doubleday Dell Publishing Group, Inc.
1540 Broadway, New York, NY 10036

ANCHOR BOOKS, DOUBLEDAY, and the portrayal of an anchor
are trademarks of Doubleday, a division of Bantam Doubleday Dell
Publishing Group, Inc.

Last edition of *The Selected Letters of William James* was
published by Nonpareil Books/David R. Godine in 1980.
First published in 1961 by Farrar, Straus and Cudahy.
The Anchor Books edition is
published by arrangement with Farrar, Straus & Giroux.

Library of Congress Cataloging-in-Publication Data

James, William, 1842–1910.
[Correspondence. Selections]
The selected letters of William James/edited with an
introduction by Elizabeth Hardwick.—1st Anchor Books ed.
p. cm.
Includes index.
1. James, William, 1842–1910—Correspondence. 2. Philosophers—
United States—Correspondence. I. Hardwick, Elizabeth.
II. Title.
B945.J24A4 1993
191—dc20
[B] 93-7107
CIP

ISBN 0-385-46941-1
Copyright © 1960, 1961 by Elizabeth Hardwick Lowell
All Rights Reserved
Printed in the United States of America
First Anchor Books Edition: July 1993

1 3 5 7 9 10 8 6 4 2

NOTE ON THE TEXT

The majority of the letters in this volume have been previously printed in *The Letters of William James*, edited by his son, Henry James, or in *The Thought and Character of William James*, by Ralph Barton Perry. Both of these large works came out of the most careful study of James's correspondence and therefore the best of his letters will usually be found in one or the other. However, there are some letters here, taken from the Houghton Library collection at Harvard, not found in either of the two well-known collections. I cannot be sure they have not been printed or referred to in other studies of William James.

When I first compared the letters in the two collections with the original manuscripts at Harvard, I was struck by the generous number of commas, dashes, periods and paragraphs that James's son, on the one hand, and Professor Perry, on the other, had added to the manuscript letters. I set about laboriously de-punctuating. I soon found that the pure originals by William James were written in such enthusiastic haste that the addition, here and there, of editorial punctuation is almost a necessity—unless, of course, one were doing a facsimile reproduction of the letters. Rather than add a third unauthorized set of punctuation marks to James's almost unmarked pages, I returned to the punctuation used by previous editors. Unfortunately Henry

James, the son, was as fat with punctuation as his father was lean, and a certain puffiness is sometimes the result; Perry's punctuation is much more acceptable.

On the matter of deletions, sometimes I have restored deleted passages, but most often the deletions of the previous editors have been retained.

I wish to thank the staff of the Houghton Library at Harvard and Mr. William James of Cambridge for their help.

CONTENTS

INTRODUCTION

The Jameses were, as Henry phrases it, almost "hotel children." They were packed and unpacked, settled and unsettled, like a band of high livers fleeing creditors—except, of course, they were seeking not fleeing. The children knew a life of sudden change, unexpected challenge, residential insecurity and educational heresy that would nowadays be thought negligent and promising to delinquency. They went from Albany to New York, from America to Europe, from New York to Boston, back and forth, without thought of continuity, without regional roots. Their father was seeking a higher continuity for his children: the old man's restlessness was cosmic and just a bit comic, with his gentle, sweet and outrageous purity of mind and spirit. Yet Henry James says that he would not have exchanged his life at "our hotel" for that of "any small person more privately bred."

It was, no doubt, the very purity of the elder Henry James that gave the family its special nature. The Jameses had tremendous natural gifts for friendship; they were talented, popular, respected always and everywhere; they were courteous and eccentric. The father was passionately devoted to his family; he adored being at home and he *was* at home, where he could make out on his considerable inheritance and be privately employed as a writer and thinker. He loved, he doted, he was completely unself-conscious and completely original. Yet the James family was shot through, too, like a piece of Irish tweed, with neurasthenia. Some of it was useful, as perhaps Henry's failure to marry was useful to his prodigious career as a creative writer; some of it was deadly, like Robertson's drinking and Alice's long, baffling invalidism which finally became cancer, providing, as William's letters interestingly reveal, a sort of relief to them all—the relief of an incapacity identified at last.

They were a gregarious family, too. Henry's dinings-out were not more plentiful than William's appearances, lecture dates, travels; Alice had her "circle." The elder Henry James knew everyone in the intellectual world. When William was born, Emerson was taken up to the nursery to bestow a nonsectarian blessing; Thackeray, popping out of the James library, asked, in the way of visitors spying a child of a friend, to see young Henry's "extraordinary jacket."

The James family life, their interior and material circumstances, their common experience have a sort of lost beauty. Their existence is a successful enterprise not easily matched. It is less difficult to understand the painful—Gosse's bleakly evangelical family, Mill's exorbitantly demanding father, or Virginia Woolf's father, Leslie Stephan, who seems to have been nervously exhausting to his daughter—than the special inheritance of the unusually loving. The memorably bitter Victorian family scenes, rich in their merciless peculiarity, are more dramatic and more quickly recoverable than the life Henry and Mary James gave to their children. Henry James writes of his father that "it was a luxury . . . to have all the benefit of his intellectual and spiritual, his religious, his philosophic and his social passion, without ever feeling the pressure of it to our direct irritation and discomfort." Compare this with Charles Francis Adams, in his *Autobiography*, and the *list* of his father's mistakes which he, the son, had never been able "sufficiently to deplore." Adams deplores, and sufficiently too, his father's lack of interest in exercise or sport, he deplores the fact that he wasn't sent to a boarding school, he deplores his parents' failure to think of definite amusements for their children; he ends by announcing, "I do not hesitate to say these mistakes of childhood have gravely prejudiced my entire life."

The Jameses are very much of the nineteenth century in the abundance of their natures, their eccentricity, the long, odd, impractical labors of the father and the steady Victorian application of at least two of the sons. And yet this family group is American, too, and of an unusually contemporary accent: the life at home is relaxed, the education "progressive," the parents, permissive. The elder Henry James was a man of religion, enthusiastically so, but his family did not go to church on a Sunday. They had private means and yet they were utterly unlike "society" people. They might go from New York to Newport to London and back with great, leisurely, upper-class frequency, but they must have done so with a good deal of simplicity and restless shabbiness—they were after all intellectual and magically indifferent to bourgeois considerations. Their style as a family was manly, bookish, absent-minded and odd, rather than correct or tasteful or elegant. They were high-minded but "bred in horror of conscious propriety." Henry certainly later struck many observers as snobbish and outlandishly refined, but at the same time there is his literally mysterious energy and grinding ambition, his devilish application like that of an obsessed prospector during the gold rush. There is a long, flowing cadence in the family tone and an elaborate, fluent expressiveness. Even when Alice and Robertson write, they have an opulent, easy command of style that seems to be a family trait. William sometimes needs to put aside this legacy, as if he felt the Jamesian manner too unpragmatic for this work; but his highest moments are drawn from it rather than from his more robust, lecturing, condensed style.

They were not the "Great James family" until the revival of interest in the novels and personality of Henry James, a revival of the last few decades. Of course, William was immensely celebrated and important, but the half-ironical interest in the elder James, the publication of Alice James's *Journal* in 1934, forty-two years after her death, seem hardly possible without the interest in Henry James. In the effort to understand the novelist, the greatness of the family as a whole somehow took shape. Even the father's Swedenborgianism has been exhaustively examined as a clue to the novelist son. The family mystery, the beasts in the jungle, the "vastations," the obscure hurts have come to have an almost mythical and allegorical meaning. The James family stands now with the Adams family as the loftiest of our native productions.

The life of William James, the eldest child, was filled with energy and accomplishment, but it was not visited by scores of dramatic happenings or by those fateful, tragic events that make some lives seem to go from year to year, from decade to decade, as if they were providing material for a lively biography to be written long after. Actually, an extraordinary biography *was* written: Henry James's *A Small Boy and Others* and *Notes of a Son and Brother*, undertaken as a memorial after William died. Nevertheless, in these surpassingly fascinating works it is always noted that William, the original protagonist, keeps vanishing from the center stage. John Jay Chapman, a friend of William's, says, "And yet it is hard to state what it was in him that gave him either his charm or his power, what it was penetrated and influenced us, what it is that we lack and feel the need of, now that he has so unexpectedly and incredibly died." Ralph Barton Perry in *The Life and Thought of William James*, gathered together with extraordinary industry and power

[XII]

of organization, all the James material in order to write a personal and intellectual biography. Perry uses James's letters, many for the first time, his diaries, his philosophical and psychological writings—everything known about him—and even then James does not quite come through as a character. An equable, successful man is not the ideal subject for portraiture, perhaps, but in the case of William James there is something more: a certain unwillingness to take form, a nature remaining open to suggestion and revision, a temperament of the greatest friendliness and yet finally elusive because of his distaste for dogmatism.

He was born in 1842 and died in 1910. He married and had four children who lived to adulthood and another who died in infancy. "William, perhaps, did not take quite so enthusiastically to parenthood as his own father," says Margaret Knight in her introduction to a Penguin selection of James's writings. No one was quite so at ease paternally as the elder Henry James, and yet William's endurance in this respect is notable when compared with that of the usual father. He began, caught up in those repetitions that persist throughout the generations, to cart his children abroad, back and forth, sending them to this school and that, and although there are a good many groans and alarms, the burden didn't seem to waste his energies or thin out his intellectual interests. When he was abroad, he missed the good, old plain America, and when he was at home, he soon got enough of the plainness and wanted the beauty of Europe once more. His family, his writing, his teaching, his lecturing, his traveling—those are about all you have to build with, biographical twigs and straw of a very commonplace kind. But no one was less commonplace than William James; his mind and sensibility were of the greatest charm, vigor and originality. He was not in the least bland or academic as the list of the pleasant little wrinkles of his nature would seem to indicate. He is usually thought to be the most significant thinker America has produced, and everyone who knew him liked him, and since his death everyone has liked him, too, because our history has not left a single man, except perhaps Jefferson, with so much wisdom and so much sheer delight, such tolerance of the embarrassments of mankind, such a high degree of personal attractiveness and spiritual generosity.

Santayana's superb description of James in *Character and Opinion in the United States* says, "He showed an almost physical horror of club sentiment and of the stifling atmosphere of all officialdom." And of course we admire him more and more for that. We commend him with our most intense feelings for not becoming a mere "professor"; we note that he did not seem interested in playing the gentleman and that he lived in Boston and Cambridge without its ever occurring to him that this meant some sort of special residential gift from the gods. Santayana adds that James was a "sort of Irishman among the Brahmins, and seemed hardly imposing enough for a great man." And for that we thank him, for his escape from dryness and thinness. He is truly a hero: courteous, reasonable, liberal, witty, expressive, a first-rate writer, a profoundly original expression of the American spirit as a thinker, inconceivable in any other country, and yet at home in other countries and cultures as few of us have been.

But James had, as we say now, "his problems." Ralph Barton Perry speaks of the "morbid traits" and the very phrase has an old-fashioned sound of something gangrenous, liverish, perforated with disease. James's "morbidity" is of a reassuring mildness and would not be remarkable at all in the dark lives of some other philosophers. In James, like a speck on the bright, polished surface of a New York State apple, it has considerable fascination, and everyone who writes about the man considers the "depression." It began in his youth, around 1867, and hung on for five or six years. James felt discouraged about the future, he experienced a kind of hopelessness and did not believe that time and change would alter the painful present—sentiments typical of the fixed convictions of a man suffering from a depressive attack. At this time he wrote of his sufferings, "*Pain, however intense, is light and life, compared to a condition where hibernation would be the ideal of conduct, and where your 'conscience,' in the form of an aspiration towards recovery, rebukes every tendency towards motion, excitement or life as a culpable excess. The deadness of spirit thereby produced 'must be felt to be appreciated.'* "

He had somatic symptoms, also—the most striking was the "dorsal insanity," as he named it, the same obscure back pains which had "long made Harry so interesting." He tell a correspondent, "on account of my back I will write but one sheet." The back, for which he went from spa to spa, is an interesting instance of a sort of family affliction in which suggestion seems to play a large part. After James's recovery, the back that had been so much cared for and bathed and warmed and rested was not heard from again. His other symptoms were insomnia, weakness, digestive disorders and eyestrain—the latter the only one usually considered to have had a physical basis.

During the two years in Germany William James felt quite lonely, homesick and much thrown back upon himself. He wrote his beautifully expressive early letters to his friends and family, letters of considerable length and great energy of feeling and observation. He speaks, in suitably stoical, manly terms of his own illness, but he also speaks of other people, shows a much truer interest in the world about him than one would expect from a man in a deep depression. His suffering is genuine, but it does not override the claims of the impersonal. A common-sense melody sings through the saddest part of the story, although some of this may be bravado or pride. It is hard to know how to estimate the depth of this early collapse.

There is no doubt that occupational uncertainty was the cause of James's low spirits. It is the usual thing of a young man in medicine or law who does not want to be in medicine or law. (Those innumerable poets who found themselves enrolled for the clergy!) Listlessness came on like a weakening fever as the absence of genuine interest became more and more obvious. "It is totally impossible for me to study now in any way, and I have at last succeeded in *genuinely* giving up the attempt to." James puts every obstacle in the way of the successful practice of medicine; there are even moral objections and he does not fail to notice the toadying young medical students must go in for with their professors, the kind of anxious flattery and unctuous activity necessary to advance professional interests. James did not want to be a doctor and yet it would have been difficult for a young man in his twenties to decide that he was going to be a "psychologist" or a "philosopher." Those one became as a culmination, as one became wise or great or full of special insight. In youth it was different, and even the novelist, Henry James, somehow incredibly found himself briefly enrolled at the Harvard Law School.

Moderate and finally benign the depression proved to be, but James *did* have it and other similar emotional disturbances, nightmarish times, and sensations approaching a state of hallucination. His special awareness of merging states of mind, of the blurred flow of consciousness, the involuntary, subconscious mental life was probably sired by the odd helplessness he experienced during his youthful struggles. The case of "The Sick Soul" in *The Varieties of Religious Experience*, an extraordinarily vivid piece of composition, has been widely called upon to give testimony to James's profound experience of the darkest corners of horror. In this dreadful vignette, attributed in the book to a Frenchman but later acknowledged by James to have come from his own experience, he tells of sitting alone in a "state of philosophic pessimism," and of then going suddenly into his dark dressing room and finding his mind involuntarily assaulted by the memory of a poor epileptic he had seen in an asylum. The remembered person was a "black-haired youth with greenish skin, entirely idiotic. . . . He sat there like a sort of sculptured Egyptian cat or Peruvian mummy, moving nothing but his black eyes and looking absolutely non-human. This image and my fear entered into a species of combination with each other. *That shape am I*, I felt, potentially. Nothing that I possess can defend me from that fate, if the hour for it should strike for me as it struck for him." This classical experience of abysmal fear, of the dreaded double, of the annihilation of the self is written with a touch of Poe and even of Henry James. The "pit of insecurity" remained long afterward, and James said the whole thing "made me sympathetic with the morbid feelings of others."

James was thirty-six years old when he married, forty-eight years old when his first important work, *The Principles of Psychology*, was completed. For all his energy and genius, there was a sort of hanging back about him, a failure of decision beginning from those first early days of anxiety about his career. He seems to have been capable of any amount of activity, but his ambition was not of the greediest sort. Inspiration and verve made it fairly easy for him to accomplish what he wished, but it was probably procrastination, in all its joy and sorrow, that made him such a great writer on the quirks of human nature. He was a sort of poet of "habit" and "will" and never able to bring himself under their pure, efficient control. A recurring hesitation to commit himself was at the very heart of his philosophical and personal nature. Santayana believed James would have been uncomfortable in the face of any decided question. "He would still have hoped that something might turn up on the other side, and that just as the scientific hangman was about to dispatch the poor convicted prisoner, an unexpected witness would ride up in hot haste, and prove him innocent." This everlasting question mark is part of James's appeal for the contemporary mind. He dreaded Germanic system-making, he feared losing touch with the personal, the subjective, the feelings of real human beings more than he feared being logically or systematically faulty. Everyone complained of the looseness of his thought. Chapman: "His mind is never quite in focus." Ralph Barton Perry speaks of James's "temperamental repugnance to the processes of exact thought." And everyone realized that it was the same openness that saved James from pedantry and egotism.

Religion: sometimes an embarrassment to James's reasonable admirers. His nuts and cranks, his mediums and table-tappers, his faith healers and receivers of communications from the dead —all are greeted by James with the purest, melting latitudinarianism, a nearly disreputable amiability, a broadness of tolerance and fascination like that of a priest at a jam session. James's pragmatism, his pluralism, his radical empiricism have been the subject of a large amount of study and comment. Reworking the sod from whence so many crops have come in their season seems profitless for the enjoyment of James's letters, letters that are nearly always personal, informal, nontechnical and rather different in this way from, for instance, Santayana's recently published correspondence in which philosophy keeps cropping up everywhere. Religion, on the other hand, was sort of addiction for James, and all of his personality is caught up in it, his unique ambivalence, his longing, as Oliver Wendell Holmes says, "for a chasm from which might appear a phenomenon without phenomenal antecedents."

Whenever someone near to him died, James could not restrain a longing for the comforts of immortality. To Charles Eliot Norton, when he was very ill in 1908, James wrote, "I am as convinced as I can be of anything that this experience of ours is only a part of the experience that is, and with which it has something to do; but *what* or *where* the other parts are, I cannot guess. It only enables one to say 'behind the veil, behind the veil!'. . ." When his sister Alice's death was obviously near, an extraordinary letter to her said, "When that which is *you* passes out of the body, I am sure that there will be an explosion of liberated force and life till then eclipsed and kept down. I can hardly imagine *your* transition without a great oscillation of both 'worlds' as they regain their new equilibrium after the change! Everyone will feel the shock, but you yourself will be more surprised than anybody else." A memorial address for his old friend, Francis Boott, ends, "Good-by, then, old friend. We shall nevermore meet the upright figure, the blue eye, the hearty laugh, upon these Cambridge streets. But in that wider world of being of which this little Cambridge world of ours forms so infinitesimal a part, we may be sure that all our spirits and their missions here will continue in some way to be represented, and that ancient human loves will never lose their own."

Immortality was a great temptation and so, also, was the tranquillity James had observed to be at least sometimes a result of religious belief. "The transition from tenseness, self-responsibility, and worry, to equanimity, receptivity, and peace

... This abandonment of self-responsibility seems to be the fundamental act in specifically religious as distinguished from moral practice." James had at hand any amount of sympathy for the believer, along with the most sophisticated knowledge of the way in which the religious experience could be treated as a neurotic symptom by the nonbeliever. At the beginning of *The Varieties* he writes, "A more fully developed example of the same kind of reasoning is the fashion, quite common nowadays among certain writers, of criticising religious emotions by showing a connection between them and the sexual life. . . . Medical materialism finishes up Saint Paul by calling his vision on the road to Damascus a discharging lesion of the occipital cortex, he being an epileptic."

Some of the enchantment of *The Varieties* comes from its being a kind of race with James running on both teams— here he is the cleverest skeptic and there the wildest man in a state of religious enthusiasm. He can call St. Theresa a "shrew," and say that the "bustle" of her style proves it, and yet he can appreciate the appeal the Roman Catholic church will often have for people of an intellectual and artistic nature. And beyond conventional religion, beyond God and immortality and belief, there is the "subliminal door," that hospitable opening through which he admits his living items of "psychical research." True his passion was instructive, scholarly and perhaps psychological in many cases, but that does not explain the stirring appeal for him in the very vulgarity of the cults, the dinginess of the seances. The Boston medium Mrs. Piper sometimes bored him; even his colleague Myers, a much more committed psychical researcher, called this lady, "that insipid Prophetess, that tiresome channel of communication between the human and the divine." But in the end, James finally said about Mrs. Piper: "In the trances of this medium, I cannot resist the conviction that knowledge appears which she has never gained by the ordinary waking use of her eyes and ears and wits." Even as late as 1893 James had eighteen sessions with a "mind-curer" and found his sleep wonderfully restored. He says, by way of testimonial to her remarkable powers, "I would like to get this woman into a lunatic asylum for two months, and have every case of chronic delusional insanity in the house tried by her."

In 1884, the American Chapter of the Society for Psychical Research was founded. James became a member and was still a member at the time of his death. Working in psychic research was not just a bit of occasional dashing about to seances and mind readings. The whole movement was filled with bickering intensity, with all the nervous, absorbing factional struggles "minority" beliefs and practices usually develop. An endless amount of work went into this research: the communications from beyond tended to be lengthy. In 1908, James wrote Flournoy, "I have just read Miss Johnson's report on the S.P.R. Proceedings, and a good bit of the proofs of Piddington's on cross-correspondence between Mrs. Piper, Mrs. Verrall, and Mrs. Holland, which is to appear in the next number. You will be much interested, if you can gather the philosophical energy, to go through with such an amount of tiresome detail. It seems to me that these reports open a new chapter in the history of automatism; and Piddington's and Johnson's ability is of the highest order." On his defense of faith healers when they were being attacked as charlatans by the medical profession, James wrote a friend, "If you think I *enjoy* this sort of thing you are mistaken."

James's son, Henry, the first editor of his letters, believed that it was only in the interest of pure research that his father gave so much time to these psychic manifestations and "not because he was in the least impressed by the lucubrations of the kind of mind" that provided such material. Ralph Barton Perry attributes the time spent to James's psychological interest in unusual cases and also to his natural liberal tendency to prefer the lowly—spiritualism, faith healing and the like—rather than the orthodox and accepted. The picturesqueness, the dishonesty even, seems to have given James the sort of delight that amounted almost to credulity. He would be fatigued and morally discouraged with such people as the famous Neapolitan medium, Eusapia Paladina, about whom he said, "Everyone agrees that she cheats in the most barefaced manner whenever she gets an opportunity," and yet he concludes optimistically that "her credit has steadily risen." He reports that in England the two daughters of a clergyman named Creery whose feats of thought-transference has much impressed certain strict investigators were later found to be signaling each other. There were many disheartening moments and infidelities. James and his fellow researcher, Hodgson, went on a trip and spent "the most hideously inept psychical night, in Charleston, over a much-praised female medium who fraudulently played on the guitar. A plague take all white-livered, anaemic, flaccid, weak-voiced Yankee frauds! Give me a full-blooded red-lipped villain like dear old D.—when shall I look upon her like again?" In the letters of a few weeks previously he had described the medium, dear old D., as a "type for Alexander Dumas, obese, wicked, jolly, intellectual, with no end of go and animal spirits . . . that woman is one with whom one would fall wildly in love, if in love at all—she is such a fat, *fat* old villain." You do not find the delight, the hospitality, the enjoyment in the other psychic researchers—only credulity and reports and statistics on "controls," those spirits who give off conversation and information to the strange vessels capable of hearing them. One control accused the psychologist Stanley Hall of having murdered his wife.

James seems to have enjoyed all this as another learned man might enjoy burlesque, but at the same time he took it with a great deal of seriousness. His yea is followed by his nay, as is usual with him, and yet he hoped that these manifestations would be scientifically validated, that the endless, wearisome, fantastic proceedings of the Society for Psychical Research would be an important contribution to knowledge. In all this James is a sort of Californian; he loves the new and unhistorical and cannot resist the shadiest of claims. He, himself, and most of the people who write piously about him felt that he died without saying all he might have said, without finishing his system, without in some grand conclusion becoming the great philosophical thinker that he was, or at least without in the end truly and thoroughly writing his final thoughts on the universe and life. Perhaps there is a sense in which this may have been the case, but perhaps it is only the usual scholarly appetite for the weighty and lengthy. William James without his gaiety, his spooks, his nuts and frauds, his credulity and his incongruous longings for something more than life, even though he was committed to testing every belief *by* life, would not be the captivating and splendid spirit he is. It is usual to remember his wit, his courtesy, his geniality, his liberalism, but in the end his image is indefinable and one does not know how to name the quality that shines in every bit of his writing, in all we know about him, in the character and spirit we believe him to have been. Perhaps it is his responsiveness, his unexpected sympathies, even his gullibility. Or his goodness. Whatever it may have been, we feel it as something simple many others might have and yet hardly anyone seems to possess. A certain flatness and repetitiveness appear in people's attempts

to define him, for he is odd but not dark, rich not in pecu-
larities but rather peculiar in the abundance of his endowment
with the qualities and dispositions we admire in all men.

About his letters the same ideas come to mind—were we
better, more gifted, more abounding in our feelings we might
have written them ourselves. James's correspondence is spontaneous and casual. Letters are not necessarily of that order;
every sort of letter, the formal, the affected, the merest scribble
or a showpiece composed with all the deliberation of a sonnet,
all these have been at some time written wonderfully by someone. Yet a special regard is given to the impulsive, free letter
because such unrevised and personal moments have an authen-
ticity utterly innocent of posthumous longings. They are the
nearest things we have to the lost conversations of memorable
persons. James's letters are felicitous, easy, genuine as talk,
hurriedly written, each for its own occasion, and yet very much
written, with all the sense of form and beauty and the natural
power to interest that come from a man with a pure gift for
the art of letter writing. They are intimate and personal; they
have a romantic fullness of emotion; they are the productions
of a social creature, a man of the world, at least in the sense of
complicated obligations and a conscientious regard for friend-
ships. They have a poetical sweetness; they delight and charm,
and they are deeply affecting, even somewhat sad, as they reveal
year by year a life and sensibility of great force and great virtue.

It certainly did not occur to William James at the beginning
of his career that he was going to be an important writer, that
this, rather than painting, was the art he going to master.
Indeed, after his first review he said, "I feel that a living is
hardly worth being gained at this price." He spoke of "sweating fearfully for three days, erasing, tearing my hair, copying,
recopying, etc." It was often hard for him to settle down to

philosophical and professional writing; yet once started, his marvelous clarity, humor, and his superb prose style carried him along rapidly enough. Letter writing, on the other hand, was a pure pleasure, a duty and an indulgence at the same time. His desire, in letters to friends, was to give happiness—compare this with D. H. Lawrence who seemed when he felt the desire to communicate with his friends to want, at best, to instruct, and, at the worst, to chastise. James's affections appear to be without limits. "Darling Belle-Mère," he addresses his mother-in-law and signs off with "oceans of love from your affectionate son." His colleagues are greeted with "Glorious old Palmer" and "Beloved Royce." James is, as his letters show, quite susceptible to women; he is their correspondent on suitable occasions with great and convincing gallantry. He has such pleasure in his friends that the reader of his letters longs to know the recipients, a condition far from being the usual one with great letter writers. (Madame de Sévigné's daughter is one of the last persons we would want to recall from the shades.) Grace Norton, Fannie Morse, Thomas Ward, Henry Bowditch, and Mrs. Whitman seem persons of the most pleasing dimensions as we meet them in James's correspondence. His attitude toward them all is benevolent, loving, loyal and completely without pompousness or self-importance. James was almost *curiously* modest. People crowded to his lectures, he was truly a public figure, and an international celebrity, too, but there is never anything of rigidity or conceit in his character. He hardly seemed to believe he had done anything unusual. His tenderness, too, was of the most luxuriant variety and stayed with him forever. John Jay Chapman thought he always liked everything and everyone too well.

NOTES ON CORRESPONDENTS

ADAMS, HENRY (1838-1918): Author of *The Education of Henry Adams*, works on American history and *Mont-St. Michel and Chartres*. Grandson of President John Quincy Adams.

BEERS, CLIFFORD (1876-   ): Author of *The Mind that Found Itself*, organizer of societies for the aid of the mentally ill.

BERGSON, HENRI (1859-1941): French philosopher, author of *Creative Evolution*.

BOWDITCH, HENRY P. (1840-1911): Life-long friend of William James, important physiologist, Harvard professor.

CHAPMAN, JOHN JAY (1862-1933): Essayist, vivid thinker and stylist.

DEWEY, JOHN (1859-1952): American philosopher of the first rank.

ELIOT, CHARLES W. (1834-1926): Scholar, President of Harvard.

EMMET, ELLEN and ROSINA: Cousins of William James.

FLOURNOY, THEODORE (1854-1920): Swiss philosopher, professor at University of Geneva.

GOLDMARK, PAULINE (1874-   ): Bryn Mawr graduate, important in welfare and social work, hiking enthusiast, friend of James's later years.

HIGGINSON, HENRY L. (1834-1919): Boston banker and philanthropist, managed James's financial affairs.

HODGSON, SHADWORTH (1832-1912): English philosopher. He and James met in 1880.

HOLMES, OLIVER WENDELL, JR. (1841-1935): Early friend of James's, later became renowned Justice of the Supreme Court.

JAMES, ALICE (Bal), (1848-1892): Sister of William James.

JAMES, GARTH WILKINSON (Wilky), (1845-1883): Brother of William James.

JAMES, HENRY, SR. (1811-1882): Father of William James.

JAMES, HENRY, JR. (1843-1916): Great novelist, brother of William James.

JAMES, MARGARET (Peg), (1887-1950): Daughter of William James.

JAMES, MARY WALSH (1810-1882): William James's mother.

JAMES, ROBERTSON (1846-1910): Brother of William James.

JAMES, WILLIAM, JR. (1882-   ): William James's son, painter.

JAMES, MRS. WILLIAM (Alice Gibbens) (1849-1922): Wife of William James.

MILLER, DICKINSON S. (1868-   ): Student of James's at Harvard. Professor of philosophy at Columbia, and later at Smith College.

MORSE, FRANCES: Boston lady, close friend of the Jameses.

NORTON, CHARLES E. (1827-1909): Editor of *North Atlantic Review*, translator of Dante.

NORTON, GRACE (1834-1926): Sister of Charles Norton. Lived in Cambridge, Mass. Friend and correspondent of both William and Henry James.

PALMER, GEORGE H. (1842-1933): Philosopher and teacher.

PEIRCE, CHARLES S. (1839-1914): Brilliant, eccentric philosopher, discoverer of "pragmatism," a concept elaborated and modified in James's work. *Collected Papers* published after his death.

PERRY, THOMAS S. (1845-1928): Editor and writer; close friend of Henry James, as well as William.

PIDDINGTON, J. G.: Member of English Society for Psychical Research.

PILLON, FRANÇOIS (1830-1914): Disciple of the philosopher, Renouvier.

RANKIN, HENRY: Resident of East Northfield, Mass. Interested in unusual psychic manifestations.

RENOUVIER, CHARLES (1815-1903): French philosopher; had early and profound influence on William James.

ROYCE, JOSIAH (1855-1916): Harvard philosopher of the Idealist school, author of *World and the Individual*.

SALTER, WILLIAM: Mrs. James's brother-in-law.

SANTAYANA, GEORGE (1863-1952): Spanish-born philosopher, lived in America, studied and taught at Harvard. Great man of letters.

SCHILLER, F. C. S. (1864-1937): Professor of Philosophy at Oxford.

STUMPF, CARL (1848-1936): German psychologist. James met him in 1882.

TAPPAN, MARY: Daughter of Mr. and Mrs. William Tappan. Mrs. Tappan carried on a brisk correspondence with the elder Henry James.

WARD, THOMAS (1844-1940): Friend of James's early years to whom some of his best youthful letters were written.

WHITMAN, MRS. HENRY (?-1904): Boston social figure, amateur painter.

THE
SELECTED LETTERS OF
WILLIAM JAMES

I

1860-1872: EARLY ARTS AND SCIENCES

AT THE age of eighteen, in 1860, William James decided that he would take up a career as a painter. Both William and Henry James felt the absolute necessity for a career, or rather for some devouring great dedication. No doubt, the elder Henry James's passionate study of the largest moral, intellectual and religious themes—a study pursued as salvation itself, but privately, personally—made the two young men wish to be somehow more clearly defined, more solidly employed. On the other hand, it was their father's absolute belief in an intellectual and philosophical life that gave his sons their tremendous indifference to a mere profession, a simple success. Henry says that when he decided to become a writer, "it was breathed upon me with the finest bewildering eloquence . . . that this too was narrowing." William sought his father's ideas on becoming a painter and learned that his father did not think such a career spiritual enough! Father and son exchanged letters on this subject which are remarkable for their lack of parental bullying and filial sulking. With an irony noted by his brother, William returned from Europe so that he might study painting with William Hunt at Newport. Then, quite suddenly, he abandoned it, after a year. Although William James had a good

[3]

deal of talent as an artist, painting was not the thing, not his life. In 1861 he entered the Lawrence Scientific School to study chemistry. But he was not endowed with a high gift for chemistry and shifted later to anatomy and physiology. In 1864 James entered the Harvard Medical School, not profoundly smitten with the profession of medicine either, but feeling the study and preparation at least *possible* to one of his mind and temperament. In 1865 he went with the Thayer Expedition to Brazil—an expedition under the direction of Agassiz. Here, too, he found himself in a situation not intolerable to his spirits and talents and yet not exhilarating: he was not a naturalist it seemed. The sensation of "not quite" and "almost" stayed with William James for a long period and in certain respects was never completely subdued. He experienced deeply the pains of versatility.

In 1867, the "famous" William James depression set in, this mysterious siege of uncertainty about the future and bodily distress of one kind and another. He went abroad in search of health, sailing in April, 1867, for Dresden. The next eighteen months were spent taking the baths at Teplitz, following lectures at the University in Berlin, reading, looking, thinking, and despairing of himself. He was not fit for laboratory work, not sturdy enough to practice medicine, not well enough adjusted to life nor financially secure enough for marriage, and so on. The enormous energy with which he describes his supposed impairments makes these letters as fascinating psychologically as they are humanly charming.

At this time James's mind began to take on its ultimate shape: he read Renouvier, became interested in psychology, and met a moment of crisis in 1870 by deciding to believe in free will! In 1868, James returned to Cambridge to live with his family and to continue his medical studies. He passed the medi-

[4]

cal examination in 1869 and in 1872 began his career as a
professor at Harvard.

To HIS FATHER

Bonn [Aug. 19, 1860]

My dearest Father,—

I got your letter on Thursday. I wish you would, as you
promise, set down as clearly as you can on paper what your idea
of the nature of art is, because I do not probably understand
it fully, and should like to have it presented in a form that I
might think over at my leisure. I wanted very much to ask
you to do so at Mrs. Livermore's, but feared you might not care
to and refrained foolishly. Now I wish you would do it as fully
as you conveniently can, so that I may ruminate it. I will not
say anything about it before I have got your next letter.

As for what your last letter did contain, what can I do but
thank you for every word of it and assure you that every word
went to the right spot! Having such a father with us, how can
we be other than in some measure worthy of him, though not
perhaps as eminently so as the distance leads his fond heart
to imagine. In regard to our self-respect and purity, I hope and
trust the day may never come when your wishes will be disappointed. I am sure that *I* should as deeply deplore any loss
of them in myself as you possibly could for me, and I hope
that with the other children the case is the same. I never value
my parents (Father especially) so much as when I am away from
them. At home I only see his faults and here he seems all
perfection, and every night I wonder why I did not value them
more when they were beside me. I beg darling old Mother's
forgiveness for the cruel and dastardly way in which I snub her,
and Aunt Kate's for the impatience and violence I have always

[5]

shown towards her. If ever I get back I will be perfect cherry cobbler to both of them, and to the little Alice, too, for the harsh way in which I have treated her....

I have just got home from dining at the boys' house.... They certainly live on the fat of the land, though they do not seem as sensible of their advantages as they should be. As I had been led to expect nothing of the kind, I was surprised at the sumptuousness of the dinner, rich beef, sausages, pigeons, capital vegetables and soup, all cooked just right, and a most delicious cherry pie, with two bottles of costly Rhine wine in honor of the day. The Doctor [Humpert] was as cordial as usual, and the two old ladies perfect characters for Dickens. They have been so shut out from the world and have been melting together so long by the kitchen fire that the minds of both have become confounded into one, and they seem to constitute a sort of two-bodied individual. I never saw anything more curious than the way in which they sit mumbling together at the end of the table, each using simultaneously the same exclamation if anything said at our end strikes their ear. The boys say they always speak together, using the same words or else one beginning a phrase, the other ending it. It is a singular life.

Harry studies pretty stoutly, but I do not think you need to be apprehensive about him. There has been no renewal of the stomach aches that I am aware of, and he looks fatter and fresher than when you left. He and Wilky appear to get on very harmoniously together. They enliven themselves occasionally by very good-natured brotherly trials of strength in their bedroom, when study has made them dull and sleepy. In these sometimes one, sometimes the other is victor. We see each other every day. They often pay me a visit here in my room in the morning when I am dressing, which is very pleasant, and I have more than once been in their room early enough to be

[6]

present at Wilky's tumble out of bed and consequent awaking, and call upon the already-at-work Harry ... We are going to put Harry through a slashing big walk daily. His old white Lordet clothes began to look so shockingly grimy that we have at last induced him to take them to be cleaned. He clung to them with such affection that it was no easy matter. I have got on very well this last week in German, am beginning to understand and to make myself tolerably understood in straightforward matters. I got a singular note from Bobby the other day. He says he wants to go into a dry goods store. "Mr. O'Conover's son" knows plenty of boys in New York knowing French, fifteen years old, getting $1000 or some $500. He wishes me to "tell Father to consider the proposition." Poor little Bobby!

Thousand thanks to the cherry-lipped, apricot-nosed, double-chinned little Bal for her strongly dashed-off letter, which inflamed the hearts of her lonely brothers with an intense longing to kiss and slap her celestial cheeks.... Mother, in her precious letter, speaks of having her photograph taken when we get there. I conjure her by all the affection she bears us and by the ties which bind her to the eldest son, not to have it done *before*. When we get there we will have a consultation about it.... Now bosom upon bosom full of love to all, from your affectionate

Willy

To HIS FATHER

Bonn, Aug. [*24, 1860*]

My dearest Father,—

Your letter came last evening too late for me to have answered it immediately. I hasten to take time to do so this morning in order to quiet your apprehensions about the time of our leaving Bonn. We have never for a moment forgotten that we were to do so on Friday, Aug. 31st. . . . With respect to the *Gazette des Beaux Arts,* I am sorry it should have caused you any uneasiness. The three numbers came punctually and in perfect condition, and I have by this time enjoyed all their contents (which are not as interesting as those of many preceding numbers, however). . . . For the abundant *Once a Weeks* too, and for an *Illustrated* which we got yesterday morning, we are most grateful. . . .

I was very glad to get your preceding letter, although its contents were not exactly what I had expected. What I wanted to ask you for at Mrs. Livermore's were the reasons why I should not be an "artist." I could not *fully* make out from your talk there what were *exactly* the causes of your disappointment at my late resolve, what your view of the nature of art was, that the idea of my devoting myself to it should be so repugnant to you. Your present letter simply points out the spiritual danger in which a man is if he allows the bent of his aesthetic nature (supposed strong) to direct his activity. It does not, therefore, cover just the ground which I had expected, unless your repugnance was in great measure merely a repugnance to my exposure to such spiritual danger, which can hardly be the case.—But now I perceive that what I was just going to say is not true, and we had better leave the matter till I get to Paris and we can talk it over.

It of course gives me a sort of gratification to see that in your letter you seem to accept the *fact* of my being an "artist," and limit yourself to showing me what you think an artist is and how he may deceive himself. In as far as you have done so I think I understand you perfectly. I had already gathered the idea from your conversation and have often thought over it and felt all its truth. I think there is small danger of my ever

[8]

forgetting it. The influence which my dealings with art and works of art hitherto have had upon me is such as would by no means tempt me to forget it. I do not see why a man's spiritual culture should not go on independently of his aesthetic activity, why the power which an artist feels in himself should tempt him to forget what he is, any more than the power felt by a Cuvier or Fourier would tempt them to do the same. Why should not a given susceptibility of religious development be found bound up in a mind whose predominant tendencies are artistic, as well as in one largely intellectual, granting, even, that the former be much the most elementary, the least dignified and useful? My experience amounts to very little, but it is all I have to go upon; and I am sure that far from feeling myself degraded by my intercourse with art, I continually receive from it spiritual impressions the intensest and purest I know. So it seems to me is my mind formed, and *I can see* no reason for avoiding the giving myself up to art *on this score*. Of course if you even agree to let this pass, there remain other considerations which might induce me to hesitate,—those of utility, of duty to society, etc. All these, however, I think ought to be weighed down by strong *inclination* towards art, and by the fact that my life would be embittered if I were kept from it. That is the way I feel *at present*. Of course I may change. I may have misapprehended your position, too, and talked quite uselessly. We will see in a week. I have no more time. Great love to all. Good-bye.

W. J.

To HIS FAMILY

Cambridge, Sunday afternoon
[Early Nov., 1861]

Dearly beloved Family,—

Wilky and I have just returned from dinner, and having completed a concert for the benefit of the inmates of Pasco Hall and the Hall next door, turn ourselves, I to writing a word home, he to digesting in a "lobbing" position on the sofa. Wilky wrote you a complete account of our transactions in Boston yesterday much better than I could have done. I suppose you will ratify our action as it seemed the only one possible to us. The radiance of Harry's visit has not faded yet, and I come upon gleams of it three or four times a day in my farings to and fro; but it has never a bit diminished the lustre of far-off shining Newport all silver and blue and this heavenly group below (all being more or less failures, especially the two outside ones),— the more so as the above-mentioned Harry could in no wise satisfy my cravings to know of the family and friends, as he did not seem to have been on speaking terms with any of them for some time past and could tell me nothing of what they did, said, or thought about any given subject. Never did I see a so much interested creature in the affairs of those about him. He is a good soul though in his way, too—much more so than the light fantastic Wilky, who has been doing nothing but disaster since he has been here, breaking down my good resolutions about eating, keeping me from any intellectual exercise, ruining my best hat wearing it while dressing, while in his night-gown, wishing to wash his face with it on, insisting on sleeping in my bed, inflicting on me thereby the pains of crucifixion, and hardly to be prevented from taking the said hat to bed with him. The odious creature occupied my comfortable armchair all the morning in the position represented in the fine plate which accompanies this letter. But one more night though and he shall be gone and no thorn shall be in the side of the serene and hallowed felicity of expectation in which I shall revel until the time comes for going home, home, home to the hearts of my infancy and budding youth.

It is not homesickness I have, if by that term be meant a sickness of heart and loathing of my present surroundings, but a sentiment far transcending this, that makes my hair curl for joy whenever I think of home, by which home comes to me as hope, not as regret, and which puts roses long faded thence in my old mother's cheeks, mildness in my father's voice, flowing graces into my Aunt Kate's movements, babbling confidingness into Harry's talk, a straight parting into Robby's hair and a heavenly tone into the lovely babe's temper, the elastic graces of a kitten into Moses's [a horse] rusty and rheumatic joints. Aha! Aha! The time will come—Thanksgiving in less than two weeks and then, oh, then!—probably a cold reception, half repellent, no fatted calf, no fresh-baked loaf of spicy bread,—but I dare not think of that side of the picture. I will ever hope and trust and my faith shall be justified.

As Wilky has submitted to you a résumé of his future history for the next few years, so will I, hoping it will meet your approval. Thus: one year study chemistry, then spend one term at home, then one year with Wyman, then a medical education, then five or six years with Agassiz, then probably death, death, death with inflation and plethora of knowledge. This you had better seriously consider. This is a glorious day and I think I must close and take a walk. So farewell, farewell until a quarter to nine Sunday evening soon! Your bold, your beautiful,

Your Blossom!!

To HIS SISTER, ALICE

Cambridge, Oct. 19, 1862

Dearest Child,—

Although unwell, such is the love I cherish for you and for all the dear folks at home that I cannot resist writing a few words this evening, in order to keep up our affectionate relations and to thank you for your nice letters, which, though rudely and coarsely executed, are rather *more* than *less* delightful for it. Father has been making such a long stay here that you at home must be beginning to think of coming on after him. I think now he will stay till Wilky leaves, *si toujours* he *does* leave, on Tuesday. I think the knocking about and excitement here is doing him good. I have been with him to the printer's, and think that between us three one of the prettiest books of modern times will be produced—plain, unadorned, but severely handsome. . . .

I have had since last Sunday a boil in my elbow. Eliot with voice of absolute certainty told me to keep painting it with iodine, and as he rarely proffers a remark, those which he does let fall have double weight. So how could I help hopefully painting away. The result has been to keep the boil about *in statu quo* until about three days ago, when my arm began to swell voluminously. The iodine seems to prevent the formation of a crater, but what else it does, heaven and Eliot alone know. It is very painful to apply, and seems only to prolong the boil, and having dropped its use I now curse it aloud. I am quite sick and feverish tonight, and sit under my lamp wrapped in my overcoat writing *à la seule que j'aime* and wishing for nothing so much as an hour or two of her voluble and senseless, though soothing and pleasing, talk. Her transparent eyes, soft step, and gentle hands, her genial voice and mood, never seemed

[12]

to me more desirable or lovable than now. And what a hallowed warmth and light environs our too fond mother's form, too, as my mind's eye now sees us; she who is always as ready to soothe us in sickness as to guide us in health, and who is as unassuming and gentle in the one function as in the other. Dear old Aunt Kate too, whose self-sacrificing zeal and devotion never seemed so angelic, and whose cool and comfortable fussing around your sickly frame never so exquisitely grateful—and the sprightly, genial Bob, with the healthy breeze of active, moving life he always bears in with him—all—all—rush over me like an aged and mellow sea at the bottom of which my soul lies faintly floating. One sofa is vacant in the parlor of my home, one place unfilled,—'t is mine. Harry just comes in, sweet child, and sends his love to each and all. You shall have Bourdon's arithmetic and anything else you please. Good night—a thousand kisses to all—*le seul qui t'aime,*

Wm. James

To HIS MOTHER

Cambridge, [*circa Sept., 1863*].

My dearest Mother,—

. . . To answer the weighty questions which you propound: I am glad to leave Newport because I am tired of the place itself, and because of the reason which you have very well expressed in your letter, the necessity of the whole family being near the arena of the future activity of us young men. I recommend Cambridge on account of its own pleasantness (though I don't wish to be invidious towards Brookline, Longwood, and other places) and because of its economy if I or Harry continue to study here much longer. . . .

I feel very much the importance of making soon a final choice of my business in life. I stand now at the place where the road forks. One branch leads to material comfort, the flesh-pots; but it seems a kind of selling of one's soul. The other to mental dignity and independence; combined, however, with physical penury. If I myself were the only one concerned I should not hesitate an instant in my choice. But it seems hard on Mrs. W. J., "that not impossible she," to ask her to share an empty purse and a cold hearth. On one side is *science*, upon the other *business* (the honorable, honored and productive business of printing seems most attractive), with *medicine*, which partakes of [the] advantages of both, between them, but which has drawbacks of its own. I confess I hesitate. I fancy there is a fond maternal cowardice which would make you and every other mother contemplate with complacency the worldly fatness of a son, even if obtained by some sacrifice of his "higher nature." But I fear there might be some anguish in looking back from the pinnacle of prosperity (*necessarily* reached, if not by eating dirt, at least by renouncing some divine ambrosia) over the life you might have led in the pure pursuit of truth. It seems as if one *could* not afford to give that up for any bribe, however great. Still, I am undecided. The medical term opens tomorrow and between this and the end of the term here, I shall have an opportunity of seeing a little into medical business. I shall confer with Wyman about the prospects of a naturalist and finally decide. I want you to become familiar with the notion that I *may* stick to science, however, and drain away at your property for a few years more. If I can get into Agassiz's museum I think it not improbable I may receive a salary of $400 to $500 in a couple of years. I know some stupider than I who have done so. You see in that case how desirable it would be to have a home in Cambridge. Anyhow, I am convinced that somewhere in this neighborhood is the place for us to rest. These matters have been a good deal on my mind lately, and I am very glad to get this chance of pouring them into yours. As for the other boys, I don't know. And that idle and useless young female, Alice, too, whom we shall have to feed and clothe! . . . Cambridge is all right for business in Boston. Living in Boston or Brookline, etc., would be as expensive as Newport if Harry or I stayed here, for we could not easily go home every day.

Give my warmest love to Aunt Kate, Father, who I hope will not tumble again, and all of them over the way. Recess in three weeks; till then, my dearest and best of old mothers, good-bye! Your loving son,

W. J.

[P.S.] Give my best love to Kitty and give *cette petite* humbug of a Minny a hint about writing to me. I hope you liked your shawl.

To HIS SISTER, ALICE

Cambridge, Sept. 13, 1863

Chérie charmante de Bal,—

Notwithstanding the abuse we poured on each other before parting and the (on *my* part) feigned expressions of joy at not meeting you again for so many months, it was with the liveliest regret that I left Newport before your return. But I was obliged in order to get a room here—drove, literally drove to it. That you should not have written to me for so long grieves me more than words can tell—you who have nothing to do besides. It shows you to have little affection and *that* of a poor quality. I have, however, heard from *others* who tell me that Wilky is doing well, "improving daily," which I am very glad indeed to hear. I am glad you had such a pleasant summer. I am nicely established in a cosy little room, with a large recess with a

window in it, containing bed and washstand, separated from
the main apartment by a rich green silken curtain and a large
gilt cornice. This gives the whole establishment a splendid look.

I found when I got here that Miss Upham had changed her
price to $5.00. Great efforts were made by two of us to raise a
club, but little enthusiasm was shown by anyone else and it fell
through. I then, with that fine economical instinct which dis-
tinguishes me, resolved to take a tea and breakfast of bread and
milk in my room and only pay Miss Upham for dinners. Miss
U. is at Swampscott. So I asked to see [her sister] Mrs. Wood,
to learn the cost of seven dinners. She, with true motherly
instinct, said that I should only make a slop in my room, and
that she would rather let me keep on for $4.50, seeing it was
me. I said she must first consult Miss Upham. She returned from
Swampscott saying that Miss U. had sworn *she* would rather
pay *me* a dollar a week than have me go away. Ablaze with
economic passion, I cried "Done!" trying to make it appear as
if she had made a formal offer to that effect. But she would not
admit it, and after much recrimination we were separated, it
being agreed that I should come for $4.50, *but tell no-one.*
(Mind *you* don't either.) I now lay my hand on my heart, and
confidently look towards my mother for that glance of approba-
tion which she *must* bestow. Have I not redeemed any weaknesses of the past? Though part of my conception failed, yet it
was boldly planned and would have been a noble stroke.

I have been pretty busy this week. I have a filial feeling towards Wyman already. I work in a vast museum, at a table all
alone, surrounded by skeletons of mastodons, crocodiles, and
the like, with the walls hung about with monsters and horrors
enough to freeze the blood. But I have no fear, as most of them
are tightly bottled up. Occasionally solemn men and women
come in to see the museum, and sometimes timid little girls

(reminding me of thee, beloved, only they are less fashionably dressed) who whisper: "Is folks allowed here?" It pains me to remark, however, that not all the little girls are of this pleasing type, *most* being boldfaced jigs. How does Wilky get on? Is Mayberry gone? How is he nursed? Who holds his foot for the doctor? Tell me all about him. Everyone here asks about him, and all without exception seem enthusiastic about the darkeys. How has Aunt Kate's knee been since her return? Sorry indeed was I to leave without seeing her. Give her my best love. Is Kitty Temple as angelic as ever? Give my best love to her and Minny and the little ones. (My little friend Elly, how often I think of her!) Have your lessons with Bradford (the brandy-witness) begun? You may well blush. Tell Harry Mr. [Francis J.] Child is here, just as usual; Mrs. C. at Swampscott. [C. C.] Salter back, but morose. One or two new students, and Prof. [W. W.] Goodwin, who is a very agreeable man. Among other students, a son of Ed. Everett [William Everett], very intelligent and a capital scholar, studying law. He took honors at Cambridge, England. Tucks, *mère & fille* away, *fils* here. . . .

I send a photograph of Gen. Sickles for yours and Wilky's amusement. It is a part of a great anthropomorphological collection which I am going to make. So take care of it, as well as of all the photographs you will find in the table drawer in my room. But isn't he a bully boy? Harry's handwriting much better. Desecrate my room as little as possible. Good-bye, much love to Wilky and all. If he wants nursing send for me without hesitation. Love to the Tweedies. Haven't you heard yet from Bobby?

Your aff. bro.,

Wm.

To HIS PARENTS

Rio, Brazil, Apr. 21, 1865

My dearest Parents,—

Every one is writing home to catch the steamer which leaves Rio on Monday. I do likewise, although, so far, I have very little to say to you. You cannot conceive how pleasant it is to feel that tomorrow we shall lie in smooth water at Rio and the horrors of this voyage will be over. O the vile Sea! the damned Deep! No one has a right to write about the "nature of Evil," or to have any opinion about evil, who has not been at sea. The awful slough of despond into which you are there plunged furnishes too profound an experience not to be a fruitful one. I cannot yet say what the fruit is in my case, but I am sure some day of an accession of wisdom from it. My sickness did not take an actively nauseous form after the first night and second morning; but for twelve mortal days I was, body and soul, in a more indescribably hopeless, homeless and friendless state than I ever want to be in again. We had a head wind and tolerably rough sea all that time. The trade winds, which I thought were gentle zephyrs, are hideous moist gales that whiten all the waves with foam. . . .

Sunday Evening. Yesterday morning at ten o'clock we came to anchor in this harbor, sailing right up without a pilot. No words of mine, or of any man short of William the divine, can give any idea of the magnificence of this harbor and its approaches. The boldest, grandest mountains, far and near. The palms and other trees of such vivid green as I never saw anywhere else. The town "realizes" my idea of an African town in its architecture and effect. Almost everyone is a negro or a negress, which words I perceive we don't know the meaning of with us; a great many of them are native Africans and tattooed.

[18]

The men have white linen drawers and short shirts of the same kind over them; the women wear huge turbans, and have a peculiar rolling gait that I have never seen any approach to elsewhere. Their attitudes as they sleep and lie about the streets are picturesque to the last degree.

Yesterday was, I think, the day of my life on which I had the most outward enjoyment. Nine of us took a boat at about noon and went on shore. The strange sights, the pleasure of walking on terra firma, the delicious smell of land, compared with the hell of the last three weeks, were perfectly intoxicating. Our Portuguese went beautifully,—every visage relaxed at the sight of us and grinned from ear to ear. The amount of fraternal love that was expressed by bowing and gesture was tremendous. We had the best dinner I ever eat. Guess how much it cost. 140,000 reis—literal fact. Paid for by the rich man of the party. The Brazilians are of a pale Indian color, without a particle of red and with a very aged expression. They are very polite and obliging. *All* wear black beaver hats and glossy black frock coats, which makes them look like *des épiciers endimanchés*. We all returned in good order to the ship at 11 P.M., and I lay awake most of the night on deck listening to the soft notes of the vampire outside of the awning. (Not knowing what it was, we'll call it the vampire.) This morning Tom Ward and I took another cruise on shore, which was equally new and strange. The weather is like Newport. I have not seen the thermometer. . . .

Agassiz just in, delighted with the Emperor's simplicity and the precision of his information; but apparently they did not touch upon our material prospects. He goes to see the Emperor again tomorrow. Agassiz is one of the most fascinating men personally that I ever saw. I could listen to him talk by the hour. He is so childlike. Bishop Potter, who is sitting opposite me writing, asks me to give his best regards to father. I am in such a state of abdominal tumefaction from having eaten bananas all day that I can hardly sit down to write. The bananas here are no whit better than at home, but *so* cheap and *so* filling at the price. My fellow "savans" are a very uninteresting crew. Except Tom Ward I don't care if I never see one of 'em again. I like Dr. Cotting very much and Mrs. Agassiz too. I could babble on all night, but must stop somewhere.

Dear old Father, Mother, Aunt Kate, Harry and Alice! You little know what thoughts I have had of you since I have been gone. And I have felt more sympathy with Bob and Wilk than ever, from the fact of my isolated circumstances being more like theirs than the life I have led hitherto. Please send them this letter. It is written as much for them as for anyone. I hope Harry is rising like a phœnix from his ashes, under the new régime. Bless him. I wish he or some person I could talk to were along. Thank Aunt Kate once more. Kiss Alice to death. I think Father is the *wisest* of all men whom I know. Give my love to the girls, especially the Hoopers. Tell Harry to remember me to T. S. P[erry] and to Holmes. Adieu.

Your loving

W. J.

Give my love to Washburn.

To HENRY JAMES

Original Seat of Garden of Eden
July 15 [*1865*]

Darling Harry,—

This place is not twenty miles from Rio, which damnable spot I left this morning at six, and now (two P.M.), am sitting on a stone resting from my walk and thinking of thee and the beloved ones in Bosting. No words, but only savage inarticulate cries, can express the gorgeous loveliness of the walk I have been taking. Houp lala! The bewildering profusion and confusion of the vegetation, the inexhaustible variety of its forms and tints (and yet they tell us we are in the winter when much of its brilliancy is lost) are *literally* such as you have never dreamt of. The brilliancy of the sky and the clouds, the effect of the atmosphere, which gives their proportional distance to the diverse planes of the landscape, make you admire the old gal Nature. I almost thought my enjoyment of nature had entirely departed, but here she strikes such massive and stunning blows as to overwhelm the coarsest apprehension. I am sitting on a rock by the side of a winding mule-path. The mule-path is made over an "erratic drift" which much delighteth Agassiz, but makes it truly erratic to the traveler. On my left, up the hill, there rises the wonderful, inextricable, impenetrable forest; on my right the hill plunges down into a carpet of vegetation which reaches to the hills beyond, which rise further back into mountains. Down in the valley I see three or four of the thatched, mud hovels of Negroes, embosomed in their vivid patches of banana trees. The hills on both sides and the path descend rapidly to the shores of a large lagoon separated by a forest-clad strip of land from the azure sea, whose surf I can hear continuously roaring at this distance. Would I could get so far, but the road is too long. A part of the path hither lay through an orange thicket where the great, hard, sweet, juicy fruit strewed the ground more than ever did apples the good old Concord turnpike. Out in the sea are a few rocky islands on which a few palm trees cut against the sky and give the whole a tropical look. How often, my dear old Harry, would I have given everything to have you by my side to enjoy the magnificent landscape of this region! As for the rest I don't enjoy it so much.

But I will write more before the next steamer. *Au revoir* at present.

To HIS BROTHER, WILKY

Boston, February 25, 1866

My dear old Wilky,

This is Sunday night and the family having just gone to bed I sit down to send you a few lines by Wednesday's steamer. We have got a note from you from Jacksonville but nothing later. There is no news at home but the political news, our president's drunken speech, and the row about his veto. I don't know how it will end, and in fact feel so fresh home that I have no opinion yet about the situation. It seems to me that if instead of suppressing papers like the Richmond Examiner, the Government would sternly punish any infringement of free speech on the other side, it would be better. Once let truth have a hearing, and, sooner or later, its victory is sure. Poor sick Ellen Washburn is going to Europe for a change of air, with Frank for a year. I'm afraid she'll have a lonesome time, and feel very sorry for her. Elly V. B. is here, but not at our house yet, older seeming and very fluent in small talk, evidently from great practice; on the whole less interesting than of yore. The other Temple girls are coming, I believe tomorrow, to pay us a visit. I went to the Watsons last night by invitation but found myself alone. I suspect they find hard work to bring those they invite up to the scratch. The old she-Watson pumped me about Brazil with a grace and charm peculiarly her own. We get constant long and admirably written letters from Bob. He is decidedly the letter writer of the family. He writes as if very much disgusted with all his circumstances, but his tone is not despondent; I am glad to see him keep such a stiff upper lip. I have just been to hear John K. Paine play on the organ with Miss Ellen Hooper. She is by far the nicest girl to me in all Boston. I help Alex Agassiz repack the fish we have sent home every morning. I don't think the Professor would have been much exhilarated at seeing the discovery by Alex and Lyman of a barrel void of fish but full of good alcohol among the lot yesterday. Verily there was more rejoicing over that one smuggled one than over the ninety and nine others.

My dear Wilky, I can't tell you any gossip, any jokes or anything else. I am sick unto death of repeating to people the same sentences about South America—so won't get them off on you, all the more as they are totally uninteresting. I am so settled down at home that I don't feel as if I'd ever been away. I think Harry much improved, he is a noble fellow—so delicate and honorable and true—and Alice has got to be a very nice girl. But everyone else seems about the same, and even a white female face can no longer charm me as it did in the first days. Everything must grow stale sometime. I wish you'd imitate Bobby and give us a long account of yourself. I forgot to say that poor Bob Temple has been sentenced to one year's hard labor at Bedlow's Island.

Your loving brother,

Wm. James

To HIS SISTER, ALICE

Cambridge, Nov. 14, 1866

CHÉRIE DE JEUNE BALLE,—I am just in from town in the keen, cold and eke beauteous moonlight, which by the above qualities makes me think of thee, to whom, nor to whose aunt, have I (not) yet written. (I don't understand the grammar of the not.)

Your first question is, "where have I been?" "To C. S. Peirce's lecture, which I could not understand a word of, but rather enjoyed the sensation of listening to for an hour." I then turned to O. W. Holmes's and wrangled with him for another hour.

You may thank your stars that you are not in a place where you have to ride in such full horse-cars as these. I rode half way out with my "form" entirely out of the car overhanging the road, my feet alone being on the same vertical line as any part of the car, there being just room for them on the step. Aunt Kate may, and probably *will*, have shoot through her prolific mind the supposish: "How wrong in him to do sich! for if, while in that posish, he should have a sudden stroke of paralysis, or faint, his nerveless fingers relaxing their grasp of the rail, he would fall prostrate to the ground and bust." To which I reply that, when I go so far as to have a stroke of paralysis, I shall not mind going a step farther and getting bruised.

Your next question probably is "*how* are and *where* are father and mother?" . . . I think father seems more lively for a few days past and cracks jokes with Harry, etc. Mother is recovering from one of her indispositions, which she bears like an angel, doing any amount of work at the same time, putting up cornices and raking out the garret-room like a little buffalo.

Your next question is "wherever is Harry?" I answer: "He is to Ashburner's, to a tea-squall in favor of Miss Haggerty." I declined. He is well. We have had nothing but invitations (6) in 3 or 4 days. One, a painted one, from "Mrs. L———," whoever she may be. I replied that domestic affliction prevented me from going, but I would take a pecuniary equivalent instead, viz: To 1 oyster stew 30 cts., 1 chicken salad 0.50, 1 roll 0.02, 3 ice creams at 20 cts. 0.60, 6 small cakes at 0.05, 0.30, 1 pear $1.50, 1 lb. confectionery 0.50.

6 glasses hock at 0.50	$3.00
3 glasses sherry at 30	0.90

Salad spilt on floor	5.00
Dish of do., broken	3.00
Damage to carpet & Miss L——'s dress frm. do	75.00
3 glasses broken	1.20
Curtains set fire to in dressing-room	40.00
Other injury frm. fire in room	250.00
Injury to house frm. water pumped upon it by steam fire-engine come to put out fire	5000.00
Miscellaneous	0.35
	5300.00

I expect momentarily her reply with a check, and when it comes will take you and Aunt Kate on a tour in Europe and have you examined by the leading physicians and surgeons of that country. Mary Lee came out here and dined with us yesterday of her own accord. I no longer doubt what I always suspected, her *penchant* for me, and I don't blame her for it. Elly Temple staid here two days, too. She scratched, smote, beat, and kicked me so that I shall dread to meet her again. What an awful time Bob & Co. must have had at sea! and how anxious you must have been about them.

With best love to Aunt Kate and yourself believe me your af. bro.

Wm. James

To HIS SISTER, ALICE

Cambridge, Dec. 12 [*1866?*]

My dearest Alice,

Mother has just got your letter, your sweet letter containing so *many nice* things about dress. I should have written to you more frequently but am growing old and more and more averse

[25]

to writing letters. I am glad you think you are doing well and are managing to live comfortably. I little thought you would be able to do so without me and my pills. As for us here, we still live. John La Farge arrived here last night and is now sitting on the sofa talking to Harry. Wilky is very stout and well, and seems to be somewhat tired of the uncivilization in which he has got to live. He says he dreads the thought of going back. . . .

The present time is a very exciting one for ambitious young men at the medical school who are anxious to get into the hospital. Their toadying the physicians, asking them intelligent questions after lectures, offering to run errands for them etc., this week reaches its climax; they call at their residences and humbly solicit them to favor their appointment, and do the same at the residence of the ten trustees. So I have sixteen visits to make. I have little fear, with my talent for flattery and fawning, of a failure. . . .

I went to Newport a fortnight ago and found the girls in remarkably fine condition, especially Minny. How is Aunt Kate's limb and how does she get about? I rather envy you having the run of the vast metropolis. John and Miss Bancroft were in here last night. She wore a small black bonnet, gored, with red band stitched well up in the back, and black ribbon to match the lace chignon. Dress of the same material in two broad folds without a tuck, and a beautiful black coat with bangles, cut bias. It was very pretty as a whole but I think a little vulgar. Still everyone dresses that way now, and gathering in around the neck without any waistband seems all the rage. Pray tell me more about the fashions in New York. You've no idea how *delightful* your letters are. I must say adieu, but will write again soon. Love to Aunt Kate. Yours affectionately,

Wm. James

To THOMAS W. WARD

Berlin, Sept. [?], *1867*

My beloved Old Tom,—

I hope you have never been tempted to infer, from my long silence that my heart has e'er grown cold towards ye! *Yours* (i.e., your silence) might have tempted *me* in moments of spleen, while hugging all my griefs, wrongs and misfortunes passionately to my breast, and solacing myself with the intoxicating thought that my *"friends"* (ha! ha!) had all shown the ingratitude which my knowledge of their base and frivolous natures ought long ago to have led me to expect, yours, I say, might have tempted me to exclaim: And my *Thomas*, him whom I loved and trusted most, is as hollow, vain, unstable, miserable as the rest! Away with him!—but I never yielded to the demon's whisper, and never said anything more severe *à ton égard, mon vieux*, than: "D—n that cuss of a Tom, if he were not so lazy, and so particularly averse to constructing a series of grammatical sentences, and perhaps so tormented and blue himself, I should by this time be receiving a good long letter from him." I have often been on the point of writing to you and two months ago had just begun a letter to you when the postman arrived with a letter from Harry from whom I learned that you had gone back to business, and as I was on the point of beginning an eloquent address encouraging you to stick to your science, this news rather threw me off the track and no more was written that day, and by a not infrequent consequence no more on any succeeding day till now. But the *envelope* in which this shall be enclosed has been lying before me for six weeks and I have over and over again filled it with interesting matter for your perusal—in imagination—so you have no right to call me an unfaithful correspondent. I have now been in Berlin six days. It likes me much, so far—but perhaps on the whole I had better begin at the beginning and lay bare to you my history from the first beginning of its present phase. I don't know whether you have heard or not that I found myself last November almost without perceptible exciting cause in possession of that delightful disease in my back, which has so long made Harry so interesting. It is evidently a family peculiarity. I said nothing about it till a couple of weeks before leaving America, as I hoped it would go over, and did not wish to inflict any avoidable pain on Harry and the rest. I thus foolishly put it out of my power to *rest* as I ought to have done, (for the damned thing showed at first a very strong tendency to disappear after repose) and the consequence was it became so confirmed that I had to throw up my hospital appointment, and fly from a home which had become loathsome. I still said nothing about it to anyone but Father, Mother and Harry, for I wanted to keep it a secret from Alice and the boys. I was strongly tempted to tell you, but was held back partly from a fear it might leak out, partly from a foolish grief and shame, but mostly from the *habit* of keeping it secret which had grown on me in the past six months. I came to Dresden where I lived a good deal the life of a hermit, getting worse rather than better till six weeks ago, when I was sent by a Doctor to a bath place, Teplitz, and in the last two weeks, since my return thence have felt a great deal better. I have no idea how far the improvement will go, but I hope still further than now. Of course, Medicine is busted, much to my sorrow, for I was beginning to get much attached to it. The future is very uncertain. I shall try to stick out the winter here and follow a few of the courses in the University. I am at all events picking up a knowledge of the German language, the possession of which gives one a sort of pleasure, even if he does not hope to make much use of it. I expect T. S. Perry in a month to come here for the winter which will be a great boon.

Sept. 12. I was a good deal surprised to hear that you had decided to go back to business where you left off, after your year's scientific experiment. I will not deny that I felt a little disappointed at first, for I had always thought that if you could get past a certain dead point in science you would be contented to go on ever after. But no one can judge for another and I don't presume to say that I regret it. I wish you would write, though, and tell me all about it, as well as about your present hopes, plans, thoughts, emotions, actions, passions, accidents, etc., etc., etc. Don't let laziness stand in the way of your writing. You have no idea what a boon a letter is to me in my solitude here, or how in particular I have longed and do long to *renouer* my old relations with *you.* I should like to display to you the list of the discoveries I have made since I left home but I have been in a deplorably inert state of mind. Sickness and solitude make a man into a mere lump of egotism without eyes or ears for anything external, and I think, notwithstanding the stimulus of the new language, etc., that I have rarely passed such an empty four months as the last. For the past six weeks, in accordance with the doctor's advice, (which I myself thought very sensible) I have taken a vacation and abstained from all intellectual labor except reading fiction in the French language, and returning yesterday to a German work on electricity was very much disheartened at finding how unfitted I had become to deal either with the language or the subject. If I were in your place, I would indulge in no foolish longings to come to Germany. The total impression of life here is not particularly new nor valuable—nature and art are somewhat bleak and unpicturesque, and too much of our own kind to have any particular instruction for us. To be sure it is good for an American to

[29]

see a race of kindly and friendly people able to enjoy the present moment, and to look at the future too, to wear the kind of clothes that please them individually, and not to feel themselves obliged if they have 500 dollars a year to spend money like their neighbor with 5000—but notwithstanding, the main value of a German culture is in its giving you command of German literature—and by doggedly translating at home, you can acquire that with really very little more trouble than here. I speak to be sure with hardly any experience of the indoor family life of the Germans. I know not a single young man here, but if I did, I doubt whether the difference in kind would be so very great as to "make creation widen to your view" in the same way that an experience of some totally foreign nature, such as Italy, or Brazil, can effect. So my advice to you is, to remain quite contented with being at home, so far as Germany is concerned, but to keep up a steady reading of German whenever you have time.—If in idle moments you want a good story, read Erckmann Chatrian's "Ami Fritz", and "Confessions d'un Joueur de Clarinette", etc. "On ne trouve point dans ces écrits cette cruelle maladie du siècle, etc." But, ass that I am, you have of course read them years ago. I am going to try this winter to stick to the study of the nervous system and psychology. Unfortunately I shall not be well enough to study the N. S. practically. There is an enormous psychological literature (from a physical and inductive point of view) in German. Berlin is a city of magnificent distances, but cabs are plenty and cheap. I saw Coutirho in Paris—he is going to North America this or next month. I hope you will see him; have you heard from Dr. Couts? Farewell, my dear old Tom, *je t'embrasse.* For heaven's sake write soon to your friend

Wm. James

P.S. Please give my best regards to your Mother and sisters.

To O. W. HOLMES, JR.

Berlin, Sept. 17, 1867

MY DEAR WENDLE,—I was put in the possession, this morning, by a graceful and unusual attention on the part of the postman, of a letter from home containing, amongst other valuable matter, a precious specimen of manuscript signed "O. W. H. Jr." covering just one page of small note paper belonging to a letter written by Minny Temple!!!!! Now I myself am not proud,—poverty, misery and philosophy have together brought me to a pass where there are few actions so shabby that I would not commit them if thereby I could relieve in any measure my estate, or lighten the trouble of living,—but, by Jove, Sir! there *is* a point, *sunt* certi denique fines, down to which it seems to me hardly worth while to condescend—better give up altogether.—I do not intend any personal application. Men differ, thank Heaven! and there may be some constituted in such a fearful and wonderful manner, that to write to a friend after six months, in another person's letter, hail him as "one of the pillars on which life rests," and after twelve lines stop short, seems to them an action replete with beauty and credit. To me it is otherwise. And if perchance, O Wendy boy, there lurked in any cranny of *thy* breast a spark of consciousness, a germ of shame at the paltriness of thy procedure as thou inditedst that pitiful apology for a letter, I would fain fan it, nourish it, till thy whole being should become one incarnate blush, one crater of humiliation. Mind, I should not have found fault with you if you had not written at all. There would have been a fine brutality about that which would have commanded respect rather than otherwise—certainly not *pity*. 'Tis that, *writing*, THAT should be the result. Bah!

But I will change the subject, as I do not wish to provoke

[31]

you to recrimination in your next letter. Let it be as substantial and succulent as the last, with its hollow hyperbolic expression of esteem, was the opposite, and I assure you that the past shall be forgotten.—I am, as you have probably been made aware, "a mere wreck," bodily. I left home without telling anyone about it, because, hoping I might get well, I wanted to keep it a secret from Alice and the boys till it was over. I thought of telling you "in confidence," but refrained, partly because walls have ears, partly from a morbid pride, mostly because of the habit of secrecy that had grown on me in six months. I dare say Harry has kept you supplied with information respecting my history up to the present time, and perhaps read you portions of my letters. My history, internal and external, since I have been in Germany, has been totally uneventful. The external, with the exception of three R.R. voyages (to and from Teplitz and to Berlin), resembles that of a sea anemone; and the internal, notwithstanding the stimulus of a new language and country, has contracted the same hue of stagnation. A tedious egotism seems to be the only mental plant that flourishes in sickness and solitude; and when the bodily condition is such that muscular and cerebral activity not only remain *unexcited*, but are *solicited*, by an idiotic hope of recovery, to crass indolence, the "elasticity" of one's spirits can't be expected to be very great. Since I have been here I have admired Harry's pluck more and more. *Pain*, however intense, is light and life, compared to a condition where hibernation would be the ideal of conduct, and where your "conscience," in the form of an aspiration towards recovery, rebukes every tendency towards motion, excitement or life as a culpable excess. The deadness of spirit thereby produced "must be felt to be appreciated."

I have been in this city ten days and hope to stay all winter. I have got a comfortable room near the University and will attempt to follow some of the lectures. My wish was to study physiology practically, but I shall not be able. The number of subjects and fractions of subjects on which courses of lectures are given here and at the other universities would make you stare. Berlin is a "live" place, with a fine, tall, intelligent-looking population, infinitely better-looking than that of Dresden. I like the Germans very much, so far (which is not far at all) as I have got to know them. The apophthegm, "a fat man consequently a good man," has much of truth in it. The Germans come out strong on their abdomens,—even when these are not vast in capacity, one feels that they are of mighty powerful construction, and play a much weightier part in the economy of the man than with us,—affording a massive, immovable background to the consciousness, over which, as on the surface of a deep and tranquil sea, the motley images contributed by the other senses to life's drama glide and play without raising more than a pleasant ripple,—while with *us*, who have no such voluminous background, they forever touch bottom, or come out on the other side, or kick up such a tempest and fury that we enjoy no repose. The Germans have leisure, kindness to strangers, a sort of square honesty, and an absence of false shame and damned pecuniary pretension that makes intercourse with them very agreeable. The language is infernal; and I seem to be making no progress beyond the stage in which one just begins to misunderstand and to make one's self misunderstood. The scientific literature is even richer than I thought. In literature proper, Goethe's "Faust" seems to me almost worth learning the language for.

I wish I could communicate to you some startling discoveries regarding our dilapidated old friend the Kosmos, made since I have been here. But I actually haven't had a fresh idea. And my reading until six weeks ago, having been all in German, covered very little ground. For the past six weeks I have, by medical order, been relaxing my brain on French fiction, and am just returning to the realities of life, German and Science. If you want to be consoled, refreshed, and reconciled to the Kosmos, the whole from a strictly abdominal point of view, read "L'Ami Fritz," and "Les Confessions d'un Joueur de Clarinette," etc., by Erckmann-Chatrian. They are books of gold, so don't read them till you are just in the mood and all other wisdom is of no avail. Then they will open the skies to you.

On looking back over this letter I perceive I have unwittingly been betrayed into a more gloomy tone than I intended, and than would convey a faithful impression of my usual mental condition—in which occur moments of keen enjoyment. The contemplation of my letter of credit alone makes me chuckle for hours. If I ever have leisure I will write an additional Bridgewater, illustrating the Beneficence and Ingenuity, etc., in providing me with a letter of credit when so many poor devils have none. There, I have again unintentionally fallen into a vein of irony—I do not mean it. I am full of hope in the future.

My back, etc., are far better since I have been in Teplitz; in fact I feel like a new man. I have several excellent letters to people here, and when they return from the country, when T. S. Perry arrives for the winter, when the lectures get a-going, and I get thinking again, when long letters from you and the rest of my *"friends"* (ha! ha) arrive regularly at short intervals— I shall mock the state of kings. You had better believe I have thought of you with affection at intervals since I have been away, and prized your qualities of head, heart, and person, and my priceless luck in possessing your confidence and friendship in a way I never did at home; and cursed myself that I didn't make more of you when I was by you, but, like the base Indian, threw evening after evening away which I might have spent in your bosom, sitting in your whitely-lit-up room, drinking in your profound wisdom, your golden jibes, your costly imagery, listening to your shuddering laughter, baptizing myself afresh, in short, in your friendship—the thought of all this makes me even now forget your epistolary peculiarities. But pray, my dear old Wendell, let me have *one* letter from you—tell me how your law business gets on, of your adventures, thoughts, discoveries (even though but of mares' nests, they will be interesting to your Williams); books read, good stories heard, girls fallen in love with—nothing can fail to please me, except your failing to write. Please give my love to John Gray, Jim Higginson and Henry Bowditch. Tell H. B. I will write to him very soon; but that is no reason why he should not write to me without waiting, and tell me about himself and medicine in Boston. Give my very best regards also to your father, mother and sister. And believe me ever your friend,

Wm. James

P.S. Why can't you write me the result of your study of the *vis viva* question? I have not thought of it since I left. I wish very much you would, if the trouble be not too great. Anyhow you could write the central formulas without explication, and oblige yours. Excuse the scrawliness of this too hurriedly written letter.

To HENRY JAMES

Berlin, Sept. 26, 1867

BELOVED 'ARRY,—I hope you will not be severely disappointed on opening this fat envelope to find it is not all *letter*. I will first explain to you the nature of the enclosed document and then proceed to personal matters. The other day, as I was sitting alone with my deeply breached letter of credit, beweeping my outcast state, and wondering what I could possibly do for a living, it flashed across me that I might write a "notice" of H. Grimm's novel which I had just been reading. To conceive with me is to execute, as you well know. And after sweating fearfully for three days, erasing, tearing my hair, copying, recopying, etc., etc., I have just succeeded in finishing the enclosed. I want you to read it, and if, after correcting the style and thoughts, with the aid of Mother, Alice and Father, and rewriting it if possible, you judge it to be capable of interesting in any degree anyone in the world but H. Grimm, himself, to send it to the "Nation" or the "Round Table."

I feel that a living is hardly worth being gained at this price. Style is not my forte, and to strike the mean between pomposity and vulgar familiarity is indeed difficult. Still, an the rich guerdon accrue, an but ten beauteous dollars lie down on their green and glossy backs within the family treasury in consequence of my exertions, I shall feel glad that I have made them. I have not seen Grimm yet as he is in Switzerland. In his writings he is possessed of real imagination and eloquence, chiefly in an ethical line, and the novel is really *distingué*, somewhat as Cherbuliez's are, only with rather a deficiency on the physical and animal side. He is, to my taste, too idealistic, and Father would scout him for his arrant moralism. Goethe seems to have mainly suckled him, and the manner of this book is precisely that of "Wilhelm Meister" or "Elective Affinities." There is something not exactly *robust* about him, but, *per contra*, great delicacy and an extreme belief in the existence and worth of truth and desire to attain it justly and impartially. In short, a rather painstaking liberality and want of careless animal spirits —which, by the bye, seem to be rather characteristics of the rising generation. But enough of him. The notice was mere taskwork. I could not get up a spark of interest in it, and I

should not think it would be *d'actualité* for the "Nation." Still,
I could think of nothing else to do, and was bound to do something.[1]. . .

I am a new man since I have been here, both from the ruddy
hues of health which mantle on my back, and from the influence
of this live city on my spirits. Dresden was a place in which it
always seemed afternoon; and as I used to sit in my cool and
darksome room, and see through the ancient window the long
dusty sunbeams slanting past the roof angles opposite down into
the deep well of a street, and hear the distant droning of the
market and think of no reason why it should not thus continue
in secula seculorum, I used to have the same sort of feeling as
that which now comes over me when I remember days passed
in Grandma's old house in Albany. Here, on the other hand, it
is just like home. Berlin, I suppose, is the most American-look-
ing city in Europe. In the quarter which I inhabit, the streets
are all at right angles, very broad, with dusty trees growing in
them, houses all new and flat-roofed, covered with stucco, and
of every imaginable irregularity in height, bleak, ugly, unset-
tled-looking—*werdend.* Germany is, I find, as a whole (I hardly
think more experience will change my opinion), very nearly
related to our country, and the German nature and ours so
akin in fundamental qualities, that to come here is not much
of an experience. There is a general colorlessness and bleakness
about the outside look of life, and in artistic matters a wide-
spread manifestation of the very same creative spirit that designs our kerosene-lamp models, for instance, at home. Nothing
in short that is worth making a pilgrimage to see. To travel in
Italy, in Egypt, or in the Tropics, may make creation widen to

---

[1] The notice of Grimm's *Unüberwindliche Mächte* appeared under the title
"A German-American Novel" in the *Nation*, 1867; vol. v, p. 432.

one's view; but to one of our race all that is *peculiar* in Germany is mental, and *that* Germany can be brought to us. . . .

(*After dinner.*) I have just been out to dine. I am gradually getting acquainted with all the different restaurants in the neighborhood, of which there there an endless number, and will presently choose one for good,—certainly not the one where I went today, where I paid 25 *Groschen* for a soup, chicken and potatoes, and was almost prevented from breathing by the damned condescension of the waiters. I fairly sigh for a home table. I used to find a rather pleasant excitement in dining "round," that is long since played out. Could I but find some of the honest, florid and ornate ministers that wait on you at the Parker House, here, I would stick to their establishment, no matter what the fare. These indifferent reptiles here, dressed in cast-off wedding-suits, insolent and disobliging and always trying to cheat you in the change, are the plague of my life. After dinner I took quite a long walk under the Linden and round by the Palace and Museum. There are great numbers of statues (a great many of them "equestrian") here, and you have no idea how they light up the place. What you say about the change of the seasons wakens an echo in my soul. Today is really a harbinger of winter, and felt like an October day at home, with a northwest wind, cold and crisp with a white light, and the red leaves falling and blowing everywhere. I expect T. S. Perry in a week. We shall have a very good parlor and bedroom, *together*, in this house, and steer off in fine style right into the bowels of the winter. I expect it to be a stiff one, as everyone speaks of it here with a certain solemnity. . . .

I wish you would articulately display to me in your future letters the names of all the books you have been reading. "A great many books, none but good ones," is provokingly vague. On looking back at what *I* have read since I left home, it shows exceeding small, owing in great part I suppose to its being in German. I have just got settled down again—after a nearly-two-months' debauch on French fiction, during which time Mrs. Sand, the fresh, the bright, the free; the somewhat shrill but doughty Balzac, who has risen considerably in my esteem or rather in my affection; Théophile Gautier the good, the golden-mouthed, in turn captivated my attention; not to speak of the peerless Erckmann-Chatrian, who renews one's belief in the succulent harmonies of creation—and a host of others. I lately read Diderot, "Œuvres Choisies," 2 vols., which are entertaining to the utmost from their animal spirits and the comic modes of thinking, speaking and behaving of the time. Think of meeting continually such delicious sentences as this,—he is speaking of the educability of beasts,—"Et peut on savoir jusqu'ou l'usage des mains porterait les singes s'ils avaient le loisir comme la faculté d'inventer, et si la frayeur continuelle que leur inspirent les hommes ne les retenait dans l'abrutissement"!!! But I must pull up, as I have to write to Father still. . . .

Adieu, lots of love from your aff.

Wilhelm

To HIS SISTER, ALICE

Berlin, Oct. 17, 1867

Your excellent long letter of September 5 reached me in due time. If about that time you felt yourself strongly hugged by some invisible spiritual agency, you may now know it was *me*. What would not I give if you could pay me a visit here! Since I last wrote home the lingual Rubicon has been passed, and I find to my surprise that I can speak German—certainly not in an ornamental manner, but there is hardly anything which I would not dare to attempt to *begin* to say and be pretty sure that a kind providence would pull me through, somehow or other. I made the discovery at my first visit to Grimm a fortnight ago, and have confirmed it several times since. I can likewise understand educated people perfectly. I feel my German as old Moses uses to feel his oats, and for ten days past have walked along the street dandling my head in a fatuous manner that rivets the attention of the public. The University lectures were to have begun this week, but the lazy professors have put it off to the last of the month.

I will describe to you the manner in which I spent yesterday. *Ex uno disce omnes*—(a German proverb). I awoke at half-past eight at the manly voice of T. S. Perry caroling his morning hymn from his neighboring bed—if the instrument of torture the Germans sleep in be worthy of that name. After some preliminary conversation we arose, performed our washing, each in a couple of tumblers full of water in a little basin of this shape [sketch], donned our clothes, and stepped into our SALON into which the morning sun was streaming and adding its genial warmth to that of the great porcelain stove, into which the maid had put the handful of fuel (which, when ignited, makes the stove radiate heat for twelve hours) the while we slumbered. T. S. P. found on the table a letter from [Moorfield] Storey, which the same vigilant maid had placed there, and I the morning paper, full of excitement about the Italian affairs and the diabolical designs of Napoleon on Germany. After a breakfast of cocoa, eggs and excellent rolls, I finished the paper, and then took up my regular reading, while T. S. P. worked at his German lesson. I finished the chapter in a treatise on Galvanism which bears the neat and concise title of [*not deciphered*].

By 10 o'clock T. S. P. had gone to his German lesson, and it was about time for me to rig up to go to Grimm's to dine, having received a kind invitation the day before. As I passed through the pleasant wood called the "Thiergarten," which was filled with gay civil and military cavaliers, I looked hard for the imposing equestrian figure of the Hon. Geo. Bancroft; but he was not to be seen. I got safely to Grimm's, and in a moment the other guest arrived. Herr Professor ——, whose name I could not catch,[1] a man of a type I have never met before. He is writing now a life of Schleiermacher of which one volume is published. A soft fat man with black hair (somewhat the type of the photographs of Renan), of a totally uncertain age between 25 and 40, with little bits of green eyes swimming in their fat-filled orbits, and the rest of his face quite "realizing one's idea" of the infant Bacchus. I, with my usual want of enterprise, have neglected hitherto to provide myself with a swallow-tailed coat; but I had a resplendent fresh-biled shirt and collar, while the Professor, who wore the "obligatory coat," etc., had an exceedingly grimy shirt and collar and a rusty old rag of a cravat. Which of us most violated the proprieties I know not, but your feminine nature will decide. Grimm wore a yellowish, greenish, brownish coat whose big collar and cuffs and enormous flaps made me strongly suspect it had been the property of the brothers Grimm, who had worn it on state occasions, and dying, bequeathed it to Herman. The dinner was very good. The Prof. was overflowing with information with regard to everything knowable and unknowable. He is the first man I have ever met of a class, which must be common here, of men to whom learning has become as natural as breathing. A learned man at home is in a measure isolated; his study is carried on in private, at reserved hours. To the public he appears as a citizen and neighbor, etc., and they know at most *about* him that he is addicted to this or that study; his intellectual occupation always has something of a put-on character, and remains external at least

1 The Herr Professor was later identified as W. Dilthey.

to some part of his being. Whereas this cuss seemed to me to be nothing if not a professor . . . [*line not deciphered*] as if he were able to stand towards the rest of society *merely* in the relation of a man learned in this or that branch—and never for a moment forget the interests or put off the instincts of his specialty. If he should meet people or circumstances that could in no measure be dealt with on that ground, he would pass on and ignore them, instead of being obliged, like an American, to sink for the time the specialty. He talked and laughed incessantly at table, related the whole history of Buddhism to Mrs. Grimm, and I know not what other points of religious history. After dinner Mrs. Grimm went, at the suggestion of her husband, to take a nap . . . [*line not deciphered*] while G. and the Professor engaged in a hot controversy about the natural primitive forms of religion, Grimm inclining to the view that the historically first form must have been monotheistic. I noticed the Professor's replies grow rather languid, when suddenly his fat head dropped forward, and G. cried out that he had better take a good square nap in the arm-chair. He eagerly snatched at the proposal. Grimm got him a clean handkerchief, which he threw over his face, and presently he seemed to slumber. Grimm woke him in ten minutes to take some coffee. He rose, refreshed like a giant, and proceeded to fight with Grimm about the identity of Homer. Grimm has just been studying the question and thinks that the poems of Homer *must* have been composed in a *written* language. From there through a discussion about the madness of Hamlet—G. being convinced that Shakespeare *meant* to mystify the reader, and intentionally constructed a riddle. The sun waned low and I took my leave in company with the Prof. We parted at the corner, *without* the Prof. telling me (as an honest, hospitable American would have done) that he would be happy to see me at his domicile, so that I knew not whether I shall be able to continue acquainted with a man I would fain know more of.

I got into a droschke and, coming home, found T. S. P. in the room, and while telling him of the events of the dinner was interrupted by the entrance of the Rev. H. W. Foote of Stone Chapel. . . . The excellent little man had presented himself a few evenings before, bringing me from Dresden a very characteristic note from Elizabeth Peabody (in which among other things she says she is "on the wing for Italy"—she is as *folâtre* a creature as your friend Mrs. W——), and we have dined together every day since, and had agreed to go to hear "Fidelio" together at the Opera that evening. Foote is really a good man and I shall prosecute his friendship every moment of his stay here; seems to have his mind open to every interest, and has a sweet modesty that endears him to the heart. He goes home next month. I advise Harry to call and see him; I know he will sympathize with him. T. S. P. never grows weary of repeating a pun of Ware's about him in Italy, who, when asked what had become of Foote (they traveled for a time together), replied: "I left him at the Hotel, hand in glove with the Bootts."

"Fidelio" was truly musical. After it, I went to Zennig's restaurant (it was over by a quarter before nine), where I had made a rendez-vous with a young Doctor to whom Mr. Thies had given me a letter. Having been away from Berlin, I had seen him for the first time the day before yesterday. He is a very swell young Jew with a gorgeous cravat, blue-black whiskers and oily ringlets, not prepossessing; and we had made this appointment. I waited half an hour and, the faithless Israelite not appearing, came home, and after reading a few hours went to bed.

Two hours later. I have just come in from dinner, a ceremony which I perform at the aforesaid Zennig's, Unter den Linden.

(By the bye, you must not be led by that name to imagine, as I always used to, an avenue overshadowed by patriarchal lime trees, whose branches form a long arch. The "Linden" are two rows of small, scrubby, abortive horse-chestnuts, beeches, limes and others, planted like the trees in Commonwealth Avenue.) Zennig's is a table-d'hôte, so-called notwithstanding the unities of hour and table are violated. You have soup, three courses, and dessert or coffee and cheese for 12½ Groschen if you buy 14 tickets, and I shall probably dine there all winter. We dined with Foote today, who spoke among other things of a new English novel whose heroine "had the bust and arms of the Venus of Milo." T. S. P. remarked that her having the arms might account for the Venus herself being without them.

I enclose you the photograph of an actress here with whom I am in love. A neat coiffure, is it not? I also send you a couple more of my own precious portraits. I got them taken to fulfill a promise I had made to a young Bohemian lady at Teplitz, the niece of the landlady. Sweet Anna Adamowiz! (pronounce—*vitch*), which means descendant of Adam.—She belongs consequently to one of the very first families in Bohemia. I used to drive dull care away by writing her short notes in the Bohemian tongue such as; "Navzdy budes v me mysli Irohm pamatkou," *i.e.*, forever bloomest thou in my memory;—"dej mne tooji bodo biznu," give me your photograph; and isolated phrases as "Mlaxik, Dicka, pritel, pritelkyne," *i.e.*, Jüngling, Mädchen, Freund, Freundinn; "mi luja," I love, etc. These were carried to her by the chambermaid, and the style, a little more florid than was absolutely *required* by mere courtesy, was excused by her on the ground of my limited acquaintance with the subtleties of the language. Besides, the sentiments were on the whole good and the error, if any, in the right direction. When she gave me her photograph (which I regret to say she spelt

[44]

"fotokraft"!!!!) she made me promise to send her mine. *Hence* mine.

I have been this afternoon to get a dress-coat measured, which will doubtless be a comfort to you to know. I must now stop. G—

I had got as far as the above G when the faithless Israelite of yesterday evening came in. He gave a satisfactory explanation of his absence and has been making a very pleasant visit. He is coming back at nine o'clock to take us (after the German mode of exercising hospitality) to a tavern to meet some of his boon companions. I reckon he is a better fellow than he seemed at first sight. I will leave this letter open till tomorrow to let you know what happens at the tavern, and whether the boon companions are old-clothes men, or Christian gentlemen. Goodnight, my darling sister! Sei tausend mal von mir geküsst. Give my best love to Father, Mother, Aunt Kate, the boys and everyone. Ever yr. loving bro.,

Wm. James

11 P.M. Decidedly the Jew rises in my estimation. He treated us in the German fashion to a veal cutlet and a glass of beer which we paid for ourselves. His boon companions were apparently Christians of a half-baked sort. One who sat next to me was half drunk [and] insisted on talking the most hideous English. T. S. P., who necessarily took small part in the conversation, endeavored to explain to Selberg that he was a "skeleton at the banquet," but could not get through. I came to his assistance, but forgot, of course, the word "Skelett," and found nothing better to say than that he was a *vertebral column* at their banquet, which classical allusion I do not think was understood by the Jew. The young men did not behave with the

politeness and attention to us which would have been shown to two Germans by a similar crowd at home. Selberg himself however improved every minute, and I have no doubt will turn out a capital fellow. Excuse these scraps of paper,

W. J.   Good night.

To HENRY P. BOWDITCH

Berlin, Dec. 12, 1867

BESTER HEINRICH,—I have arrived safely on this side of the ocean and hasten to inform you of the fact.—What a fine pair of young men we are to write so punctually and constantly to each other!—I will not gall you by any sarcasms, however (I naturally think you are more to blame than myself), because (as you naturally are of a similar way of thinking) you might recriminate at great length in your next and much other to-me-more-agreeable matter be crowded out of your letter. Suffice [it] to say that I have thought of you continually, and with undiminished affection, since that bright April morn when we parted; but I am of such an invincibly inert nature as regards letter-writing that it takes a combination of outward and inward circumstances and motives that hardly ever happens, to start me. I wrote you a letter last summer, but destroyed it because I was in such doleful dumps while writing it that it would have given you too unpleasant an impression. . . .

I live near the University, and attend all the lectures on physiology that are given here, but am unable to do anything in the Laboratory, or to attend the cliniques or Virchow's lectures and demonstrations, etc. Du Bois-Raymond, an irascible man of about forty-five, gives a very good and clear, yea, brilliant, series of five lectures a week, and two ambitious young Jews give six more between them which are almost as instruc-

[46]

tive. The opportunities for study here are superb, it seems to me. Whatever they may be in Paris, they can*not* be better. The physiological laboratory, with its endless array of machinery, frogs, dogs, etc., etc., almost "bursts my gizzard," when I go by it, with vexation. The German language is not child's play. I have lately begun to understand almost everything I hear said around me; but I still speak "with a slight foreign accent," as you may suppose—and, with all my practice in reading, do not think I can read more than half as fast as in English. It is very discouraging to get over so little ground. But a steady boring away is bound to fetch it, I suppose; and it seems to me it is worth the trouble.

The general level of thoroughness and exactness in scientific work here is beyond praise; and the abundance of books on every division of every subject something we English have no idea of. It all comes from the thorough mode of educating the people from childhood up. The *Staats Examina*, before passing which no doctor can practise here in Prussia, exact an amount of physiological, and what we at home call "merely theoretical" knowledge of the candidate, which a young doctor at home would claim and receive especial distinction for having made himself master of. But the men here think it but fair; gird about their loins and set about working their way through. The general impression the Germans make on me is not at all that of a remarkably intellectually gifted people; and if they are not so, their eminence must come solely from their habits of conscientious and plodding work. It may be that their expressionless faces do their minds injustice. I don't know enough of them to decide. But I know the work is a large factor in the result. It makes one repine at the way he has been brought up, to come here. Unhappily most of us come too late to profit by what we see. Bad habits are formed, and life hurries us on too much to stop and drill. But it seems to me that the fact of so many American students being here of late years (they outnumber greatly all other foreign students) ought to have a good influence on the training of the succeeding generation with us. Tuck, Dwight, Dick Derby, Quincy, Townsend, and Heaven knows how many more are in Vienna. Tuck and Dwight write me that they are getting on remarkably well. I saw them both here in September and think T. D. improves a good deal as he grows older.

Berlin is a bleak and unfriendly place. The inhabitants are rude and graceless, but must conceal a solid worth beneath it. I only know seven of them, and they are of the *élite*. It is very hard getting acquainted with them, as you have to make all the advances yourself; and your antagonist shifts so between friendliness and a drill sergeant's formal politeness that you never know exactly on what footing you stand with him. These Prussians bow in the most amusing way you ever saw,—as if an invisible hand suddenly punched them in the abdomen and an equally invisible foot forthwith kicked them in the rear,—one time and two motions, and they do it 100 times a day.

But enough of national gossip—let us return to that about individuals. Oh! that I could see thy prominent nose and thy sagacious eyes at this moment relieved against the back of that empty arm-chair that stands opposite this table. Oh! that we might once again sit apart from the fretful and insipid herd of our congeners, and take counsel together concerning the world and life—our lives in particular, and all life in general. How the shy goddess would tremble in her hiding-places at the sound of our unerringly approaching voices. And how you would pour into my astonished ear all that is new and wonderful about pathology and microscopical research, all that is sound and neat about operative surgery, while I would recite the most thrilling chapters of Kolliker's "Entwickelungs-geschichte," or Helm-holtz's "Innervationsfortpflanzungsgeschwindigkeitsbestimmun-gen"! I suppose you have been rolling on like a great growing snowball through the vast fields of medical knowledge and are fairly out of the long tunnel of low spirits that leads there by this time. It is only three months since I have taken up medical reading, as I made all sorts of excursions in the language when I came here, and, owing to the slowness of progression I spoke of above, I have not got over much ground. Of course I can never hope to practise; but I shall graduate on my return, and perhaps pick up a precarious and needy living by doing work for medical periodicals or something of that kind—though I hate writing as I do the foul fiend. But I don't want to break off connexion with biological science. I can't be a teacher of physiology, pathology, or anatomy; for I can't do laboratory work, much less microscopical or anatomical. I may get better, but hardly before it will be too late for me to begin school again.

I'll tell you what let's do! Set up a partnership, you to run around and attend to the patients while I will stay at home and, reading everything imaginable in English, German, and French, distil it in a concentrated form into your mind. This division of labor will give the firm an immense advantage over all of our wooden-headed contemporaries. For, in your person, it will have more experience than any one else has time to acquire; and in mine, more learning. We will divide the profits equally, of course; and he who survives the other (you, proba-bly) will inherit the whole. Does not the idea tempt you? If you don't like it, I'll go you halves in the profits in any other feasible way. Seriously, you see I have no very definite plans for the future; but I have enough to keep body and soul together for some years to come, and I see no need of providing for more. This talk of course is only for your "private ear." I want you to write immediately on receipt of this,—for if you don't then, you never will,—and tell me all about what you've been doing and learning and what your future plans are. Also, gossip about the School and Hospital. I have not had a chance to talk medicine with any one but Dwight and Tuck (for a week), and hunger thereafter. . . . Believe me, ever til deth, your friend

Wm. James

T. S. Perry of '66, who lives with me here, reminds me of a story to tell you. He lived with Architect Ware in Paris, and Ware received a visit from Dr. Bowditch and Mr. Dixwell last summer. The concierge woman was terribly impressed by the personal majesty of your uncles, particularly of Dr. Bowditch, of whom she said: "Il a le grand air, tout à fait comme Christophe Colomb!" It would be curious to understand exactly who and what she thought C. C. was, or whether she would have thought Mr. Dixwell like Americus Vespucius if she had known *him.*

To THOMAS W. WARD

Berlin, Jan. —, 1868

My beloved old Tom,

I received your second letter December 8th, and sending to the Caitiff's Baring Bros. & Co. for your first received it in company with others, one of which had been for six months in their possession. The confidence you place in me goes to my heart. I destroyed, as you requested, your first letter; I could not help involuntarily casting about to recognize the lady you speak of, but no gleam of light dawned on me, and I conclude we are strangers to each other. The episode of your history was very interesting, though I confess much of it, from your necessarily not supplying links, was quite obscure. If you have *any* doubts as to the absolute integrity of your feelings, or see any macula *whatever* in the young female, my advice (grounded on a long and deep experience in such matters!!) is to drop the concern entirely; especially if you have at all got into a *habit* of thinking about it. I think your mother's saying a very sound one, and would refer you for another to the last lines of a poem by R. W. Emerson: "Give all to love." Damn it, Tom, a little fleck hardly visible to the naked eye at first in the being of a girl we are attracted to, ends by growing, when we are bound to her in any way, bigger than the whole world, so that it mixes with everything and nauseates it for our enjoyment. You've had a pretty valuable experience, I should think, but I imagine not an uncommon one. It has made you change one plan of life for another, and in that way may stretch its influence into your future more than otherwise it might have done. . . . It made me feel quite sad to hear you talk about the inward deadness and listlessness into which you had again fallen in New York. Bate not a jot your heart nor hope, but steer right onward. Take for granted that you've got a temperament from which you must make up your mind to expect twenty times as much anguish as other people need to get along with. Regard it as something as external to you as possible, like the curl of your hair. Remember when old December's darkness is everywhere about you, that the world is really in every minutest point as full of life as in the most joyous morning you ever lived through; that the sun is whanging down, and the waves dancing, and the gulls skimming down at the mouth of the Amazon, for instance, as freshly as in the first morning of creation; and the hour is just as fit as any hour that ever was for a new gospel of cheer to be preached. I am sure that one can, by merely thinking of these matters of fact, limit the power of one's evil moods over one's way of looking at the Kosmos.

[51]

I am very glad that you think the methodical habits you must stick to in book-keeping are going to be good discipline to you. I confess to having had a little feeling of spite when I heard you had gone back on science; for I had always thought you would one day emerge into deep and clear water there—by keeping on long enough. But I really don't think it so *all*-important what our occupation is, so long as we do respectably and keep a clean bosom. Whatever we are *not* doing is pretty sure to come to us at intervals, in the midst of our toil, and fill us with pungent regrets that it is lost to us. I have felt so about zoölogy whenever I was not studying it, about anthropology when studying physiology, about practical medicine lately, now that I am cut off from it, etc., etc., etc.; and I conclude that that sort of nostalgia is a necessary incident of our having imaginations, and we must expect it more or less whatever we are about. I don't mean to say that in some occupations we should not have less of it though.

My dear old Thomas, you have always sardonically greeted me as the man of calm and clockwork feelings. The reason is that your own vehemence and irregularity was so much greater, that it involuntarily, no matter what my private mood might have been, threw me into an outwardly antagonistic one in which I endeavored to be a clog to your mobility, as it were. So I fancy you have always given me credit for less sympathy with you and understanding of your feelings than I really have had. All last winter, for instance, when I was on the continual verge of suicide, it used to amuse me to hear you chaff my animal contentment. The appearance of it arose from my reaction against what seemed to me your unduly *noisy* and demonstrative despair. The fact is, I think, that we have both gone through a good deal of similar trouble; we resemble each other in being both persons of rather wide sympathies, not particularly logical in the processes of our minds, and of mobile temperament; though your physical temperament being so much more tremendous than mine makes a great quantitative difference both in your favor, and against you, as the case may be.

Well, neither of us wishes to be a mere loafer; each wishes a work which shall by its mere *exercise* interest him and at the same time allow him to feel that through it he takes hold of the reality of things—whatever that may be—in some measure. Now the first requisite is hard for us to fill, by reason of our wide sympathy and mobility; we can only choose a business in which the evil of feeling restless shall be at a minimum, and then go ahead and make the best of it. That minimum will grow less every year.—In this connection I will again refer to a poem you probably know: "A Grammarian's Funeral," by R. Browning, in "Men and Women." It always strengthens my backbone to read it, and I think the feeling it expresses of throwing upon eternity the responsibility of making good your one-sidedness somehow or other ("Leave *now* for dogs and apes, Man has forever") is a gallant one, and fit to be trusted if one-sided activity is in itself at all respectable.

The other requirement is hard theoretically, though practically not so hard as the first. All I can tell you is the thought that with me outlasts all others, and onto which, like a rock, I find myself washed up when the waves of doubt are weltering over all the rest of the world; and that is the thought of my having a will, and of my belonging to a brotherhood of men possessed of a capacity for pleasure and pain of different kinds. For even at one's lowest ebb of belief, the fact remains empirically certain (and by our will we can, if not *absolutely* refrain from looking beyond that empirical fact, at least practically and *on the whole* accept it and let it suffice us)—that men suffer and enjoy. And if we have to give up all hope of seeing into the

[53]

purposes of God, or to give up theoretically the idea of final causes, and of God anyhow as vain and leading to nothing for us, we can, by our will, make the enjoyment of our brothers stand us in the stead of a final cause; and through a knowledge of the fact that that enjoyment on the whole depends on what individuals accomplish, lead a life so active, and so sustained by a clean conscience as not to need to fret much. Individuals can add to the welfare of the race in a variety of ways. You may delight its senses or "taste" by some production of luxury or art, comfort it by discovering some moral truth, relieve its pain by concocting a new patent medicine, save its labor by a bit of machinery, or by some new application of a natural product. You may open a road, help start some social or business institution, contribute your mite in *any* way to the mass of the work which each generation subtracts from the task of the next; and you will come into *real* relations with your brothers—with some of them at least.

I know that in a certain point of view, and the most popular one, this seems a cold activity for our affections, a stone instead of bread. We long for sympathy, for a purely *personal* communication, first with the soul of the world, and then with the soul of our fellows. And happy are they who think, or know, that they have got them! But to those who must confess with bitter anguish that they are perfectly isolated from the soul of the world, and that the closest human love incloses a potential germ of estrangement or hatred, that all *personal* relation is finite, conditional, mixed (*vide* in Dana's "Household Book of Poetry," stanzas by C. P. Cranch, "Thought is deeper than speech," etc., etc.), it may not prove such an unfruitful substitute. At least, when you have added to the property of the race, even if no one knows your name, yet it is certain that, without what you have done, some individuals must needs be acting now in a somewhat different manner. You have modified their life; you are in *real* relation with them; you have in so far forth entered into their being. And is that such an unworthy stake to set up for our good, after all? Who are these men anyhow? Our predecessors, even apart from the physical link of generations, have made us what we are. Every thought you now have and every act and intention owes its complexion to the acts of your dead and living brothers. *Everything* we know and are is through men. We have no revelation but through man. Every sentiment that warms your gizzard, every brave act that ever made your pulse bound and your nostril open to a confident breath was a man's act. However mean a man may be, man is *the best we know;* and your loathing as you turn from what you probably call the vulgarity of human life—your homesick yearning for a *Better,* somewhere—is furnished by your manhood; your ideal is made up of traits suggested by past men's words and actions. Your manhood shuts you in forever, bounds all your thoughts like an overarching sky—and all the Good and True and High and Dear that you know by virtue of your sharing in it. They are the Natural Product of our Race. So that it seems to me that a sympathy with men as such, and a desire to contribute to the weal of a species, which, whatever may be said of it, contains All that we acknowledge as good, may very well form an external interest sufficient to keep one's moral pot boiling in a very lively manner to a good old age. The idea, in short, of becoming an accomplice in a sort of "Mankind its own God or Providence" scheme is a *practical* one.

I don't mean, by any means, to affirm that we must come to that, I only say it is *a* mode of envisaging life; which is capable of affording moral support—and may at any rate help to bridge over the despair of skeptical intervals. I confess that, in the lonesome gloom which beset me for a couple of months last summer, the only feeling that kept me from giving up was that by waiting and living, by hook or crook, long enough, I might make my *nick*, however small a one, in the raw stuff the race has got to shape, and so assert my reality. The stoic feeling of being a sentinel obeying orders without knowing the general's plans is a noble one. And so is the divine enthusiasm of moral culture (Channing, etc.), and I think that, successively, they may all help to ballast the same man.

What a preacher I'm getting to be! I had no idea when I sat down to begin this long letter that I was going to be carried away so far. I feel like a humbug whenever I endeavor to enunciate moral truths, because I am at bottom so skeptical. But I resolved to throw off *"views"* to you, because I know how stimulated you are likely to be by any accidental point of view or formula which you may not exactly have struck on before (*e.g.*, what you write me of the effect of that sentence of your mother's about marrying). I had no idea this morning that I had so many of the elements of a Pascal in me. Excuse the presumption.—But to go back. I think that in business as well as in science one can have this philanthropic aspiration satisfied. I have been growing lately to feel that a great mistake of my past life—which has been prejudicial to my education, and by telling me which, and by making me understand it some years ago, some one might have conferred a great benefit on me—is an impatience of *results*. Inexperience of life is the cause of it, and I imagine it is generally an American characteristic. I think you suffer from it. Results should not be too voluntarily aimed at or too busily thought of. They are *sure* to float up of their own accord, from a long enough daily work at a given matter; and I think the work as a mere occupation ought to be the primary interest with us. At least, I am sure this is so in the intellectual realm, and I strongly suspect it is the secret of German prowess therein. Have confidence, even when you seem to yourself to be making no progress, that, if you but go on in your own uninteresting way, they must bloom out in their good time. Ouf, my dear old Tom! I think I must pull up. I have no time or energy left to gossip to thee of our life here. . . .

To HENRY P. BOWDITCH

Teplitz, May 5, 1868

My dear Henry,—

I was very much pleased to get your letter of January 12th some time ago. I had despatched a letter to you not many days previously which I hope you have also received. I got Dr. Holmes's pamphlet with the letter, and was much obliged to you for it—it was a real treat to me. Our excellent Professor may be lacking in practical sense, and his style of writing may be heavy and dull, but for the genuine scientific *furor* he can't be beat (subtle joke). . . .

In ten days I start for Dresden, where I shall stay at least one month, and perhaps longer, trying to husband the good effects of this bathing by rest and not work them right off as I have hitherto done. Then it is most probable that I shall go to Heidelberg. I have by this time dropped all hope of doing anything at physiology, for I'm not fit for laboratory work, and even if that were not the only reputable way of cultivating the science at all (which it is), it would be for *me* with my bad memory and slack interest in the details, the only practicable way of getting any honest knowledge of the subject. I go to Heidelberg because Helmholtz is there and a man named Wundt, from whom I think I may learn something of the physiology of the senses without too great bodily exertion, and may perhaps apply the knowledge to some use afterwards. The immortal Helmholtz is such an ingrained mathematician that I suppose I shall not profit much by him. How long I stay in Heidelberg will depend on what I find I can gain there, and on the state of my back. It's a delicious place to live in, people say, although the Swabian German is laughed at by those of the North. So if you are intending to come to Germany this summer and to devote yourself first to the language, which is the common plan, you would hardly choose it for a residence. For my part, I think this universal fastidiousness on the part of Americans about hearing good German the first three months is the most ludicrous phenomenon of the 19th Century. The common people you won't understand, no matter where you are, and your own dialect is so certain to be worse than the very worst you can possibly hear from educated people, that to be particular is as absurd as for a chimney sweep to refuse to sit down because there's dust on the bench. . . .

I have been totally demoralized for more than two months past, what with sickness and weakness from these baths, and general disgust at my prospects, and have let medical science almost totally slide. I feel as if I had forgotten all I ever learned on the subject of disease and treatment, etc., since I left home, and would have to begin another three years' course of study to take my degree. For that reason would I so gladly be with you to hear you talk over your studies. But on the other hand my brain has not been totally idle, although occupied with literary matters that can't be used for anything. . . . Good-bye and good luck to you till we meet. Yours,

Wm. James

May 7

P.S. I got letters from home this morning and among them is incidentally mentioned that you have been to Florida lately.

To O. W. HOLMES, JR. [*1868*]

You will be very glad when you get here that you already have seen so much of your own country. Most Germans have read a good deal about the U. S. and have a great curiosity. I have often wished I had travelled more at home so as to be able to answer questions that have been asked me here. . . . Ever yours,

Wm. James

To O. W. HOLMES, Jr.

Dresden, May 15, 1868

My dear Wendell,—

Your unexpected letter has just burst into my existence like a meteor into the sphere of a planet, and here I go for an answer while the heat developed by the impact is at its highest. I have got so accustomed to thinking of you as not a writing animal that such an event rather dislocates my mind from its habitual "sag" in contemplating the world. I have of late been repeatedly on the point of writing to you but have paused ere slipping o'er the brink. It is easy to write people whom you have been steadily writing to, for one letter seems to continue the previous ones. But to fire off a letter point blank at a man once in six months has an arbitrary savor. There are so many things of about equal importance for you to tell him that there is no reason for you to begin with any particular one and leave off the rest. Consequently you don't begin at all. However, heaven reward you for this inspired effusion and help you to another some time. It runs through the whole circle of human energy, Shelley, Kant, Goethe, Walt Whitman, all being fused in the unity of your fiery personality. Were I only in the vein, O! friend, I would answer in the same high strain, but today I grovel in prose. That you firmly embrace like a *Bothriocephalus latus* the very bowels of the law and grapple them to your soul with hooks of steel, is

good. That the miasmas thence arising do not forever hide the
blue Jove above, is better. I am firmly convinced that by going
straight in almost any direction you can get out of the woods
in which the young mind grows up, for I have an idea that the
process usually consists of a more or less forcible reduction of
the other elements of the chaos to a harmony with the terms
of the one on which one has taken his particular stand. I think
I might have fought it out on the line of practical medicine
quite well. Your image of the ideals being vanishing points
which give a kind of perspective to the chaos of events, tickleth
that organ within me whose function it is to dally with the in-
effable. I shall not fail to remember it, and if I stay long enough
in Germany to make the acquaintance of ary a philosopher, I
shall get it off as my own, you bet!

Your letter last winter I got and acknowledged on the cover
of one I had just written you. Your criticism of Kant seems
perfectly sound to me. I hoped to have got at him before now
but have been interfered with. I have read only his *Prolego-
mena* and his little *Anthropology* (a marvellous, biting little
work), and Cousin's exposé of him (and of himself at the same
time, darn him and the likes of him!—he is a mere politician).
I hope soon to begin with the *Kritik*, for which I feel myself
now quite prepared. And I reserve any half-ripe remarks I may
have made on Kant till after that is done. I think a good five
hours' talk with you would probably do me more good than
almost any other experience I can conceive of. I have not had
any contact out of books with any soul possessed of *reason* since
I left home, except, perhaps, Grimm—and I did not, owing to
the linguistic wall between us, succeed in putting myself into
communication with him. And in personal contact, Wendell,
lies a deep dark power. I say "reason," but I have no idea what
the thing is. I have slipped so gradually out of sight of it in

people that I did not know any particular thing was gone, till the day before yesterday I made the acquaintance of a young female from New York who is here in the house, and suddenly noticed that an old long-forgotten element was present (I mean in her way of accepting the world). It has been a beneficent discovery, and the suddenness and quasi-definiteness of it almost shatters one's empirical philosophy. But probably it, too, may be resolved into other more vulgar elements.

The fact is, my dear boy, that I feel more as if you were my ally against what you call "the common enemy" than anyone I know. As I am writing a grave statement of facts and not an effusion of friendliness, I may say that Tom Ward seems to me to have as great an intuition of the length and breadth of the enemy (which is the place in which most people fail), and perhaps a greater animal passion in his feeling about it, but poor Tom is so deficient in power of orderly thought that intercourse with him hardly ever bears fruit. With Harry and my Dad I have a perfect sympathy "personally," but Harry's orbit and mine coincide but part way, and Father's and mine hardly at all, except in a general feeling of philanthropy in which we both indulge. I have no idea that the particular point of view from which we spy the fiendish enemy has *per se* any merit over that of lots of other men. Such an opinion we recognize in other people as "conceit." But merely because it is common to both of us, I have an esteem for you which is *tout particulier,* and value intercourse with you. You have a far more logical and orderly mode of thinking than I (I stand between you and T. Ward), and whenever we have been together I have somehow been conscious of a reaction against the ascendancy of this over my ruder processes—a reaction caused by some subtle deviltry of egotism and jealousy, whose causes are untraceable by myself, but through whose agency I put myself involuntarily into a position of self-defense, as if you threatened to overrun my territory and injure my own proprietorship. I don't know whether you ever noticed any such thing,—it is hard to define the subtleness of it. *Some* of it may have been caused by the feeling of a too "cosmo-centric" consciousness in you. But most of it was pure meanness. I *guess* that were we to meet now I should be less troubled with it. I have grown into the belief that friendship (including the highest half of that which between the two sexes is united under the single name of love) is about the highest joy of earth, and that a man's rank in the general scale is well indicated by his capacity for it. So much established, I will try in a few brief strokes to define my present condition to you. If asked the question which all men who pretend to know themselves ought to be able to answer, but which few probably could offhand,—"What reason can you give for continuing to live? What ground allege why the thread of your days should not be snapped *now*?"

May 18th. Wendell of my entrails! At the momentous point where the last sheet ends I was interrupted by the buxom maid calling to tea and through various causes have not got back till now. As I sit by the open window waiting for my breakfast and look out on the line of *Droschkes* drawn up on the side of the Dohna Platz, and see the coachmen, red-faced, red-collared, and blue-coated, with varnished hats, sitting in a variety of indolent attitudes upon their boxes, one of them looking in upon me and probably wondering what the devil I am,—when I see the big sky with a monstrous white cloud battening and bulging up from behind the houses into the blue, with a uniform copper film drawn over cloud and blue, which makes ones anticipate a soaking day—when I see the houses opposite with their balconies and windows filled with flowers and greenery—Ha! on the topmost balcony of one stands a maiden, black-jacketed, red-

petticoated, fair and slim under the striped awning, leaning
her elbow on the rail and her peach-like chin upon her rosy
finger tips! Of whom thinkest thou, maiden, up there aloft?
Here, *here!* beats that human heart for which in the drunken-
ness of the morning hour thy being vaguely longs, and tremu-
lously, but recklessly and wickedly, posits elsewhere, over those
distant housetops which thou regardest. Out of another window
hangs the form, seen from behind and centre of gravity downwards, of an intrepid servant girl, washing the window. Blue
frocked is she, and like a spider fast holding to his thread, or
one that gathers samphires on a dizzy promontory, she braves
the danger of a fall. Against the lamp-post leans the *Dienstman*
or *commissionaire*, cross-legged and with tin-badged cap, smok-
ing his cheap morning cigar. Far over the *Platz* toils the big
country wagon with high-collared horses, and the still pavement
rings with the shuffling feet of broad-backed wenches carrying
baskets, and of short-necked, wide-faced men. The day has in
fact begun, and when I see all this and think that at the same
moment thou art probably in a dead sleep whirled round
through the black night with rocks and trees and monuments
like an inanimate thing, when I think all this, I feel—*how?*—
I give it up myself? After this interruption, which on the ground
of local color and my half-awake condition you will excuse, I
return to the former subject. But here's the breakfast! Excuse
me! Man eats in Germany a very light breakfast, chocolate and
dry bread, so it won't take me long.

'T is done, and a more genial glow than ever fills my system.
Having read over what I wrote the day before yesterday I feel
tempted not to send it, for I cannot help thinking it does not
represent with perfect sincerity the state of the case. Still, if I
do not write to you now, it may postpone itself a good while,
and I let it go for the general spirit which animates it rather

than for the particular propositions it contains. The point which seems to me unwarranted was my assumption of any special battle I was fighting against the powers of darkness, and of your being allied with me therein as the ground of my esteem for you. The truth is painfully evident to me that I am but little interested in any particular battle or movement of progress, and the ground of my friendship for you is more a sort of physical relish for your wit and wisdom, and passive enjoyment of the entertainment they afford, than anything else. Much would I give for a constructive passion of some kind. As it is, I am in great measure in the hands of Chance. Your metaphysical industry and the artistic satisfaction you take in the exercise of it, gives you an immeasurable advantage. In the past year if I have learned little else, I have at least learned a good deal that I previously did not suspect about the limits of my own mind. They are not exhilarating. I will not annoy you by going into the details, but they all conspire to give my thoughts a vague emptiness wherever feeling is, and to drive feeling out wherever the thought becomes good for anything. Bah! My answer to the question I asked at the end of sheet two would be vague indeed; it would vary between the allegation of a dogged desire to assert myself at certain times, and the undermined hope of making *some* nick, however minute, in the pile which humanity is fashioning, at others. Of course I would beg for a *temporary* respite from the inevitable shears, for different reasons at different times. If a *particular* and passionate reason for wishing to live for four hours longer were *always* forthcoming, I should think myself a very remarkable man, and be quite satisfied. But in the intervals of absence of such a reason, I could wish that my general grounds are more defined than they are. . . .

I am tending strongly to an empiristic view of life. I don't know how far it will carry me, or what rocks insoluble by it

will block my future path. Already I see an ontological cloud
of absolute idealism waiting for me far off on the horizon, but
I have no passion for the fray. I shall continue to apply empirical principles to my experiences as I go on and see how
much they fit. One thing makes me uneasy. *If* the end of all is
to be that we must take our sensations as simply given or as
preserved by natural selection for us, and interpret this rich
and delicate overgrowth of ideas, moral, artistic, religious and
social, as a mere mask, a tissue spun in happy hours by creative
individuals and adopted by other men in the interests of their
sensations,—how long is it going to be well for us not to "let
on" all we know to the public? How long are we to indulge the
"people" in their theological and other vagaries so long as such
vagaries seem to us more beneficial on the whole than otherwise? How long are we to wear that uncomfortable "air of
suppression" which has been complained of in Mr. Mill? Can
any men be trusted to dole out from moment to moment just
that measure of a doctrine which is consistent with utility? I
know that the brightest jewel in the crown of Utilitarianism is
that every notion hatched by the human mind receives justice
and tolerance at its hands. But I know that no mind can trace
the far ramifications of an idea in the mind of the public; and
that any idea is at a disadvantage which cannot enlist in its favor
the thirst for conquest, the love of absoluteness, that have
helped to found religions; and which cannot open a *definite*
channel for human sympathies and affections to flow in. It
seems exceedingly improbable that any new *religious* genius
should arise in these days to open a fresh highway for the masses
who have outgrown the old beliefs. Now ought not we (supposing we become indurated sensationalists) to begin to smite the
old, hip and thigh, and get, if possible, a little enthusiasm
associated with our doctrines? If God is dead or at least irrele-

vant, ditto everything pertaining to the "Beyond." If happiness is our Good, ought we not to try to foment a passionate and bold will to attain that happiness among the multitudes? Can we not conduct off upon our purposes from the old moralities and theologies a beam which will invest us with some of the proud absoluteness which made them so venerable, by preaching the doctrine that Man is his own Providence, and every individual a real God to his race, greater or less in proportion to his gifts and the way he uses them? The sentiment of philanthropy is now so firmly established and apparently its permanence so guaranteed by its beneficent nature, that it would be bold to say it could not take its place as an ultimate motive for human action. I feel no *confidence* (even apart from my doubts as to the theoretical finality of "sensationalism") that society is as yet ripe for it as a popular philosophy and religion combined, but as I said above, no one can measure the effects of an idea, or distribute exactly the shares which different ideas have in our present social order. And certainly there is something disheartening in the position of an esoteric philosopher. The conscientious prudence which would wish to educate mankind gradually instead of throwing out the line, and letting it educate itself, may be both presumptuous and timid. Do you take? I only throw out these as doubts, and would like to know whether you have been troubled by any similar ones on the matter of policy. The breath of my nostrils is doubt, and that is what makes me so the slave of chance. . . .

I have been reading lately in Teplitz in Schiller and Goethe. The possession of those two men's lives and works by a people gives them a great advantage over neighboring nations. Goethe at last has shot into distinct individual shape for me, which is a great relief, and an enormous figure he is. . . . I am sensible to your expression of sympathy with my stove-in condition of

back. I shall *endeavor* (by jerks) to keep the upper lip rigid even
if the vertebral column yields. An account of a man in a
western settlement which I heard from a traveler on the ship
coming over has afforded me much satisfaction ever since, and
served as a good example. The traveler stopped at a grocery
store to get some whiskey, and alarmed at the woebegone appearance of the storekeeper, asked him what was the matter.
"Do you see that man sitting in the back shop?" said the other.
"He's the sheriff, and has attached all my goods." He then
went on to tell his other misfortunes, ending with the story of
his wife having run away the day before with another man, but
presently wiped his eyes, and with a smile of sweet recollection
said: "I don't know, though, as I have any right to complain—
I've done pretty well on the whole since I came to this settlement." Comment is needless.

There, my dear boy, I hope you have not begun to thank
your stars I don't write oftener, since I write at such lengths.
I wanted to give you a report of my mental condition, I have
done so more or less, and trust you will respect the affection
and confidence which dictated it. I'd rather my father should
not see it. Use your own judgment about showing it to Harry.
I leave here in a month or so for Heidelberg. Get my address
from Harry whenever you write. And for God's sake do so
again before too long. I got a letter in Teplitz from Miss Fanny
Dixwell which was a great godsend. Please remember me to all
your family, and believe me thy friend

                                                    Wm. James

To THOMAS W. WARD

2 Dohna Platz, parterre.
Dresden, May 24, 1868.

My well beloved Tom,—

I got your short letter in February last while I was at Teplitz.
I could have wished it longer, and of more cheerful contents,
but whatever they may be, your letters are welcome. I have
been several times on the point of writing to you, but have
always waited in the desperate hope that a few days later I
might have some important discovery on the problem of life
to communicate. I have no such thing now and never will have
perhaps—but as you find hints in all sorts of unlikely places,
and I am in the dark entirely as to your own particular industry
at this moment I will briefly tell you what has happened to me
since my last letter. In January, finding the activity of Berlin
was hurting my back, I escaped to Teplitz, took a severe course
of treatment combined with "faradization" for a month and
found myself so much the worse for it that I judged it prudent
to stay another month before coming away. I then spent a
month at Dresden and got as well as I was before leaving Berlin, then went back again to Teplitz to risk a mild course, and
finally have been back here again for two weeks. The effects of
the "mild course" are dubious, but I am going to keep rigidly
still for a couple of months and give the damned old muscles
a fair chance. When I was last here I hurt myself by running
about too much in the Picture Gallery, being in a frantic and
insatiable mood of mind generated by eight mortal sick weeks
cooped up in a house in a Bohemian village in winter. I have
now given up all idea of ever doing anything at physiology, and
for the last two months my mind has been off the tolerably
steady mechanical track in which I had succeeded in keeping it

in Berlin. Consequence: dissatisfaction and general listlessness and skepticism, with however a few random gleams of light that would not have met me if I had kept on reading physiology. First of these is a better insight into that which makes the Greek things so peculiar to us. I looked at the casts here in the museum and read a great part of Homer (in Dutch) over again. Second. The beginning of a real acquaintance with Goethe as an Individual, and the acquaintance of Schiller. Third. The friendship of a young American lady here in the house, who has stirred chords in this desiccated heart which I long thought had turned to dust.—To begin with no. 3. First let me disclaim sincerely anything like flirtation. I soar in a region above that, I think. The young woman is a prey to her nerves and is in a sort of hysterical hypochondriac state, but her mind is perfectly free from sentimentality and disorder of any sort—and she has really genius for music. I never heard a piano speak as she makes it. Now what is beautiful and so to speak absolute and finished about her has struck into me so deeply as quite to rejuvenate my feeeling. I am naturally almost as skeptical as you and not having come into contact for the past year with any living human Reason, had sunk ever deeper into the drifting slough of indifference and disrespect for individual manifestations of life which seem to me to be the Devil's own drug with which he benumbs our souls before catching them. Now to the phenomena of this young lady—my eyes happened not to be clogged and blurred as they were to almost all other phenomena —for I reckon that every phenomenon can be seen, if the sight is sound, hanging by some sort of a navel-string to the Infinite womb. And I was seized, as I saw an absoluteness in the phenomena of this young person, (a something whereby their place in the phenomenal series of which they were members seemed *not* to exhaust their significance,) with a horror of the hideous waste of life that I was wallowing in. "Life is *such*! And what have *I* been making it? About! my heart, my brain. This *Auseinandersetzen* of the every day occurrence of a man having his soul aroused and inspired at the sight of the good, true, or beautiful, may amuse you. But it is nevertheless a goodly experience. The only trouble is that the reverberation dies away so soon in the soul and the bag closes around one again. Nothing is so efficacious as the actual sensible intuition of these portions of the unveiled absolute. (Pardon my rude phraseology.) But when the young lady goes away (in a week) and I probably see her in this life no more, I shall try to kick and spur my sluggish senses by contemplating the lives of Schiller and Goethe, which brings me to my second point. I am just beginning to break through to the skin of Goethe's personality and to grasp it as an unity. Hitherto he has always annoyed me by apparent contradictions, such as a want of humor and (absurd as it may sound) a want of *intuition* in aesthetical things and in the matter of personal character. The tedious clinging to minute details of apparently no essential importance que tu as du remarquer chez lui pour peu que tu l'aies lu, une certaine *conscientiousness* pénible et terre à terre dans sa manière de rendre compte des choses, comme un homme qui n'a pas le don de pénétrer du premier coup d'oeil au coeur du sujet, qui a pourtant peur de rien perdre qui soit bon, et qui ramasse tout, l'essentiel et l'insignifiant en un seul et même faisceau. Cette impression qu'il m'avait faite s'est dernièrement complètement évanouie sans que je puis m'en rendre un compte exact de la manière dont cela est arrivé. He *is* a perfect natural born *collector*, as much as Agassiz, and he does hate to lose *anything* in creation—but he has the intelligent glance none the less which takes no time to discern the relative values of the different planes of being, and when he gives you chaff, it is only

[70]

thrown in extra out of his superabundance. The man lived at every pore of his skin, and the tranquil clearness and vividness with which *every* thing printed itself on his sensorium, and found a cool nook in his mind without interfering with any of the other denizens thereof, must have been one of the most exquisite spectacles ever on exhibition on this planet. Apart from that general and undefined refreshment and encouragement which accrue to us from the sight of great resources and possibilities in human nature of any kind, I have drawn from Goethe a special lesson lately which is not easy for me to define in black and white but which may be called a lesson of theoretical patience and respect towards the Objective. Contrasted with the attention he vouchsaved to every phenomenon that impinged upon his senses, with the deep and worthy stillness in which every voice of Nature seemed to be listened to by his soul, *our* petulance and worry, our love of taking short cuts to the truth, making quick generalizations, our resorting to "summary" views of the great outspread Universe seem trivial and frivolous, to say the least, and the partiality and disrespect which almost all of us show towards *some* department of Experience, our rooted habit of not being able to raise x in our estimation except by lowering y, of "setting off" one thing *against* another in our judgments seem low traits. Goethe of course had his task made easy for him by the unexampled perfection of his faculties, by the undistractedness with which his attention could turn itself to every thing in turn and the smoothness with which all his mental processes worked. But over and above these natural gifts he had a deep belief in the reality of Nature as she lies developed and a contempt for bodyless formulas. Through every individual fact he came in contact with the world and he strove and fought without ceasing ever to lay his mind more and more wide open to Nature's teaching—more

[71]

and more to efface those subjective wrinkles in which we all force the objective matter Nature gives us to lie in our minds. The judging of things by a subjective standard which we all are born with he seems to have hated as if it were the very brand of original sin within us. Of course his Natural gifts cannot be communicated to the reader but this enthusiasm can in some measure, and I think that the glimpse of it I have got in reading his *Wilhelm Meister* again, and especially his 'Annalen" (a sort of autobiography of his later years) and some other things I cannot signalize, is one of the important experiences of my own mind.—Of course, an optimistic faith lies at the bottom of it; but if one can set out with the supposition of Harmony among phenomena as the *summum bonum* and look upon the world as a progressive development, I don't know whether such a faith be not the best. It seems to be so practically at any rate. And if the philosophy of Mill, Bain, etc., ever becomes victorious a terrestrial harmony *must* become our summum bonum. Perhaps a new simple and classical era may so be inaugurated for us after the fever of the Christian and barbarous period. This brings me to point one. I remember your saying on the ship coming from Parà after reading that little book, *du Polythéisme*, that the characteristic of the Greek "Weltanschauung" was its optimism. And since then it seems to me more and more to have been a deep-reaching remark. This world in so far forth as it stood was good to them. Evil was synonymous with perishability. And the peculiarity to us of the Greek attitude is that it accepted these two hostile elements of creation as simply given, without feeling that unquenchable desire to reconcile them which we barbarians are beset with. We seek in some way to "get around" the contradiction between good and evil, and to fuse them both in some higher unity. The naïve natural good of the Greek is not *the*

[72]

good, but holds a subtle poison—the justness of the just man is not a final fact as it was for the Greeks, but, under the name of self-righteousness or what not, merely throws open an endless realm of evil more subtle and strong than that of the senses. And so the evil of the senses is not *the* evil for us. Altogether the wiping out of border lines, the fantastic creations and devices which are made necessary as soon as men refuse to accept the two elements in their primitive contradictory shape, introduce the confusion, the irony, the sickliness and general absence of distinctness which separate us from the Greeks. You will be able to furnish examples of the difference in detail for yourself.—I think you will understand and agree with what I have said about the Greeks with very little trouble. I don't know whether I have expressed myself so clearly with regard to Goethe, but it is hard to define such a broad way of looking at that so as to make it intelligible. One must see it work in details. For my own part I do not feel like giving adhesion to the whole of what I understand Goethe's philosophy to be, any more than I feel like rejecting it. I merely feel far better than hitherto what a respectable rationality it has—and how eminent its claims will be if it is ever decided that our standpoint for contemplating the World must always be more or less of a *parti-pris.* I have grown up partly from education and the example of my Dad, partly I think from a natural tendency in a very non-optimistic view of Nature, going so far as to have some years ago a perfectly passionate aversion to all moral praise etc., etc.,—an anti-nomian tendency in short. I have regarded the affairs of human life to be only a phantasmagoria, which had to be *interpreted* elsewhere in the Kosmos into its real significance. But of late the sturdy realism of Goethe and the obdurate beauty and charm of the Greeks have shaken my complexion more than anything else. If we can only bring

[73]

ourselves to accept evil as an ultimate inscrutable fact, the way may be open towards a great practical reform on earth, as our aims will be clearly defined, and our energies concentrated. But enough of this rather windy speculation. I have written it to thee, Thomas, because nothing else occurred to me fit for thy perusal. I should like to know very much what you are busying yourself with now, and if the clouds are breaking about you. Whatever happens my dear Tom, keep a stiff upper lip, and don't drop that courage . . . in pursuit of the Best that you have always shown, and by which you have so often sent me away with a fresh fire in my gizzard and determination in my breast. The longer I live it seems to me the more worthily I think of personal good qualities whether they be immediately successful or not. I think your demands of the Universe are wider than those of anyone I know, and I hope to Heaven you'll hang on like grim Death to the end. Happiness is an outside consideration. I feel *certain* looking at you as I do from without and comparing you with others, that if you go on in *any* line of life, bringing your other requirements as much as possible into harmony with those which it comports, that you will reach solid ground some day and at any rate deal with the "realities" in some manner, which is after all enough to satisfy one.—I am going to stay on here as long as I can stand it for the sake of resting my back. Probably in six weeks I shall go to Heidelberg; and it is likely that I stay there all winter studying Psychology in some shape or other. I don't know now exactly what practical use I can put it to, but something may turn up. I feel a sort of confidence in these thick Germans, in their honesty and earnestness at a [not decipherable].

May 26. Yesterday afternoon at this point I was interrupted by a message from the young lady who was going a-driving, and asked if I'd like to go along. I naturally accepted. The young

Lady has many foibles—but the spirit of Goethe which still reëchoes through my being forbids any impatient rejection of a whole on account of defectiveness in the parts. Grapple to your soul with hooks of steel all the good points, and with patience and enduring courage gradually mould and forge the rest into harmony with them. Thus is nought wasted in the world. As for me I shall never give up the young lady.

Young Thies came in last night bringing me Mrs. Agassiz's book which he had borrowed for me from the dentist. I looked through it for an hour or so, and was very much pleased, having expected to find it bulkier and duller. I think much more might have been made of it though. She can't describe landscape, or in fact anything worth a damn. I shall proceed to read the scientific part with care. But I feel humiliated at the weakness of my memory. So many of those fish names which were so familiar to me call up no image of what they represent now. And altogether a queer atmosphere rises from the book. The nostalgic way in which I have so often thought of Brazil, is replaced by a feeling of loneliness and intellectual and moral deadness that makes me feel as if I did not want to go there again, as I read. This is unexpected and I can't trace the cause of it. The fact is there was plenty to justify both modes of feeling in the experience of all of us.—But this letter is getting too long, and besides it must be posted within an hour. I wish, my dear Tom, you would write to me, even if it is an effort and you have to re-write your letter twice. It will do you good to try to "define your position" whatever it may be, and in this breast beats a heart which thou knowest to be ever responsive. Your last short letter made me feel sad. For heavens sake don't give up the fight *even if you are getting licked*. If you go to Boston, I wish you would try to get in with Wendell Holmes— I'm pretty sure when you get to understand each other you will like each other. You and he are my best friends so far, and he has heard me talk a great deal about you. He is particularly alive to everyone's good points especially the various degrees of excellence and expression with which one reacts against the mystery of the Kosmos, and you will each profit by the other's experience and ideas.—I have written a few book noices lately, to earn a few dollars—two or three in the *Nation* of no account. In the next *North American Review* will probably be two, one of Darwin's new book, one of Bernard's *Report on Physiology*. In the *Atlantic* . . . one of Darwin, which I sent to the *Nation* but was forestalled. I sent the other day a notice of a book on Sleep by one Liébault to Dr. Hammond's Quarterly, but doubt if he will print it. I tell you of these not because they contain anything of interest that you don't know but because it seems fraternal to let you know what I'm about. Adieu, my dear Tom. Pray write soon. Address here; if I'm gone, it will be sent to me. Remember me to your family and believe me ever your affectionate friend

Wm. James

To O. W. HOLMES, JR., AND JOHN C. GRAY, JR.

[*Winter of 1868-69.*]

Gents!—entry-thieves—chevaliers d'industrie—well-dressed swindlers—confidence men—wolves in sheep's clothing—asses in lion's skin—gentlemanly pickpockets—beware! The hand of the law is already on your throats and waits but a wink to be tightened. All the resources of the immensely powerful Corporation of Harvard University have been set in motion, and concealment of your miserable selves or of the almost equally miserable (though not *as such* miserable) goloshes which you stole from our entry on Sunday night is as impossible as would be the concealment of the State House. The motive of your precipitate departure from the house became immediately evident to the remaining guests. But they resolved to *ignore* the matter provided the overshoes were replaced within a week; if not, no *considerations whatever* will prevent Messrs. Gurney & Perry from proceeding to treat you with the utmost severity of the law. It is high time that some of these genteel adventurers should be made an example of, and your offence just comes in time to make the cup of public and private forbearance overflow. My father and self have pledged our lives, our fortunes and our sacred honor to see the thing through with Gurney and Perry, as the credit of our house is involved and we might ourselves have been losers, not only from you but from the aforesaid G. & P., who have been heard to go about openly declaring that "if they had known the party was going to be *that* kind of an affair, d—d if they would not have started off earlier themselves with some of those aristocratic James overcoats, hats, gloves and canes!"

So let me as a friend advise you to send the swag back. No questions will be asked— Mum's the word.

Wm. James

To HENRY P. BOWDITCH

Cambridge, Jan. 24-25, 1869

My dear Henry,—

. . . I have just been quit by Charles S. Peirce, with whom I have been talking about a couple of articles in the St. Louis *Journal of Speculative Philosophy* by him which I have just read. They are exceedingly bold, subtle and incomprehensible and I can't say that his vocal elucidations helped me a great deal to their understanding, but they nevertheless interest me strangely. The poor cuss sees no chance of getting a professorship anywhere, and is likely to go into the Observatory for good. It seems a great pity that as original a man as he is, who is willing and able to devote the powers of his life to logic and metaphysics, should be starved out of a career, when there are lots of professorships of the sort to be given in the country, to "safe," orthodox men. He has had goood reason, I know, to feel a little discouraged about the prospect, but I think he ought to hang on, as a German would do, till he grows gray. . . .

I continue to "bide my time" here. I have a shrewd suspicion (which I will not put in the form of a categoric declaration, lest the blasted thing should hear it and go back on me as it has done before) that I have begun to get better. But I have discovered that I must not only drop exercise, but also mental labor, as it immediately tells on my back. I have consequently made up my mind to lose at least a year now in vegetating and doing nothing but survive. So I can't report to you any discoveries. I shall not make any experiments for my thesis but just compile what I find in the books under my hand. . . . Wendell Holmes comes out and we jaw once a week. I have been out two or three times in a buggy with Miss Fanny Dixwell, and derived no mean amount of joy therefrom. I am going again through the old medical textbooks, taking small doses daily, so as not to get *interested* and so fall into *study*—a poor business. . . . My brother Harry goes abroad in the spring, and will, I hope, strike Paris before you leave. His back is in a queer condish. He can walk and stand about all day without detriment, sitting and reading on the other hand go right to his back. What's your opinion? I hope this letter is *décousue* enough for you. What is a man to write when a reef is being taken in his existence, and absence from thought and life is all he aspires to. Better times will come, though, and with them better letters. Good-bye, ever yours,

Wm. James

To THOMAS W. WARD

Cambridge, March 1869

My dear Tom,—

Your letter of March 22nd and the one before it gave me great pleasure. What you say about my letter from Berlin amuses me muchly. I should like to read it myself sometime— I've entirely forgotten everything I said in it except that the gulls were still flying about the mouth of the Amazon in the sunshine. I remember the sour black Berlin afternoon in which I wrote it and that I was chiefly moved to do so by way of working off my own despair.—I should have written to you any time within the past twelve days as I had a longing to do so, but the state of my back made me refrain from writing. I had been getting on so bully that I broke bounds and rushed about for four or five days heedless of the consequences with the result of throwing me away back. I'm well on the rise again now however, with a lesson gained for prudence.—What you say of Burnouf's articles is interesting, and if your analysis is comprehensible to anyone but yourself, I should well like to see it or a copy of it as it would save me the time of a second reading of the originals. I read 'em all as they appeared and remember their suggestiveness. But there's a priggish tone about the cuss in his way of talking in the name of *"la Science"* as if in *these* matters there was as yet much beside *opinions*. Moreover it struck me in the late articles that there was a certain pedantic silliness in his assumption that no particular religion existing has any right to quarrel with the results of "Science", since these results are the same as the essential feature of the primitive Vedic religion from which later religions have derived. This latter fact is no argument. The Vedic doctrine seems to have been both a doctrine of nature and of men's fates, conglomerated or harmonized, and is the germ of the philosophy, science and religion of later times. But in developing, the Nature-lore and the individual-fate-lore or religion have become so differentiated as to be antagonistic; and to say they are not really so because both sprout of one stem seems as vain as to say Cain couldn't kill Abel because one womb bore them.—I had great movings of my bowels towards thee lately—the distant cynical isolation in which we live with our hearts' best brothers sometimes comes over me with a deep bitterness, and I had a little while ago an experience of life which woke up the spiritual monad within me as has not happened more than once or twice before in my life. "Malgré la vue des misères où nous vivons et qui nous tiennent par la gorge—" there is an inextinguishable spark which will when we least expect it flash out, and reveal the existence—at least—of something real—of reason at the bottom of things. I can't tell you how it was now. I'm swamped in an empirical philosophy—I feel that we are Nature through and through, that we are *wholly* conditioned, that not a wiggle of our wile happens save as the result of physical laws, and yet notwithstanding we are en rapport with reason.—How to conceive it? Who knows? I'm convinced that the defensive tactics of the French "spiritualists" fighting a steady retreat before materialism will never do anything.—It is not that we are all nature *but* some point which is reason, but that all is Nature *and* all is reason too. We shall see, damn it, we shall see.—I will beg you to send me the rapports on Surgery and medicine and the philosophy of Shakespeare's sonnets. I have time for them. I have read nothing lately of any interest. Your affectionate

W.J.

To HENRY P. BOWDITCH

Cambridge, May 22, 1869

My dear Henry,—

I am mortified at the long silence I have kept towards you. I have thought of you often enough with *Sehnsucht*, but I have lacked that cheerful and definite news to give you without which writing does not seem a natural act. . . . It is totally impossible for me to study now in any way, and I have at last succeeded in *genuinely* giving up the attempt to. With all this, I never was so cheerful—I've done what I can, and it's a mean thing for a man to fret about what is accidentally and externally imposed upon him. I took in my thesis and tickets to Hodges yesterday. The examination takes place on June 21st, and I suppose my star will guide me through it, though I'm ashamed of the fewness of the medical facts I know. I wrote a thesis on cold, nary experiment and nary chance of consulting any books on the subject but those I had, and a few I could send for by name to the library,—so it's of no value. I shall keep quiet till the examination is over, and then go with my family to the country (Pomfret, Conn.) and try whether almost perfect cessation from reading and some degree of exercise out of doors will make a change in my physical condition. If not, no matter.

So much for myself. I heard from Vienna, via Henry Tuck, that Warren was considering his winter in Paris as so much time wasted. . . . There's a dash of lawless and godless impatience in the French character,—an abandonment to merely physical capriciousness, a hatred of whatever bores them, com-

[81]

bined with that subjection of theirs to merely gregarious sentiment (I hardly know how to characterize the damned thing) which, especially since I have become acquainted with the German nature, is exceedingly unpleasant to me. You will find extending through everything in Germany a deep allegiance to principles as such, which gives you a feeling of confidence and security in the critters that I know of nowhere else. They are not willing to rest on arbitrary personal likes and dislikes— while the French rather glory in their impatience; and however erring men's ideas may be, so long as they admit the existence of *discipline* in life, of something external really existing, which it is the duty of a man to bring his will into harmony with, there is hope for him, and you feel secure in his presence. You never know when the irresponsible Frenchman's contemptuous monkeyhood may flash out and get the upper hand in him. I am convinced you'll feel this and enjoy it very much as soon as you begin to be at home in German books and among German people. I have been reading three or four German literary books this winter at odd hours and have realized more than I ever did before what a real intellectual gain it is to a man to have the freedom of the German tongue bestowed upon him. In all matters of thought (if not of form) the English and French literatures are provincial in comparison. . . . I have read no medical books this winter but the old textbooks. . . . I shall be glad to wash my hands of the subject, now that I know it is *to* lead to nothing for me.

Charles S. Peirce has been writing some very acute and original psychologico-metaphysical articles in the St. Louis philosophic *Journal,* though they are so crabbedly expressed that one can hardly get their exact sense. He is an original fellow, but with a capacity for arbitrariness that makes one mistrust him. C. W. Eliot was confirmed President yesterday. His great personal defects, tactlessness, meddlesomeness, and disposition to cherish petty grudges seem pretty universally acknowledged; but his ideas seem good and his economic powers first-rate,— so in the absence of any other possible candidate, he went in. It seems queer that such a place should go begging for candidates.

Our Senate and people generally, judging by newspapers, seem to me to have stultified themselves in first-class style about the Alabama question; we will of course back down; but so long as the good old American belief is not extinct that it is more creditable and "smart" to get out of a scrape unscathed than to keep clear of getting into one, backing out will not be popularly regarded as humiliating. National *dignity* for its own sake is something the existence of which has not yet risen on the horizon of the great popular heart here; perhaps our growing intercourse with the effete governments of Europe may gradually make us aware of it. Meanwhile, our buoyant way of doing things has on the whole great practical domestic advantages. "Buoyant" seems to me *the* adjective for us, nationally.

My brother Harry is now in England, enjoying the sights thereof mightily. I hope you may soon meet. . . . Wendell Holmes pays me a weekly visit. John Ropes told me the other night he had never known of anyone in the law who studied anything like as hard as Wendell. (This must lead to Chief Justice, U. S. Supreme Court.) Wendell amuses me by being composed of at least two and a half different people rolled into one, and the way he keeps them together in one tight skin, without quarreling any more than they do, is remarkable. I like him and esteem him exceedingly. . . .

My dear old boy, write soon to a cove and give him your budget of the winter's progress. You don't know how much I want to hear from you. Ever your friend,

Wm. James

[83]

To HENRY JAMES

Cambridge, Jan. 19, 1870

Dear Harry,—

Your letter from Naples the twenty-first of December and Rome the twenty-third, arrove yesterday morning. We were all heartily glad to have a tolerably cheerful report of your health, though it did not descend into details. . . I write now a few words only, being impeded these days by an inflammation of the eyelids, produced in a remarkable way by an overdose of chloral (a new hypnotic remedy which I took for the fun of it as an experiment, but whose effects are already on the wane). I write mainly to undo the impression my last letter written about Christmas-tide must have made on you. Those days marked the turning point, and the unaccountable symptoms which have been bothering me for many months began to combine themselves about the New Year in a way which gives me the strongest suspicion that they have formed but the transition to a second stage of the complaint. . . . Had I the somewhat mystical faith of a Hosmer, I suppose I should feel an inward conviction that I was from henceforth to rise; as it is, I only strongly suspect that it *may* be so. It will need another month or two to make me feel sure; and meanwhile failure will not hurt my feelings as much as if my hopes had been more confident.

What a pity that the weather, which is, I suppose, the mainspring of Naples's power to charm, failed you when there. Your wanderings and sight-seeings are beginning to foot up to quite a respectable sum, and the tolerably simple conception that it has been possible to frame of your life since you were reft from us, is fading to a many-hued chaos, with a gradually widening gulf between it and the grasping-power of our imagination.

[84]

But it doeth my very gizzard good to think of your being able to lay all those meaty experiences to your soul. . . .

Father has been writing a couple of articles on women and marriage in the *Atlantic*. I can't think he shows himself to most advantage in this kind of speculation. I will send you . . . the January number of the *Atlantic*, with a long and good poem by Lowell. . . . I enjoyed last week the great pleasure of reading *The House of the Seven Gables*. I little expected so *great* a work. It's like a great symphony, with no touch alterable without injury to the harmony. It made a deep impression on me and I thank heaven that Hawthorne was an American. It also tickled my national feeling not a little to note the resemblance of Hawthorne's style to yours and Howells's, even as I had earlier noted the converse. That you and Howells with all the models in English literature to follow, should needs involuntarily have imitated (as it were) this American, seems to point to the existence of some real American mental quality. But I must spare my eyes and stop. Ever your devoted

Wms.

P.S. It's a burning shame that all the while you were in Italy you should not have been able to write any "notes" for the *Nation*. Is it now too late? . . .

II

1872-1896: TEACHING, MARRIAGE, *THE PRINCIPLES OF PSYCHOLOGY*

STUDENTS of William James's career feel a certain relief when, at last, in 1872, he accepts an appointment as a lecturer in physiology at Harvard. He is now *settled*—painting, dilettantism, European spa treatments for obscure aches and pains, illusions of weakness and incapacity will disappear, we expect, to be replaced by that busy, brisk air young scholars want in their instructors. And in 1878, further relief: James married Alice Gibbens of Weymouth, Massachusetts. Still, marriage and Harvard did not entirely destroy the restlessness. Atlantic crossings continued, undertaken with the optimistic mobility and energy that made father and son set out with hope and return with relief, only to set out again, and again return.

During this period James had been writing reviews and short essays on psychological and philosophical subjects. In 1878, he signed a contract with Holt and Company to do a volume on psychology. The work was enthusiastically promised for 1880 and was actually delivered in 1890. This tardiness was serious: a prodigious amount of experience, thought and scholarship went into the two volumes of *The Principles of Psychology*. For all his modesty, James felt himself very much a pioneer in psychological study and defended his priority to G. Stanley Hall in 1895 when Hall implied that his own investigations and those of his students were the first in America. James wrote, "... some little regard should be paid to the good will with which I have tried to force my nature, and to the actual things I have done. One of them, for example, was inducting YOU into experimental investigation, with very naïve methods, it is true, but you may remember that there was no other place but Harvard where during those years you could get even that."

The elder Henry James died in 1882. William's last letter to his father, written when he learned of his father's serious illness, shows, as if by some magical condensation or distillation, that special James family blending of dignity and richness of feeling. Also in the letters of this period and the later ones, too, William James's superb gift for intellectual friendship is shown. His lack of malice or jealousy and his powers to recognize excellence in his colleagues, even when he disagreed or felt antipathetic, are astonishing. This uniquely appealing aspect of James's character was recently noted by Lionel Trilling in an address to the American Academy of Arts and Letters. "There is in James's superb manners in disagreement (as in agreement) a certain innocence, now lost from American life, a certain respect for his fellow man that transcends any question of mere status or prestige in the social or intellectual community."

The following letter to the French philosopher, Charles Renouvier—the beginning of their correspondence—is usually given considerable attention in James's intellectual biography. The reading of Renouvier's work had a large effect upon James and is even thought to have cured his mental depression by giving the sufferer the notion of the subtle relationship between mental states and bodily reactions. In 1911, even though differences of temperament and attitude had developed, James wrote about Renouvier: "He was one of the greatest of philosophic characters, and but for the decisive impression made upon me in the seventies by his masterly advocacy of pluralism, I might never have got free from the monistic superstition under which I had grown up."

To CHARLES RENOUVIER[1]

Cambridge, Nov. 2, 1872

Monsieur,—

I have just learned from your *Science de la morale* that the work of M. Lequier, to which you allude in your second *Essai de critique*, has never been placed on sale. This explains the failure of my long-continued efforts to obtain it through the library. If you still have copies would it be too much to ask you to send me one, which, after I have read it, I shall present in your name to the university library here? If the edition is already exhausted, do not take the trouble to reply. I hope that the keen interest which I take in your ideas will serve as an excuse for my request.

I must not lose this opportunity of telling you of the admiration and gratitude which have been excited in me by the reading of your *Essais* (except the third, which I have not yet read). Thanks to you I possess for the first time an intelligible and reasonable conception of freedom. I accept it almost entirely. On other points of your philosophy I still have doubts, but I can say that through that philosophy I am beginning to experience a rebirth of the moral life; and I assure you, Monsieur, that this is no small thing!

[1] This translation into English is reprinted from *The Thought and Character of William James*, by Ralph Barton Perry. James's original letter was in French.

With us it is the philosophy of Mill, Bain, and Spencer which just now carries everything before it. This philosophy has done good work in psychology, but from the practical point of view it is deterministic and materialistic; and already, I think, I can discern in England the symptoms of a revival of religious thought. Your philosophy seems, on its phenomenist side, to be peculiarly qualified to appeal to minds trained in the English empirical school, and I have no doubt that when it is a little better known in England and this country it will attract a good deal of attention. It appears to make its way slowly, but I am convinced that each year will bring us nearer to the time when it will be recognized by everybody as the most powerful philosophical effort of the century in France, and that it will always count as one of the great landmarks in the history of speculation. As soon as my health (which has been very bad for several years) allows me to undertake serious intellectual work, I mean to make a more thorough and critical study of it, and to write a report of it for one of our reviews. So if, Monsieur, there is still an available copy of the *Recherche d'une première vérité*, I take the liberty of asking you to send it to the enclosed address of the library, writing my name on the wrapper. M. Galette will pay the charges, if there are any. I again beg you, dear Monsieur, to be assured of the feelings of admiration and of high respect with which I remain your most obedient servant,

Wm. James

To HENRY JAMES

Cambridge, Nov. 24, 1872

Dear Harry,—

On this saintly Sabbath morn I take up my long unwonted pen to make you a report of progress at home ensheathed in other gossip. I sit at your old table facing the Lowell's empty house which has grown to look more tumble down than ever during the absence of the family in the country—(they are still there, old Mrs. L. being sick)—the double sashes just put up in front and a sickly mist-swathed November sunshine pouring through the back window on the right. . . . I send you today the last *Nation* with your letter about Chambéry, etc.,—a very delightful light bit of work, and perhaps the best of all for commercial newspaporial purposes. I must, however, still protest against your constant use of French phrases. There is an order of taste, and certainly a respectable one, to which they are simply maddening. I have said nothing to you about "Guest's Confession" which I read and enjoyed, admiring its cleverness though not loving it exactly. I noted at the time a couple of blemishes, one of the French phrase *les indifférents* at the end of one of her sentences which suddenly chills one's very marrow. The other the expression: "to whom I had dedicated a sentiment," earlier in the story,—I cannot well look up the page, but you will doubtless identify it. Of the people who experience a personal dislike, so to speak, of your stories, the most I think will be repelled by the element which gets expression in these two phrases, something cold, thin-blooded and priggish suddenly popping in and freezing the genial current. And I think that is the principal defect you have now to guard against. In flexibility, ease, and light power of style you clearly continue to gain—"Guest's Confession" and this last letter in the *Nation* are proofs of it; but I think you should fight shy of that note of literary reminiscence in the midst of what ought to be pure imagination absorbed in the object, which keeps every now and then betraying itself, as in these French phrases. I criticize you so much as perhaps to seem a mere caviler, but I think it ought to be of use to you to have any detailed criti-

cism from even a wrong judge, and you don't get much from
anyone else. I meanwhile say nothing of the great delight which
all your pieces give me by their insight into the shades of being,
and their exquisite diction and sense of beauty and expression
in the sights of the world. I still believe in your greatness as a
critic and hope you will send home something good of that kind.
Alice said you were going to do *Middlemarch*. . . . I have been
reading with deep pleasure though not *pure* pleasure three
chapters from Morley's forthcoming life of Rousseau which
have appeared in the *Fortnightly*. . . . I think I'll try to sling a
notice of it for Howells, and keep the book. I gave him a rather
ill-considered notice of M's Voltaire, contrasting M. favorably
with Tyndall and Huxley and in the heat of composition calling
T. a coxcomb, which Howells did not alter and which seemed
rather uncourteous as T. and the magazine made their appearance at the same moment and the Boston Globe said it made
one despair of the future of American letters to find such criti-
cisms in the *Atlantic*. But Morley is, I think, a very Great
Moralist and if he would only be less redundant a very great
writer.

Your letter describing your intimacy with J. R. Lowell, and
your dinner with the irascible Frenchmen at the Hôtel de
Lorraine, was received a few days ago and was very entertaining.
But can't you find out a way of knowing any good French
people? It seems preposterous that a man like you should be
condemned to the society of washer-women and café waiters.
I envy you, however, even the sight of such. Massive and teeming Paris, with all its sights, sounds and smells, is so huge and
real in the world, that from this insubstantial America one longs
occasionally for it with a mighty yearn. Just about nightfall at
this season with drizzle above and mud-paste beneath, and gas-

blazing streets and restaurants, is the time that particularly appeals to me with thick-wafted associations. . . .

Wendell Holmes spent an evening here this week. He grows more and more concentrated upon his law. His mind resembles a stiff spring, which has to be abducted violently from it, and which every instant it is left to itself flies tight back. . . . Charles Peirce and wife are going to Washington again for the winter and perhaps for good. He says he is appreciated there, and only tolerated here, and would be a fool not to go there. He read us an admirable introductory chapter to his book on logic the other day. I go in to the Medical School nearly every morning to hear Bowditch lecture, or paddle round in his laboratory. It is a noble thing for one's spirits to have some responsible work to do. I enjoy my revived physiological reading greatly, and have in a corporeal sense been better for the past four or five weeks than I have been at all since you left.

You may be surprised that I have as yet not mentioned the fire. But it was so snug and circumscribed an affair that one felt no *horror* at all about it. Rich men suffered, but upon the community at large I should say its effect had been rather exhilarating than otherwise. Boston feels rather proud that the fire of youth and prodigality yet smoulders in her. Harvard College has lost nearly a quarter of a million, but last night the subscriptions to aid her footed eighty-odd thousand so that she may lose nothing in the end. And I am convinced now that each occasion for giving in charity strengthens the habit and makes it easier. No one that we know intimately seems to have lost much. But Mother will have told you already the "personalities" connected with the affair, so I hush up. Adieu! adieu! I am glad to hear that you are so well, and hope it will last. . . . Write more now about what you read and think. . . . Ever yours affectionately, 				W. J.

To HENRY JAMES

Isles of Shoals, July 14-16 [1873]

Dear Harry,—

It occurs to me as I wait, this July 14, six P.M., on board the little steamer *Major* going to the Isles of Shoals, for her to start, that I may as well begin a letter to you in pencil, and be so much advanced on my way towards finishing that impending task. I left home four hours ago, where I had spent three days with Father and Mother after my visit to the coast at Magnolia, and am now off again till August, proposing to touch at various points. Today Father got your second from Berne, I getting at Magnolia your answer to my prudential inquiry. Your account of Rome was more satisfactory than anything I anticipated. I earnestly, hope, however, not to have to verify it next winter, as such a step would be about equivalent to desperation of any continuous professional development, and would leave my future quite adrift again. I shall let July and August shape my decision, and bear whatever comes with as equal a mind as I can. What weighs on me perhaps as much as anything now is the ignominy of my parasitic life on the family, in view of the sweating existence of Bob and Wilky and their need of money as married men. Every hundred dollars I take or don't earn is so much less that Father can give them. The only thing with me is my health; my ideas, my plans of study, are all straightened out. But I have no clue to the future of my strength, nor can I be *sure* what course is safest for that. I alternate between fits, lasting from four or five days to three weeks, of the most extreme languor and depression, weakness of body and head and pain in back—during which, however, I sleep well—and fits of equally uneven duration of great exhilaration of spirits, restlessness, comparative bodily and mental activity—coupled, however, with wakefulness of the most distressing sort that makes me absolutely ill. . . .

Next day, noon. The far-famed Isles of Shoals are absolutely barrel rocks with a great and first-class hotel on two of them. This one, Appledore, the biggest, may be walked round in half an hour. I performed the feat after breakfast . . . but the place does not yet tempt me to settle upon it for a long time. . . . I have enjoyed the vacation intensely so far. I got to Magnolia feeling pretty seedy. After five days there I had revived the spirits I used to possess at Newport. I did not know such a deep revulsion of mind was possible in so short a time. *Von allen Wissensqualm entladen*, I just lay around drinking the air and the light and the sounds. I succeeded in reading no word for three days, and then took Goethe's *Gedichte* out on my walks, and with them in my memory, the smell of the laurels and pines in my nose, and the rhythmic pounding of the surf upon my ear, I was free and happy again. How people can pass years without a week of that *normal* life I can't imagine—life in which your cares, responsibilities and thoughts for the morrow become a far-off dream, and you are, simply, floating on from day to day, and "boarded" you don't know how, by what Providence—washed clean, without and within, by the light and the tender air. It ought to do me good. Unluckily I can only enjoy its plenitude for ten days more. I must then do a little daily task of study, as I have to deliver about thirty new lectures next year and have hardly yet made a stroke of preparation. No joke! There were two nice girls, the Miss Wards, at Magnolia, who have spent much time in Europe and were "cultivated" and at the same time jolly and not devoid of the principle of sexual fascination. The day before I left Mrs. Ernest Longfellow lay on the beach, backed by a rock, reading your "Roman Holiday" to her Mamma aloud. Her looks lose their magic by being seen in conjunction with her family, whose faces are so many half-way houses, gropings as it were after hers, and awful failures, her sister being polly-wog faced and her mother *unique dans son genre.*

Another night—good sleep, and another shining day. The world recedes; and I can begin to understand Mrs. Celia Thaxter's ravings about the beauty of these rocks. Yesterday afternoon I took a long sail with a fresh breeze which quite recalled the Newport days ten years ago, as I sailed the boat myself. I will close this letter here—you perceive I have not *multa* to say. I have read nothing of late except a few of Goethe's poems which make me feel like living entirely on poetry for the rest of my days. . . . Good-bye! Perhaps, in case I should go abroad, you had better send me a list of books or other furniture you would like me to bring you. Affectionately yours,

Wm. James

To HIS SISTER, ALICE

Florence, Nov. 23, 1873

Beloved Sisterkin,—

Your "nice long letter," as you call it, of Oct. 26 reached me five days ago, Mother's of November 4th yesterday, and with it one from Father to Harry. Though you will probably disbelieve me, I cannot help stating how agreeable it is to me to be once more in regular communication with that which, in spite of all shortcomings, is all that has ever been vouchsafed to me in the way of a "home" (and a mother). The hotel in which we live here is anything but home-like. In fact, when the heart aches for cosiness, etc., all it can do is to turn out into the street.

I begin to feel, too, strongly that at my time of life, with such a set of desultory years behind, what a man most wants is to be settled and concentrated, to cultivate a patch of ground which may be humble but still is his own. Here all this dead civilization crowding in upon one's consciousness forces the mind open again even as the knife the unwilling oyster—and what my mind wants most now is practical tasks, not the theoretical digestion of additional masses of what to me are raw and disconnected empirical materials. I feel like one still obliged to eat more and more grapes and pears and pineapples, when the state of the system imperiously demands a fat Irish stew, or something of that sort. I knew it all before I came, however; and I hope in a fortnight to be able comparatively to disregard what lies about me and get interested in the physiological books I brought. So far I find the pictures, etc., drive my thoughts far away. I have just been reading a big German octavo, Burkhardt's "Renaissance in Italy," with the title of which you may enrich your historical consciousness, though I hardly think you need read the book. This is the place for history. I don't see how, if one lived here, historical problems could help being the most urgent ones for the mind. It would suit you admirably. Even art comes before one here much more as a problem—how to account for its development and decline —than as a refreshment and an edification. I really think that end is better served by the stray photographs which enter our houses at home, finding us in the midst of our work and surprising us.

But here I am pouring out this one-sided splenetic humor upon you without having the least intended it when I sat down. Your pen accidentally slips into a certain vein and you must go on till you get it out clearly. If you had heard me telling Harry two or three times lately that I feared the fatal fascination of this place,—that I began to feel it taking little stitches in my soul,—you would have a different impression of my state than my above written words have left upon you. . . . I went out intending to stroll in the Boboli Garden, a wonderful old piece of last-century stateliness, but found it shut till twelve. So I returned to Harry's room, where I sit by the pungent wood fire writing this letter which I did not expect to begin till the afternoon, while he, just at this moment rising from the table where his quill has been busily scratching away at the last pages of his Turguenieff article, comes to warm his legs and puts on another log. . . .

Good-bye beloved Sister, and Father and Mother. . . . Write repeatedly such nice long letters, and make glad the heart of both the Angel and the other brother,

W. J.

To HENRY JAMES

Cambridge, April 18, 1874

Dear Harry,—

. . . Any gossip about Florence you can still communicate will be greedily sucked in by me, who feel towards it as I do towards the old Albany of our childhood, with afternoon shadows of trees, etc. Not but that I am happy here,—more so than I ever was there, because I'm in a permanent path, and it shows me how for our type of character the thought of the *whole* dominates the particular moments. All my moments here are inferior to those in Italy, but they are parts of a long plan which is good, so they content me more than the Italian ones which only existed for themselves. I have been feeling uncommonly strong for almost three weeks . . . and [have] done a good deal of work in Bowditch's laboratory. . . . I went yesterday to dine with Mrs. Tappan and did not get out till midnight through the snow storm. She lives on Beacon Street looking down Dartmouth, and Emerson and Ellen, Dr. Holmes, and Miss Georgiana Putnam were the guests. None oped the mouth save Holmes, at table. Emerson looks in magnificent health, but the refined idiocy of his manner seems as if it must be affectation. After dinner I had a long and drastic dose of Miss Putnam, then was relieved by the incoming of Miss Bessie Lee who is very "nice." The Tappan girls are improved. Ellen longed for Europe, Boston being so "tame"(!) and they probably will go next fall. After all, Mrs. Tappan's eagerness for intellectual sensations, her passion, more than atone for all her crimes, and make her the most nutritious person I have yet struck here. I confess that we seem a poor lot on the whole. My short stay abroad has given me quite a new sense of what you used to call the provinciality of Boston, but that is no harm. What displeases me is the want of stoutness and squareness in the people, their ultra quietness, prudence, slyness, intellectualness of gait. Not that their intellects amount to anything, either. You will be discouraged, I remain happy!

But this brings me to the subject of your return, of which I have thought much. It is evident that you will have to eat your bread in sorrow for a time here; it is equally evident that time ... will provide a remedy for a great deal of the trouble, and you will attune your at present coarse senses to snatch a fearful joy from wooden fences and commercial faces, a joy the more thrilling for being so subtly extracted. Are you ready to make the heroic effort? ... This is your dilemma: The congeniality of Europe, on the one hand, plus the difficulty of making an entire living out of original writing, and its abnormality as a matter of mental hygiene ... on the other hand, the dreariness of American conditions of life plus a mechanical, routine occupation possibly to be obtained, which from day to day is *done* when 't is done, mixed up with the writing into which you distil your essence. . . . In short, don't come unless with a *resolute* intention. If you come, your worst years will be the first. If you stay, the bad years may be the later ones, when, moreover, you can't change. And I have a suspicion that if you come, too, and *can* get once acclimated, the quality of what you write will be higher than it would be in Europe. . . . It seems to me a very critical moment in your history. But you have several months to decide. Good-bye. . . .

[W. J.]

To HIS BROTHER, ROBERTSON

Cambridge, Sept. 20, 1874

My dear Bob,—

I received your letter some time since and read it with much pleasure. I can't say that I altogether congratulate you on having become a householder at Prairie du Chien, as it seems prophetic of a prolonged stay there, and from all you say of the place I do not think that is a consummation to be devoutly wished by you or anyone else. But I'm glad you, so long as you are there, are contented enough not to seem to worry for a change. I don't know, however, what you may do inwardly. Next June I trust to know better, for I think there is little doubt that I shall then be your guest.

We are established for the winter, Harry very well indeed and seeming glad to be back. The only event that has happened of any interest is the marriage of Edward Emerson and Miss Keyes yesterday at the Keyes' house. I went up with half a car load of people from town,—the Forbes crowd, and various other relatives. The day was warm, drizzly and dripping, bringing out the moist green of the country beautifully. The wedding was a delightful thing, being, with the exception of Aunt Kate's and Wendell Holmes's—which latter took place in a church—the first I ever attended. All my friends have been so high-toned of late, T. S. Perry, Ellen Gurney, John La Forge, Clover Adams, etc., as to get married in secret, so that no mortal eye should profane the ceremony, and I had passively accepted that as the only fitting way for a person of "culture" who respected himself. But the affair of yesterday entirely opened my eyes and when I get married I shall have a cheerful sociable crowd round me. The crowd there all had the worthy, reliable, Concord look—all called each other by their first names, and you felt that the men and especially the woman standing next you, though you did not know them, were people worthy of your esteem. Tom Ward was there, and the famous Miss Lizzie Simmons who is very good looking; the Bartlett family looking all like baked apples; and old Mr. Emerson more gaunt and lop-sided than ever; Mr. Sanborn, who supported himself by leaning his hand against the ceiling and who sent his regards to you and Wilky. All the people seem to remember you, for more asked about you than I can now remember—Miss Elizabeth Hoar, for example, and Mrs. Simmons. Ellen Emerson looked beautiful in a white dress and lilac crape shawl, and Edith Forbes was there sumptuously attired, with three magnificent looking children. The person that pleased me most was Malcolm Forbes's young wife, who is as pretty faced and voiced as she can be, and a very bright little talker. Edward looked and behaved very well, while Miss Keyes, who had just recovered from a sharp illness, looked a little too bony and had two bright crimson spots on her cheek bones. Will Forbes has asked me to Naushon for a few days at the end of the week. Edward and his bride will be there, and they will have a deer hunt. I will write to Wilky about it.

Today I went on my regular Sunday morning visit to the Sedgwicks and dined with the Bootts off roast beef and potatoes baked in the drippings of the joint under the beef, a mode of cooking them which I earnestly recommend to Mary as a means of securing forever your affection. I am glad to hear such good accounts of your baby, and only hope that the half promise you made in the spring of getting on here this winter will be kept. It will be a great disappointment to us if it is not. A few of the photographs Harry brought home would interest you.

I see Tilton is out with a new "statement" which Heaven forbid that I should read. Between the supposition of a villainy more fiendish than that of Iago and Richard III rolled into one on the part of Moulton, or of a cheek and brazen genius for hypocrisy on Beecher's part almost as incredible, it seems hard to choose. Either horn of the dilemma is an improbability.

Cambridge is washing up and preparing for the winter's work, and I with it. I hope and expect it will sit lightly on me if I take it easy, which is perhaps hard to do. How are your eyes now? Give my best love to Mary and a kiss to the *brat* and believe me, dear Bob, always your loving

W. J.

To HENRY JAMES

Cambridge, Dec. 12, 1875

My dear Harry,—

We have received your first letter from Paris, and last night the *Tribune* arrived with your first official one blazoned forth, as you will no doubt see before you get this. I am amused that you should have fallen into the arms of C. S. Peirce, whom I imagine you find a rather uncomfortable bedfellow, thorny and spinous, but the way to treat him is after the fabled "nettle" receipt: grasp firmly, contradict, push hard, make fun of him, and he is as pleasant as anyone; but be overawed by his sententious manner and his paradoxical and obscure statements—wait upon them, as it were, for light to dawn—and you will never get a feeling of ease with him any more than I did for years, until I changed my course and treated him more or less chaffingly. I confess I like him very much in spite of all his peculiarities, for he is a man of genius, and there's always something in that to compel one's sympathy. I got a letter from him about Chauncey Wright in which he said he had just seen you. . . . How long does he stay in Paris and when does he return? I may feel like asking him to bring me back an instrument or two when he comes. Please tell him I got his letter and enjoyed it, and that a subscription paper is now passing round to defray the cost of publishing Wright's remains,—forty names at $20 each are what is hoped for. Norton will be editor, and if it is decided to have any extended introductory notice, I will tell him that Peirce is willing to write an account of his [Wright's] philosophical ideas. Norton did intend giving it to Fiske, who would make a very inferior thing of it.

Roderick Hudson seems to be a very common theme of conversation. . . . In looking through the volume it seems to me even better than it did, but I must tell you that I am again struck unfavorably by the tendency of the personages to reflect on themselves and give an acute critical scientific introspective classification of their own natures and states of mind, *à la* G. Sand. Take warning once more!

Yesterday Howells and wife and Godkin and Aunt dined here. Plenty of laughter, but not much else. . . . The only other thing I have done except mind my anatomy is the squib in the *Nation* which I enclose. In the interval between sending it and seeing it appear in print, I have dipped into Baudelaire and am reluctantly obliged to confess that Scherer is quite as wrong as Saintsbury. It is a pity that every writer in France is bound to do injustice to the opposite "camp." Baudelaire is really, in his *Fleurs du Mal*, original and in a certain sense elevated, and on the whole I can bear no rancor against him, although at times he writes like a person half-awake and groping for words. The most amusing thing about it all is the impression one gets of the innocence of a generation in which the *Fleurs du Mal* should have made a *scandal*. It is a mild and spiritualistic book today. Get it and write about it in the *Nation* or *Atlantic*, if you like, and especially read a letter of Sainte-Beuve's at the end of it, which is the *ne plus ultra* of his diabolic subtlety and malice.

I had an interview with C. W. Eliot the other day, who smiles on me and lets me expect $1200 this year and possibly hope for $2000 the next, which will be a sweet boon if it occurs. As the term advances I become sensible that I am really better than I was last year in almost every way; which gives me still better prospects for the future. . . . Good-bye! Heaven bless you,—get as much society as you can. Your first letter was a very good beginning, though one sees that you are to a certain extent fishing for the proper tone or level. I should like to accompany you to some of the theatres. Adieu!

W. J.

P.S. Latest American humor, quoted last night by Godkin—child (lost at fair): "Where's my mother? I told the darned thing she'd lose me."

To HENRY JAMES

Newport, June 3, 1876

My Dear H.,—

I write you after [a] considerable interval filled with too much work and weariness to make letter-writing convenient.

. . . I ran away three days ago, the recitations being over for the year, in order to break from the studious associations of home. I have been staying at the Tweedies with Mrs. Chapman, and James Sturgis and his wife, and enjoying extremely, not the conversation indoors, but the lonely lying on the grass on the cliffs at Lily Pond, and four or five hours yesterday at the Dumplings, feeling the moving air and the gentle living sea. There is a purity and mildness about the elements here which purges the soul of one. And I have been as if I had taken opium, not wanting to do anything else than the particular thing I happened to be doing at the moment, and feeling equally good whether I stood or walked or lay, or spoke or was silent. It's a spendid relief from the overstrain and stimulus of the past few scholastic months. I go the day after tomorrow (Monday) with the Tweedies to New York, assist at Henrietta Temple's wedding on Tuesday, and then pass on to the Centennial for a couple of days. I suppose it will be pretty tiresome, but I want to see the English pictures, which they say are a good show. . . . I fancy my vacationizing will be confined to visits of a week at a time to different points, perhaps the pleasantest way after all of spending it. Newport as to its villas, and all that, is most repulsive to me. I really didn't know how little charm and how much shabbiness there was about the place. There are not more than three or four houses out of the whole lot that are not offensive, in some way, externally. But the mild nature grows on one every day. This afternoon, God willing, I shall spend on Paradise.[1]

The Tweedies keep no horses, which makes one walk more or pay more than one would wish. The younger Seabury told me yesterday that he was just reading your "Roderick Hudson,"

[1] The name of a rocky promontory near Newport.

but offered no [comment]. Colonel Waring said of your "American" to me: "I'm not a blind admirer of H. James, Jr., but I said to my wife after reading that first number, 'By Jove, I think he's hit it this time!' " I think myself the thing opens very well indeed, you have a first-rate datum to work up, and I hope you'll do it well.

Your last few letters home have breathed a tone of contentment and domestication in Paris which was very agreeable to get. . . . Your accounts of Ivan Sergeitch are delightful, and I envy you the possession of the young painter's intimacy. Give my best love to Ivan. I read his book which you sent home (foreign books sent by mail pay duty now, though; so send none but good ones), and although the vein of "morbidness" was so pronounced in the stories, yet the mysterious depths which his plummet sounds atone for all. It is the amount of life which a man feels that makes you value his mind, and Turguenieff has a sense of worlds within worlds whose existence is unsuspected by the vulgar. It amuses me to recommend his books to people who mention them as they would the novels of Wilkie Collins. You say we don't notice "Daniel Deronda." I find it extremely interesting. Gwendolen and her spouse are masterpieces of conception and delineation. Her ideal figures are much vaguer and thinner. But her "sapience," as you excellently call it, passes all decent bounds. There is something essentially womanish in the irrepressible garrulity of her moral reflections. Why is it that it makes women feel so good to moralize? Man philosophizes as a matter of business, because he must,—he does it to a purpose and then lets it rest; but women don't seem to get over being tickled at the discovery that they have the faculty; hence the tedious iteration and restlessness of George Eliot's commentary on life. The La Farges are absent. Yours always,

W. J.

To CHARLES RENOUVIER

Cambridge, July 29, 1876

My dear Sir,—

I am quite overcome by your appreciation of my poor little article in the "Nation." It gratifies me extremely to hear from your own lips that my apprehension of your thoughts is accurate. In so despicably brief a space as that which a newspaper affords, I could hardly hope to attain any other quality than that, and perhaps clearness. I had written another paragraph of pure eulogy of your powers, which the editor suppressed, to my great regret, for want of room. I need not repeat to you again how grateful I feel to you for all I have learned from your admirable writings. I do what lies in my feeble power to assist the propagation of your works here, but *students* of philosophy are rare here as everywhere. It astonishes me, nevertheless, that you have had to wait so long for general recognition. Only a few months ago I had the pleasure of introducing to your "Essais" two *professors* of philosophy, able and learned men, who hardly knew your name!! But I am perfectly convinced that it is a mere affair of time, and that you will take your place in the general History of Speculation as the classical and finished representative of the tendency which was begun by Hume, and to which writers before you had made only fragmentary contributions, whilst you have fused the whole matter into a solid, elegant and definitive system, perfectly consistent, and capable, by reason of its moral vitality, of becoming popular, so far as that is permitted to philosophic systems. After your Essays, it seems to me that the only important question is the deepest one of all, the one between the principle of contradiction, and the *Sein und Nichts*. You have brought it to that clear issue; and extremely as I value your logical attitude, it would be uncandid

of me (after what I have said) not to confess that there are
certain psychological and moral facts, which make me, as I
stand today, unable wholly to commit myself to your position,
to burn my ships behind me, and proclaim the belief in the
one and the many to be the Original Sin of the mind. I long
for leisure to study up these questions. I have been teaching
anatomy and physiology in Harvard College here. Next year,
I add a course of physiological psychology, using, for certain
practical reasons, Spencer's "Psychology" as a textbook. My
health is not strong; I find that laboratory work and study, too,
are more than I can attend to. It is therefore not impossible
that I may in 1877–8 be transferred to the philosophical department, in which there is likely to be a vacancy. If so, you may
depend upon it that the name of Renouvier will be as familiar
as that of Descartes to the Bachelors of Arts who leave these
walls. Believe me with the greatest respect and gratitude, faithfully yours

Wm. James

. . . I must add a *vivat* to your "Critique Philosophique,"
which keeps up so ably and bravely! And although it is probably an entirely superfluous recommendation, I cannot refrain
from calling your attention to the most robust of English
philosophic writers, [Shadworth] Hodgson, whose "Time and
Space" was published in 1865 by Longmans, and whose "Theory
of Practice," in two volumes, followed it in 1870.

The following fragment from a letter to his wife was written in 1878, some months after their marriage. As James's son, Henry, says, "It is an unusual bit of self-analysis . . ."

To MRS. JAMES

. . . I have often thought that the best way to define a man's character would be to seek out the particular mental or moral attitude in which, when it came upon him, he felt himself most deeply and intensely active and alive. At such moments there is a voice inside which speaks and says: "*This* is the real me!" And afterwards, considering the circumstances in which the man is placed, and noting how some of them are fitted to evoke this attitude, whilst others do not call for it, an outside observer may be able to prophesy where the man may fail, where succeed, where be happy and where miserable. Now as well as I can describe it, this characteristic attitude in me always involves an element of active tension, of holding my own, as it were, and trusting outward things to perform their part so as to make it a full harmony, but without any *guaranty* that they will. Make it a guaranty—and the attitude immediately becomes to my consciousness stagnant and stingless. Take away the guaranty, and I feel (provided I am *überhaupt* in vigorous condition) a sort of deep enthusiastic bliss, of bitter willingness to do and suffer anything, which translates itself physically by a kind of stinging pain inside my breast-bone (don't smile at this—it is to me an essential element of the whole thing!), and which, although it is a mere mood or emotion to which I can give no form in words, authenticates itself to me as the deepest principle of all active and theoretic determination which I possess. . . .

W. J.

To JOSIAH ROYCE

Cambridge, Feb. 3, 1880

Beloved Royce!—

So far was I from having forgotten you that I had been revolving in my mind, on the very day when your letter came, the rhetorical formulas of objurgation with which I was to begin a page of inquiries of you: whether you were dead and buried or had become an idiot or were sick or blind or what, that you sent no word of yourself. *I* am blind as ever, which may excuse my silence.

First of all *Glückwünsche* as to your *Verlobung!* which, like the true philosopher that you are, you mention parenthetically and without names, dates, numbers of dollars, etc., etc. I think it shows great sense in her, and no small amount of it in you, whoe'er she be. I have found in marriage a calm and repose I never knew before, and only wish I had done the thing ten years earlier. I think the lateness of our usual marriages is a bad thing, and hope your engagement will not last very long.

It is refreshing to hear your account of philosophic work. ... I'm sorry you've given up your article on Hodgson. He *is* obscure enough, and makes me sometimes wonder whether the *ignotum* does not pass itself off for the *magnifico* in his pages. I enclose his photograph as a loan, trusting you will return it soon. I will never write again for Harris's journal. He refused an article of mine a year ago "for lack of room," and has postponed the printing of two admirable original articles by T. Davidson and Elliot Cabot for the last ten months or more, in order to accommodate Mrs. Channing's verses and Miss [G. Garrigus's] drival about the school of Athens, etc., etc. It is too loathsome. Harris has resigned his school position in St. Louis and will, I am told, come East to live. I know not whether he means to lay siege to the Johns Hopkins professorship. My ignorant prejudice against all Hegelians, except Hegel himself, grows wusser and wusser. Their sacerdotal airs! and their sterility! Contemplating their navels and the syllable *oum!* My dear friend Palmer, assistant professor of philosophy here, is already one of the white-winged band, having been made captive by Caird in two summers of vacation in Scotland. Palmer is an *extremely* able man, or rather person, in many ways, but a born prig, and such are I suppose all bound to be Hegelians. Caird didn't strike one as a prig, but the ineffectiveness and impotence of the ending of [Caird's] work on Kant seem to me simply scandalous, after its pretentious (and able) beginning. What do you think of Carveth [Reid]'s Essay on Shadworth [Hodgson]? I haven't read it. Our Philosophic Club here is given up this year—I think we're all rather sick of each other's voices. My teaching is small in numbers, though my men are good. I've tried Renouvier as a text-book—for the last time! His exposition offers too many difficulties. I enjoyed your Rhapsody on Space, and hereby pledge myself to buy two copies of your work ten years hence, and to devote the rest of my life to the propagation of its doctrines. I despise my own article, which was dashed off for a momentary purpose and published for another. But I don't see why its main doctrine, from a psychologic and sublunary point of view, is not sound; and I think I can, if my psychology ever gets writ, set it down in decently clear and orderly form. All *deducers* of space are, I am sure, mythologists. You are, after all, not so very much isolated in California. We are all isolated—"columns left alone of a temple once complete," etc. Books are our companions more than men. But I wish nevertheless, and firmly expect, that somehow or other you will get a call East, and within my humble sphere of power I will do what I can to further that end. My accursed eye-sight balks me always about study and production. *Ora pro me!* With most respectful and devout regards to the fair Object, believe me always your

Wm. James

To CHARLES RENOUVIER

Cambridge, Dec. 27, 1880

My dear Monsieur Renouvier,—

   Your note and the conclusion of my article in the "Critique" came together this morning. It gives me almost a feeling of pain that you, at your age and with your achievements, should be spending your time in translating my feeble words, when by every principle of right *I* should be engaged in turning your invaluable writings into English. The state of my eyes is, as you know, my excuse for this as for all other shortcomings. I have not even read the whole of your translation of [my] "Feeling of Effort," though the passages I have perused have seemed to me excellently well done. My exposition strikes me as rather complicated now. It was written in great haste and, were I to rewrite it, it should be simpler. The omissions of which you speak are of no importance whatever.

   I have read your discussion with Lotze in the "Revue Philosophique" and agree with Hodgson that you carry off there the honors of the battle. *Quant au fond de la question*, however, I am still in doubt and wait for the light of further reflexion to settle my opinion. The matter in my mind complicates itself with the question of a universal ego. If time and space are not *in se*, do we not need an enveloping ego to make continuous the times and spaces, not necessarily coincident, of the partial egos? On this question, as I told you, I will not fail to write again when I get new light, which I trust may decide me in your favor.

[112]

To JOSIAH ROYCE [1882]

My principal amusement this winter has been resisting the inroads of Hegelism in our University. My colleague Palmer, a recent convert and a man of much ability, has been making an active propaganda among the more advanced students. It is a strange thing, this resurrection of Hegel in England and here, after his burial in Germany. I think his philosophy will probably have an important influence on the development of our liberal form of Christianity. It gives a quasi-metaphysic backbone which this theology has always been in need of, but it is too fundamentally rotten and charlatanish to last long. As a reaction against materialistic evolutionism it has its use, only this evolutionism is fertile while Hegelism is absolutely sterile.

I think often of the too-short hours I spent with you and Monsieur Pillon and wish they might return. Believe me with the warmest thanks and regards, yours faithfully,

Wm. James

To JOSIAH ROYCE

Cambridge, April 23, 1882

My dear Royce,—

I have read your Saratoga paper with even more than my usual pleasure in your style. The preliminary critical part of it is first-rate in all respects. As for your "recasting" attempt, without saying I disagree, I find certain things obscure, and cannot but think that the attempt you make is destined to receive further elaboration at your own hands.

But the object of this writing is not to bandy compliments or the reverse with you, but to ask you a practical question. I have received leave of absence on half-pay for next year and must find a substitute to do my work on the remaining half, which makes the dwarfish figure of $1250. Schurman of Nova Scotia, who is a fine fellow and perfectly safe man, will undoubtedly do the job if asked; but inasmuch as whoever does it gets the inside track for promotion here on Bowen's withdrawal; inasmuch, too, as I may safely say that you and Schurman are the only men the College Corporation has its eyes on for filling a vacancy (G. Stanley Hall has just been appointed to the Johns Hopkins University for three years, and I am disposed to doubt of a vacancy here being tendered him); inasmuch, moreover, as I think you would be the highest prize we could permanently gain; inasmuch, also, as I know the President does not feel convinced of your teaching powers being first-class, partly because they don't yet offer you the new professorship in your own university; partly because no accounts either favorable or unfavorable have yet been received here; inasmuch as all this, you see that if you could manage to come for a year at your own risks, many questions of the highest concern to you *might* be settled at a stroke. The President, I think, would rather try you than Schurman because it gives him the chance of capturing a larger prize, but he has an impression that with you he also runs larger risks; and he does not believe that you could afford to drop your permanent appointment at Berkeley and travel all this way for $1250 without a guarantee of something beyond one year. . . .

Should your teaching during my absence give satisfaction, and yet the looked-for vacancy not occur at the end of the year, it is probable but not certain, that there will be vacancies in the English rhetoric and theme department in which you could bide your time, which certainly can't be long, as good old Bowen hints at resignation constantly and seems very feeble. I think you see clearly just what the chances and the risks are. I write without the President's knowledge to ask you whether, knowing them all, you still feel as if you might like to take my place. I feel sure the President would then officially invite you. There is a chance of a good little furnished house here for $360 rent. First-class board would cost you and your wife $30 a week. I ought to say that your work would consist of Psychology, three hours a week (a beginner's course with Taine or Spencer as textbook); of Locke, Berkeley and Hume, three hours a week; and of a graduate course in "Advanced Psychology" of one or two hours, for which there will probably be no applicants and out of which, even if there are, you can easily wriggle.

I would give anything to have you safe within our fold, but I should think your own university must now advance you. You have no doubt heard of their sounding Palmer and of his refusing to be a candidate. I don't know what first-class man they can get to go from the East—possibly poor John Watson with his transcendental ego might, possibly George S. Morris, but you are worth Palmer, Watson and Morris together for one who really enjoys the living movement of philosophizing. If your answer is affirmative, as I hope it may be, *telegraph* it immediately. No time is to be lost. Yours always,

Wm. James

P.S. I ought to say as my *private* opinion, that I cannot myself imagine why you should *not* succeed as a teacher here, and that I should suppose your coming for the next year would be practically tantamount to perpetuity. . . But the *risks*, such as they are, are yours.

W. J.

The following remarkable letter was written from London when James got news of his father's serious illness. The elder Henry James died a few days later, on the 19th of December.

To HIS FATHER

Bolton St., London, Dec. 14, 1882

Darling old Father,—

Two letters, one from my Alice last night, and one from Aunt Kate to Harry just now, have somewhat dispelled the mystery in which the telegrams left your condition; and although their news is several days earlier than the telegrams, I am free to suppose that the latter report only an aggravation of the symptoms the letters describe. It is far more agreeable to think of this than of some dreadful unknown and sudden malady.

We have been so long accustomed to the hypothesis of your being taken away from us, especially during the past ten months, that the thought that this may be your last illness conveys no very sudden shock. You are old enough, you've given your message to the world in many ways and will not be forgotten; you are here left alone, and on the other side, let us hope and pray, dear, dear old Mother is waiting for you to join her. If you go, it will not be an inharmonious thing. Only, if you are still in possession of your normal consciousness, I should like to see you once again before we part. I stayed here only in obedience to the last telegram, and am waiting now for Harry—who knows the exact state of my mind, and who will know yours—to telegraph again what I shall do. Meanwhile, my blessed old Father, I scribble this line (which may reach you though I should come too late), just to tell you how full of the tenderest memories and feelings about you my heart has for the last few days been filled. In that mysterious gulf of the past into which the present soon will fall and go back and back, yours is still for me the central figure. All my intellectual life I derive from you; and though we have often seemed at odds in the expression thereof, I'm sure there's a harmony some- where, and that our strivings will combine. What my debt to you is goes beyond all my power of estimating,—so early, so penetrating and so constant has been the influence. You need be in no anxiety about your literary remains. I will see them well taken care of, and that your words shall not suffer for being concealed. At Paris I heard that Milsand, whose name you may remember in the "Revue des Deux Mondes" and elsewhere, was an admirer of the "Secret of Swedenborg," and Hodgson told me your last book had deeply impressed him. So will it be; especially, I think, if a collection of *extracts* from your various writings were published, after the manner of the ex- tracts from Carlyle, Ruskin, & Co. I have long thought such a volume would be the best monument to you.—As for us; we shall live on each in his way,—feeling somewhat unprotected, old as we are, for the absence of the parental bosoms as a refuge, but holding fast together in that common sacred memory. We will stand by each other and by Alice, try to transmit the torch in our offspring as you did in us, and when the time comes for being gathered in, I pray we may, if not all, some at least, be as ripe as you. As for myself, I know what trouble I've given you at various times through my peculiar- ities; and as my own boys grow up, I shall learn more and more of the kind of trial you had to overcome in superintend- ing the development of a creature different from yourself, for whom you felt responsible. I say this merely to show how my *sympathy* with you is likely to grow much livelier, rather than to fade—and not for the sake of regrets.—As for the other side, and Mother, and our all possibly meeting, I *can't* say anything.

More than ever at this moment do I feel that if that *were* true, all would be solved and justified. And it comes strangely over me in bidding you good-bye how a life is but a day and expresses mainly but a single note. It is so much like the act of bidding an ordinary good-night. Good-night, my sacred old Father! If I don't see you again—Farewell! a blessed farewell! Your

William

To MRS. JAMES

December, 1882

. . . Father's boyhood up in Albany, Grandmother's house, the father and brothers and sister, with their passions and turbulent histories, his burning, amputation and sickness, his college days and ramblings, his theological throes, his engagement and marriage and fatherhood, his finding more and more of the truths he finally settled down in, his travels in Europe, the days of the old house in New York and all the men I used to see there, at last his quieter motion down the later years of life in Newport, Boston and Cambridge, with his friends and correspondents about him, and his books more and more easily brought forth—how long, how long all these things were in the living, but how short their memory now is! What remains is a few printed pages, us and our children and some incalculable modifications of other people's lives, influenced this day or that by what he said or did. For me, the humor, the good spirits, the humanity, the faith in the divine, and the sense of his right to have a say about the deepest reasons of the universe, are what will stay by me. I wish I could believe I should transmit some of them to our babes. We all of us have some of his virtues and some of his shortcomings. Unlike the cool, dry thin-edged men who now abound, he was full of the fumes of the *ur-sprünglich* human nature; things turbid, more than he could formulate, wrought within him and made his judgments of rejection of so much of what was brought [before him] seem like revelations as well as knock-down blows. . . . I hope that rich soil of human nature will not become more rare! . . .

To CHARLES RENOUVIER

Keene Valley, Aug. 5, 1883
Adirondacks

My dear Monsieur Renouvier,—

My silence has been so protracted that I fear you must have wondered what its reasons could be. Only the old ones!—much to do, and little power to do it, obliging procrastination. You will doubtless have heard from the Pillons of my safe return home. I have spent the interval in the house of my mother-in-law in Cambridge, trying to do some work in the way of psychologic writing before the fatal day should arrive when the College bell, summoning *me* as well as my colleagues to the lecture-room, should make literary work almost impossible. Although my bodily condition, thanks to my winter abroad, has been better than in many years at a corresponding period, what I succeeded in accomplishing was well-nigh zero. I floundered round in the morasses of the theory of cognition,—the Object and the Ego,—tore up almost each day what I had written the day before, and although I am inwardly, of course, more aware than I was before of where the difficulties of the subject lie, outwardly I have hardly any manuscript to show for my pains. Your unparalleled literary fecundity is a perfect wonder to me. You should return pious thanks to the one or many gods who had a hand in your production, not only for endowing you with so clear a head, but for giving you so admirable a working temperament. The most rapid piece of literary work I ever did was completed ten days ago, and sent to "Mind," where it will doubtless soon appear. I had promised to give three lectures at a rather absurd little "Summer School of Philosophy," which has flourished for four or five years past in the little town of Concord near Boston, and which has an audience of from twenty to fifty persons, including the lecturers themselves; and, finding at the last moment that I could do nothing with my much meditated subject of the Object and the Ego, I turned round and lectured "On Some Omissions of Introspective Psychology," and wrote the substance of the lectures out immediately after giving them—the whole occupying six days. I hope you may read the paper some time and approve it—though it is out of the current of your own favorite topics and consequently hardly a proper candidate for the honours of translation in the "Critique."

I understand now why no really good classic manual of psychology exists; why all that do exist only treat of particular points and chapters with any thoroughness. It is impossible to write one at present, so infinitely more numerous are the difficulties of the task than the means of their solution. Every chapter bristles with obstructions that refer one to the next ten years of work for their mitigation.

With all this I have done very little consecutive reading. I have not yet got at your historic survey in the "Critique Religieuse," for which my brain nevertheless itches. But I have read your articles apropos of Fouillée, and found them—the latest one especially—admirable for clearness and completeness of statement. Surely nothing like them has ever been written—no such stripping of the question down to its naked essentials. Those who, like Fouillée, have the intuition of the Absolute

Unity, will of course not profit by them or anything else. Why can all others view their own beliefs as *possibly* only hypotheses —*they* only not? Why does the Absolute Unity make its votaries so much more *conceited* at having attained it, then any other supposed truth does? This inner sense of superiority to all antagonists gives Fouillée his *fougue* and adds to his cleverness, and no doubt increases immensely the effectiveness of his writing over the average reader's mind. But it also makes him careless and liable to overshoot the mark.

I have just been interrupted by a visit from Noah Porter, D.D., President of Yale College, whose bulky work on "The Human Intellect" you may have in your library, possibly. An American college president is a very peculiar type of character, partly man of business, partly diplomatist, partly clergyman, and partly professor of metaphysics, armed with great authority and influence if his college is an important one—which Yale is; and Porter is the paragon of the type—*bonhomme et rusé*, learned and simple, kindhearted and sociable, yet possessed of great decision and obstinacy. He is over seventy, but comes every summer here to the woods to refresh himself by long mountain walks and life in "camp," sleeping on a bed of green boughs before a great fire in the open air. He looks like a farmer or a fisherman, and there is no sort of human being who does not immediately feel himself entirely at home in his company.

I have been here myself just a week. The virgin forest comes close to our house, and the diversity of walks through it, the brooks and the ascensions of hilltops are infinite. I doubt if there be anything like it in Europe. Your mountains are grander, but you have nowhere this carpet of absolutely primitive forest, with its indescribably sweet exhalations, spreading in every direction unbroken. I shall stay here doing hardly any work till late in September. I need to lead a purely animal life for at least two months to carry me through the teaching year. My wife and two children are here, all well. I would send you her photograph and mine, save that hers—the only one I have —is too bad to send to anyone, and my own are for the moment exhausted. I find myself counting the years till my next visit to Europe becomes possible. Then it shall occur under more cheerful circumstances, if possible; and I shall stay the full fifteen months instead of only six. As I look back now upon the winter, I find the strongest impression I received was that of the singularly artificial, yet deeply vital and soundly healthy, character of the English social and political system as it now exists. It is one of the most *bizarre* outbirths of time, one of the most abnormal, in certain ways, and yet one of the most success-ful. I know nothing that so much confirms your philosophy as this spectacle of an accumulation of individual initiatives *all preserved*. I hope both you and the Pillons are well. I shall never forget their friendliness, nor the spirit of human kindness that filled their household. I am ashamed to ask for letters from you, when after so long a silence I can myself give you so little that is of philosophic interest. But we must take long views; and, if life be granted, I shall do something yet, both in the way of reading and writing. Ever truly yours,

Wm. James.

To SHADWORTH H. HODGSON

Cambridge, Feb. 20, 1885

My dear Hodgson,—

Your letter of the 7th was most welcome. Anything responsive about my poor old father's writing falls most gratefully upon my heart. For I fear he found *me* pretty unresponsive during his lifetime; and that through my means any post-mortem response should come seems a sort of atonement. You would have enjoyed knowing him. I know of no one except Carlyle who had such a smiting *Ursprünglichkeit* of intuition, and such a deep sort of humor where human nature was concerned. He bowled one over in such a careless way. He was like Carlyle in being no *reasoner* at all, in the sense in which philosophers are reasoners. Reasoning was only an unfortunate necessity of exposition for them both. His *ideas*, however, were the exact inversion of Carlyle's; and he had nothing to correspond to Carlyle's insatiable learning of historic facts and memory. As you say, the world of his thought had a few elements and no others ever troubled him. *Those* elements were very deep ones, and had theological names. Under "Man" he would willingly have included all flesh, even that resident in Sirius or ethereal worlds. But he felt no need of positively looking so far. He was the humanest and most genial being in his impulses whom I have ever personally known, and had a bigness and power of nature that everybody felt. I thank you heartily for your interest. I wish that somebody could *take up* something from his system into a system more articulately scientific. As it is, most people will feel the *presence* of something real and true for the while they read, and go away and presently, unable to dovetail [it] into their own framework, forget it altogether.

I am hoping to write you a letter ere long, a letter philosophical. I am going over Idealism again, and mean to review your utterances on the subject. You know that, to quote what Gurney said one evening, to attain to assimilating your thought is the chief purpose of one's life. But you know also how hard it is for the likes of me to write, and how much that is felt is unthought, and that as thought [it] goes and must go unspoken. Brother Royce tells me he has sent you his "Religious Aspect of Philosophy." He is a wonderfully powerful fellow, not yet thirty, and this book seems to me to have a real fresh smell of the Earth about it. You will enjoy it, I know. I am very curious to hear what you think of his brand-new argument for Absolute Idealism.

I and mine are well. But the precious time as usual slips away with little work done. Happy you, whose time is all your own!

Wm. James.

To CARL STUMPF

Cambridge, Jan. 1, 1886

My dear Stumpf,—

. . . Let me tell you of my own fate since I wrote you last. It has been an eventful and in some respects a sad year. We lost our youngest child in the summer—the flower of the flock, 18 months old—with a painful and lingering whooping-cough complicated with pneumonia. My wife has borne it like an angel, however, which is something to be thankful for. Her mother, close to whom we have always lived, has had a severe pulmonary illness, which has obliged her to repair to Italy for health. She is now on the Ocean, with her youngest and only unmarried daughter, the second one having only a month ago become the wife of that [W. M.] Salter whose essays on ethics have lately been translated by von Gizycki in Berlin. So I have gained him as a brother-in-law, and regard it as a real gain. I have also gained a full Professorship with an increase of pay, and have moved into a larger and more commodious house. My eyes, too, are much better than they were a year ago, and I am able to do more work, so there is plenty of sweet as well as bitter in the cup.

I don't know whether you have heard of the London "Society

for Psychical Research," which is seriously and laboriously investigating all sorts of "supernatural" matters, clairvoyance, apparitions, etc. I don't know what you think of such work; but I think that the present condition of opinion regarding it is scandalous, there being a mass of testimony, or apparent testimony, about such things, at which the only men capable of a critical judgment—men of scientific education—will not even look. We have founded a similar society here within the year,—some of us thought that the publications of the London society deserved at least to be treated as if worthy of experimental disproof,—and although work advances very slowly owing to the small amount of disposable time on the part of the members, who are all very busy men, we have already stumbled on some rather inexplicable facts out of which something may come. It is a field in which the sources of deception are extremely numerous. But I believe there is no source of deception in the investigation of nature which can compare with a fixed belief that certain kinds of phenomenon are *impossible*.

My teaching is much the same as it was—a little better in quality, I hope. I enjoy very much a new philosophic colleague, Josiah Royce, from California, who is just thirty years old and a perfect little Socrates for wisdom and humor. I still try to write a little psychology, but it is exceedingly slow work. No sooner do I get interested than bang! goes my sleep, and I have to stop a week or ten days, during which my ideas get all cold again. Nothing so fatiguing as the eternal hanging on of an uncompleted task. . . . I try to spend two hours a day in a laboratory for psycho-physics which I started last year, but of which I fear the *fruits* will be slow in ripening, as my experimental aptitude is but small. But I am convinced that one must guard in some such way as that against the growing tendency to *subjectivism* in one's thinking, as life goes on. I am hypnotizing, on a large scale, the students, and have hit one or two rather pretty unpublished things of which some day I hope I may send you an account. . . . Ever faithfully yours,

Wm. James.

To HENRY JAMES

Cambridge, May 9, 1886

My dear Harry,—

I seize my pen the first leisure moment I have had for a week to tell you that I have read "The Bostonians" in the full flamingness of its bulk, and consider it an exquisite production. My growling letter was written to you before the end of Book I had appeared in the "Atlantic"; and the suspense of narrative in that region, to let the relation of Olive and Verena grow, was enlarged by the vacant months between the numbers of the magazine, so that it seemed to me so slow a thing had ne'er been writ. Never again shall I attack one of your novels in the magazine. I've only read one number of the "Princess Casamassima" —though I hear all the people about me saying it is the best thing you've done yet. To return to "The Bostonians"; the two last books are simply sweet. There isn't a hair wrong in Verena, you've made her neither too little nor too much—but absolutely *liebenswürdig*. It would have been so easy to spoil her picture by some little excess or false note. Her moral situation, between Woman's rights and Ransom, is of course deep, and her discovery of the truth on the Central Park day, etc., inimitably given. Ransom's character, which at first did not become alive to me, does so, handsomely, at last. In Washington, Hay told me that Secretary Lamar was delighted with it; Hay himself ditto, but especially with "Casamassima." I enclose a sheet from a letter of Gurney's but just received. You see how seriously he takes it. And I suppose he's right from a profoundly serious point of view,—*i.e.*, he would be right if the characters were real,—but as the story stands, I don't feel his objection. The *fancy* is more tickled by R.'s victory being complete. I hear very little said of the book, and I imagine it is being less read than its predecessors. The truth about it, combining what I said in my previous letter with what I have just written, seems to be this, that it is superlatively well done, provided one admits that method of doing such a thing at all. Really the *datum* seems to me to belong rather to the region of fancy, but the treatment to that of the most elaborate realism. One can easily imagine the story cut out and made into a bright, short, sparkling thing of a hundred pages, which would have been an absolute success. But you have worked it up by dint of descriptions and psychologic commentaries into near 500—charmingly done for those who have the leisure and the peculiar mood to enjoy that amount of miniature work—but perilously near to turning away the great majority of readers who crave more matter and less art. I can truly say, however, that as I have lain on my back after dinner each day for ten days past reading it to myself, my enjoyment has been complete. I imagine that inhabitants of other parts of the country have read it more than natives of these parts. They have bought it for the sake of the information. The way you have touched off the bits of American nature, Central Park, the Cape, etc., is exquisitely true and calls up just the feeling. Knowing you had done such a good thing makes the meekness of your reply to me last summer all the more wonderful.

I cannot write more—being much overloaded and in bad condition. The spring is opening deliciously—all the trees half out, and the white, bright, afternoon east winds beginning. Our household is well. . . .

Don't be alarmed about the labor troubles here. I am quite sure they are a most healthy phase of evolution, a little costly, but normal, and sure to do lots of good to all hands in the end. I don't speak of the senseless "anarchist" riot in Chicago, which has nothing to do with "Knights of Labor," but is the work of a lot of pathological Germans and Poles. I'm amused at the anti-Gladstonian capital which the English papers are telegraphed to be making of it. All the Irish names are among the killed and wounded policemen. Almost every anarchist name is Continental. Affectly.,

W. J.

To HIS SISTER, ALICE

Cambridge, Feb. 5, 1887

Dearest Alice,—

Your card and, a day or two later, K. P. L.'s letter to A. K., have made us acquainted with your sad tumble-down, for which I am sorrier than I can express, and can only take refuge in the hope, incessantly springing up again from its ashes, that you will "recuperate" more promptly than of late has been the case. I'm glad, at any rate, that it has got you into Harry's lodgings for a while, and hope your next permanent arrangement will prove better than the last. When, as occasionally happens, I have a day of headache, or of real sickness like that of last summer at Mrs. Dorr's, I think of you whose whole life is woven of that kind of experience, and my heart sinks at the horizon that opens, and wells over with pity. But when all is over, the longest life appears short; and we had better drink the cup, whatever it contains for, it *is* life. But I will not moralize or sympathize, for fear of awakening more "screams of laughter" similar to those which you wrote of as greeting my former attempts.

We have had but one letter from Harry—soon after his arrival at Florence. I hope he has continued to get pleasure and profit from his outing. I haven't written to him since he left London, nor do I now write him a special letter, but the rest of this is meant for him as well as you, and if he is still to be away, you will forward it to him. We are getting along very well, on the whole, I keeping very continuously occupied, but not seeming to get ahead much, *for the days grow so short* with each advancing year. A day is now about a minute—hardly time to turn round in. Mrs. Gibbens arrived from Chicago last night, and in ten days she and Margaret will start, with our little Billy, for Aiken, S.C., to be gone till May. B. is asthmatic, she is glad to go south for her own sake, and the open-air life all day long will be much better for him than our arduous winter and spring. He is the most utterly charming little piece of human nature you ever saw, so packed with life, impatience, and feeling, that I think Father must have been just like him at his age. . . .

I have been paying ten or eleven visits to a mind-cure doctress, a sterling creature, resembling the "Venus of Medicine," Mrs. Lydia E. Pinkham, made solid and veracious-looking. I sit down beside her and presently drop asleep, whilst she disentangles the snarls out of my mind. She says she never saw a mind with so many, so agitated, so restless, etc. She said my *eyes*, mentally speaking, kept revolving like wheels in front of each other and in front of my face, and it was four or five sittings ere she could get them *fixed*. I am now, *unconsciously to myself*, much better than when I first went, etc. I thought it might please you to hear an opinion of my mind so similar to your own. Meanwhile what boots it to be made unconsciously better, yet all the while consciously to lie awake o'nights, as I still do?

Lectures are temporarily stopped and examinations begun. I seized the opportunity to go to my Chocorua place and see just what was needed to make it habitable for the summer. It is a goodly little spot, but we may not, after all, fit up the buildings till we have spent a summer in the place and "studied" the problem a little more closely. The snow was between two and three feet deep on a level, in spite of the recent thaws. The day after I arrived was one of the most crystalline purity, and the mountain simply exquisite in gradations of tint. I have a tenant in the house, one Sanborn, who owes me a dollar and a half a month, but can't pay it, being of a poetic and contemplative rather than of an active nature, and consequently excessively poor. He has a sign out "Attorney and Pension Agent," and writes and talks like one of the greatest of men. He was working the sewing machine when I was there, and talking of his share in the war, and why he didn't go to live in Boston, etc. (namely that he wasn't known), and my heart was heavy in my breast that so rich a nature, fitted to inhabit a tropical dreamland, should have nothing but that furnitureless cabin within and snow and sky without, to live upon. For, however spotlessly pure and dazzlingly lustrous snow may be, pure snow, always snow, and naught but snow, for four months on end, is, it must be confessed, a rather lean diet for the human soul—deficient in variety, chiaroscuro, and oleaginous and medieval elements. I felt as I was returning home that some intellectual inferiority *ought* to accrue to all populations whose environment for many months in the year consisted of pure snow.—You are better off, better off than you know, in that great black-earthed dunghill of an England. I say naught of politics, war, strikes, railroad accidents or public events, unless the departure of C. W. Eliot and his wife for a year in Europe be a public event. . . .

Well, dear old Alice, I hope and pray for you. Lots of love to Harry, and if Katharine is with you, to her. Yours ever,

W. J.

To HENRY JAMES

Cambridge, Feb. 15, 1891

Dear Harry,—

. . . Last Sunday I dined with Howells at the Childs', and was much delighted to hear him say that you were both a friend and an admirer of Rudyard Kipling. I am ashamed to say that I have been ashamed to write of my adoration of that infant phenomenon, not knowing, with your exquisitely refined taste, how you might be affected by him and fearing to *jar*. The more rejoiced am I at this, but why didn't you say so ere now? He's more of a Shakespeare than anyone yet in this generation of ours, as it strikes me. And seeing the new effects he lately brings in in "The Light That Failed," and that Simla Ball story with Mrs. Hauksbee in the *Illustrated London News*, makes one sure now that he is only at the beginning of a rapidly enlarging career, with indefinite growth before him. Much of his present coarseness and jerkiness is youth only, divine youth. But *what* a youth! Distinctly the biggest literary phenomenon of our time. He has such human entrails, and he takes less time to get under the heartstrings of his personages than anyone I know. On the whole, bless him.

All intellectual work is the same,—the artist feeds the public on his own bleeding insides. Kant's *Kritik* is just like a Strauss waltz, and I felt the other day, finishing "The Light That Failed," and an ethical address to be given at Yale College simultaneously, that there was no *essential* difference between Rudyard Kipling and myself as far as that sacrificial element goes. I gave the address last Monday to an audience of about

[131]

a hundred, absolutely mute. Professor Ladd, who was my host, did not by a single syllable allude to the address after it was delivered, either on our walk home or the following morn. Apparently it was unmentionable.

Speaking of the unmentionable, it may interest Alice to hear that I have had this afternoon a two hours' visit from Mrs. H. of Princeton, Mass., where she and the family boarded in the '60s. I didn't know it till Mrs. H. reminded me, and asked about Alice and Mrs. Walsh. Her husband is the victim of one of those hideous mockeries of our civilization, and now serves out a two years' sentence in state prison for sending obscene matter through the mails; the matter consisting in a minute sheet called the *Voice,* which, of all imaginable causes of oppressed things, has taken up that of defending certain Saxon words not usually mentioned in polite society. These few words are martyrs and victims of injustice and prejudice, and one must die to reinstate them! *Grandeur et Néant de l'Homme!* Could anyone imagine such a crusade? Mrs. H. is a gifted creature in her way but practically quite mad. The Almighty must have laughed to see her *aux prises* with Dr. Peabody whilst the trial was going on. She came out here to get some scholars to stand up for her husband. Knowing no names she called at a house, and asked who were "liberal" in the college. "Do you mean in the way of *giving?*" "No, in the way of thought." Peabody and C. C. Everett were named. She goes to Peabody. He says "Your husband is a *bad,* a very *bad* man. He deserves to be imprisoned." . . . She told him she hated to cry, and forgave him. Outside the door the tears rained on the ground. . . . The two opposite lacks of humor, for her "the words" absolutely good, for Peabo "the words" absolutely bad,—what fools we all are! . . . Love to all. . . .

W. J.

To HIS SISTER, ALICE

Chocorua, N.H., July 6, 1891

Dearest Alice,

Tonight there comes another letter from Katherine telling everything about Dr. Clark's visit, especially the tumor in your poor breast and the pain which you have suffered there. I don't myself see very well how such a heart-defect as you could now be having could account for anything like the "heft" of your symptoms and condition; and so far from being shocked I am, although made more compassionate, yet (strange to say) rather relieved than shaken by this more tangible and immediately menacing source of woe. Katherine describes you as being so too; and I don't wonder. Vague nervousness has a character of ill about it that is all its own, and in comparison with which any organic disease has a good side. Of course, if the tumor should turn out to be cancerous, that means, as all men know, a finite length of days; and then, good-bye to neurasthenia and neuralgia and headache, and weariness and palpitation and disgust all at one stroke—I should think you would be reconciled to the prospect with all its pluses and minuses! I know you've never cared for life, and to me, now at the age of nearly fifty, life and death seem singularly close together in all of us— and life a mere farce of frustration in all, so far as the realization of the innermost ideals go to which we are made respectively capable of feeling an affinity and responding. Your frustrations are only rather more flagrant than the rule; and you've been saved many forms of self-dissatisfaction and misery which appertain to such a multiplication of responsible relations to different people as I, for instance, have got into. Your fortitude, good spirits and unsentimentality have been simply unexampled in the midst of your physical woes; and when you're relieved from your post, just *that* bright note will remain behind, together with the inscrutable and mysterious character of the doom of nervous weakness which has chained you down for all these years. As for that, there's more in it than has ever been told to so-called science. These inhibitions, these split-up selves, all these new facts that are gradually coming to light about our organization, these enlargements of the self in trance, etc., are bringing me to turn for light in the direction of all sorts of despised spiritualistic and unscientific ideas. Father would find in me today a much more receptive listener—all *that* philosophy has got to be brought in. And what a queer contradiction comes to the ordinary scientific argument against immortality (based on body being mind's condition and mind going *out* when body is gone), when one must believe (as now, in these neurotic cases) that some infernality in the body *prevents* really existing parts of the mind from coming to their effective rights at all, suppresses them, and blots them out from participation in this world's experiences, although they are *there* all the time. When that which is *you* passes out of the body, I am sure that there will be an explosion of liberated force and life till then eclipsed and kept down. I can hardly imagine *your* transition without a great oscillation of both "worlds" as they regain their new equilibrium after the change! Everyone will feel the shock, but you yourself will be more surprised than anybody else.

It may seem odd for me to talk to you in this cool way about your end; but, my dear little sister, if one has things present to one's mind, and I know they are present enough to *your* mind, why not speak them out? I am sure you appreciate that best. How many times I have thought, in the past year, when my days were so full of strong and varied impression and activities, of the long unchanging hours in bed which those days stood for with you, and wondered how you bore the slow-paced monotony at all, as you did! You can't tell how I've pitied you. But you *shall* come to your rights erelong. Meanwhile take things gently. Look for the little good in each day as if life were to last a hundred years. Above all things, save yourself from bodily pain, if it can be done. You've had too much of that. Take all the morphia (or other forms of opium if that disagrees) you want, and don't be afraid of becoming an opium-drunkard. What was opium created for except for such times as this? Beg the good Katharine (to whom *our* debt can never be extinguished) to write me a line every week, just to keep the currents flowing, and so farewell until I write again. Your ever loving,

W. J.

To HENRY JAMES

Asheville, N.C., Aug. 20, 1891

My dear Harry,—

... Of poor Lowell's death you heard. I left Cambridge the evening of the funeral, for which I had waited over, and meant to write to you about it that very afternoon. But as it turned out, I didn't get a moment of time. . . . He had never been ill in his life till two years ago, and didn't seem to understand or realize the fact as most people do. I doubt if he dreamed that his end was approaching until it was close at hand. Few images in my memory are more touching than the picture of his attitude in the last visits I paid him. He was always up and dressed, in his library, with his velvet coat and tobacco pipes, and ready to talk and be talked to, alluding to his illness with a sort of apologetic and whimsical plaintiveness that had no querulousness in it, though he coughed incessantly, and the last time I

[135]

was there (the last day of June, I think) he was strongly nar-
cotized by opium for a sciatica which had lately supervened.
Looking back at him, what strikes one most was his singularly
boyish cheerfulness and robustness of temperament. He was a
sort of a boy to the end, and makes most others seem like pre-
mature old men. . . .

To HIS SISTER, ALICE

Roan Mountain, Aug. 23, 1891

Dearest Sister,—

. . . I walked up here yesterday, and this peaceful sunny
morning, with the billowy mountain-world spread out all round
and beneath, the air is as round-edged and balmy (in spite of
its vitality) as if we were on the plain instead of at a height
of 6300-odd feet. Very different from the Mount Washington
air!

I got your admirable, inspired and inspiring letter before I
left home. It is good to hear you speak of this year as one of
the best of your life. It is good to hear you speak of life and
death from a standpoint so unshaken and serene, with what
one of the Adirondack guides spoke of as such "heaven-up-
histedness" in the point of view. A letter from Harry, received
only a few days later, confirmed me in this impression. He says
he is less "anxious" about you than at any former time, and I
think we ought all to be so together now. Poor Lowell's disease
was cancer. He never knew what it was, and in the shape of
positive pain, suffered comparatively little, although he had no
end of various discomforts. Now that he is gone, he seems a
much more unique and rare individual than before. What a
pity it is always so. I do hope that you will leave some notes on
life and English life which Harry can work in hereafter, so as

to make the best book he ever wrote. Charles Norton, I see, receives the bequest of Lowell's manuscripts, etc. The way that man gets his name stuck to every greatness is fabulous—Dante, Goethe, Carlyle, Ruskin, Fitzgerald, Chauncey Wright, and now Lowell! His name will dominate all the literary history of this epoch. 100 years hence, the *Revue des deux mondes* will publish an article entitled "La Vie de l'esprit aux États-Unis vers la fin du XIXme siècle; étude sur Charles Norton." He is our *foyer de lumières*; and the worst of it is that he does all the chores therewith connected, and practically fills the position rather better, than if he were the genuine article. . . .

I appear to be tougher physically and capable of more continuous head work than in many a long year. The *Psychology* turns out to be a much "bigger" book than I though it was; and reviews in the technical periodicals (I am given to understand) are erelong to inform the world of its true greatness. . . . Our children grow lovelier every year and more confidence-inspiring. . . . God bless you, dearest sister. Your loving

W. J.

Alice James, William's sister, died in 1892, at the age of 44.

To MISS MARY TAPPAN

Cambridge, April 29, 1892

My dear Mary,—

Your kind letter about poor Alice came today, and makes me do what I have long been on the *point* of doing—write a friendly word to you. Yes, Alice's death is a great release to her; she longed for it; and it is in a sense a release to all of us. In spite of its terrific frustrations her life was a triumph all the same, as I now see it. Her particular burden was borne well. She never whimpered or complained of her sickness, and never seemed to turn her face towards it, but up to the very limit of her allowance attended to outer things. When I went to London in September to bid her good-bye, she altogether refused to waste a minute in talking about her disease, and conversed only of the English people and Harry's play. So her soul was not subdued! I wish that mine might ever be as little so! Poor Harry is left rather disconsolate. He habitually stored up all sorts of things to tell her, and now he has no ear into which to pour their like. He says her talk was better than anyone's he knew in London. Strange to say, altho' practically bedridden for years, her mental atmosphere, barring a little over-vehemence, was altogether that of the *grand monde,* and the information about both people and public affairs which she had the art of absorbing from the air was astonishing.

We are probably all going to Europe on the 25th of May —[SS.] Friesland [to] Antwerp. Both Alice and I need a "year off," and I hope we shall get it. Our winter abode is yet unknown. I wish you were going to stay and we could be near you. I wish anyhow we might meet this summer and talk things over. It doesn't pay in this short life for good old friends to be nonexistent for each other; and how can one write letters of friendship when letters of business fill every chink of time? I *do hope* we shall meet, my dear Mary. Both of us send you lots of love, and plenty to Ellen too. Yours ever,

W. J.

To JOSIAH ROYCE

Florence, Dec. 18, 1892

Beloved Josiah,—

Your letter of Oct. 17, with "missent Indian mail" stamped upon its envelope in big letters, was handed in only ten days ago, after I had long said in my heart that you were no true friend to leave me thus languishing so long in ignorance of all that was befalling in Irving St. and the country round about. Its poetical hyperboles about the way I was missed made amends for everything, so I am not now writing to ask you for my diamonds back or to return my ringlet of your hair. It was a beautiful and bully letter and filled the hearts of both of us with exceeding joy. I have heard since then from the Gibbenses that you are made Professor—I fear at not more than $3000. But still it is a step ahead and I congratulate you most heartily thereupon. What I most urgently wanted to hear from you was some estimate of Münsterberg, and when you say "he is an immense success" you may imagine how I am pleased. He has his foibles, as who has not; but I have a strong impression that that youth will be a great man. Moreover, his naïveté and openness of nature make him very lovable. I do hope that [his] English will go—of course there can be no question of the students liking him, when once he gets his communications open. He has written me exhaustive letters, and seems to be out-doing even you in the amount of energizing which he puts forth. May God have him in his holy keeping!

From the midst of my laziness here the news I get from Cambridge makes it seem like a little seething Florence of the XVth Century. Having all the time there is, to myself, I of course find I have no time for doing any particular duties, and the consequence is that the days go by without anything very serious accomplished. But we live well and are comfortable by means of sheet-iron stoves which the clammy quality of the cold rather than its intensity seems to necessitate; and Italianism is "striking in" to all of us to various degrees of depth, shallowest of all I fear in Peg and the baby. When *Gemüthlichkeit* is banished from the world it will still survive in this dear and shabby old country; though I suppose the same sort of thing is really to be found in the East even more than in Italy, and that we shall seek it there when Italy has got as tram-roaded and modernized all over as Berlin. It is a curious smell of the past, that lingers over everything, speech and manners as well as stone and stuffs!

I went to Padua last week to a Galileo anniversary. It was splendidly carried out, and great fun; and they gave all of us foreigners honorary degrees. I rather like being a doctor of the University of Padua, and shall feel more at home than hitherto in the *Merchant of Venice*. I have written a letter to the *Nation* about it, which I commend to the attention of your gentle partner. Allan Marquand was there, just returning from a very thorough hunting up of all the specimens of Della Robbia pottery in Italy, for a monograph which he is preparing. He didn't strike me as having any special sympathy with the aesthetic side of art, but I find that nowadays the critical cataloguer regards the man whose interest in art is artistic as a most miserable and ignorant worm. Denman Ross seems to *me* a saint in this matter, with great love and acquaintance, but little scholarship and no humbug or conceit of knowledge. Mark Twain is here for the winter in a villa outside the town, hard at work writing something or other. I have seen him a couple of times—a fine, soft-fibred little fellow with the perversest twang and drawl, but very human and good. I should think that one might grow very fond of him, and wish he'd come and live in Cambridge.

I am just beginning to wake up from the sort of mental palsy that has been over me for the past year, and to take a little "notice" in matters philosophical. I am now reading Wundt's curiously long-winded *System*, which, in spite of his intolerable sleekness and way of *soaping* everything on to you by plausible transitions so as to make it run continuous, has every now and then a compendiously stated truth, or *aperçu*, which is nourishing and instructive. Come March, I will send you proposals for my work next year, to the "Cosmology" part of which I am just beginning to wake up. Benn, of the history of Greek philosophy, is here, a shy Irishman (I should judge) with a queer manner, whom I have only seen a couple of times, but with whom I shall probably later take some walks. He seems a good and well-informed fellow, much devoted to astronomy, and I have urged your works on his attention. He lent me the *New World* with your article in it, which I read with admiration. Would that belief would ensue! Perhaps I shall get straight. I have just been "penning" a notice of Renouvier's *Principes de la Nature* for Schurman. Renouvier cannot be *true*—his world is so much *dust*. But that conception is a *zu überwindendes Moment*, and he has given it his most energetic expression. There is a theodicy at the end, a speculation about this being a world fallen, which ought to interest you much from the point of view of your own cosmology.

Münsterberg wrote me, and I forgot to remark on it in my reply, that Scripture wanted him to contribute to a new Yale psychology review, but that he wished to publish in a volume. I confess it disgusts me to hear of each of these little separate college tin-trumpets. What I should really like would be a philosophic *monthly* in America which would be all-sufficing, as the *Revue philosophique* is in France. If it were a monthly, Münsterberg could find room for all his contributions from the laboratory. But I don't suppose that Scripture will combine with Schurman any more than Hall would, or for the matter of that, I don't know whether Schurman himself would wish it.

I hear that Mrs. Palmer is to go to Chicago. Is this to end by drawing Palmer gradually thither, or not? I also hear that they have 250 graduates, which might well account for any amount of depletion elsewhere. Have you heard of their filling out Palmer's philosophic program at all? What are you working at? Is the Goethe work started? Is music raging round you both as of yore? . . . We heard last night the new opera by Mascagni, *I Rantzau*, which has made a furore here and which I enjoyed hugely. How is Santayana, and what is he up to? You can't tell how thick the atmosphere of Cambridge seems over here. "Surcharged with vitality," in short. Write again whenever you can spare a fellow a half-hour, and believe me, with warmest regards from both of us to both of you, yours always,

Wm. James

To DICKINSON S. MILLER

London, July 8, 1893

Darling Miller,—

I must still for a while call you darling, in spite of your Toryism, ecclesiasticism, determinism, and general diabolism, which will probably result in your ruthlessly destroying me both as a man and as a philosopher some day. But sufficient unto that day will be its evil, so let me take advantage of the hours before "black-manhood comes" and still fondle you for a while upon my knee. And both you and Angell, being now colleagues and not students, had better stop Mistering or Professoring me, or I shall retaliate by beginning to "Mr." and "Prof." you. . . .

What you say of Erdmann, Uphues and the atmosphere of German academic life generally, is exceedingly interesting. If we can only keep our own humaner tone in spite of the growing complication of interests! I think we shall in great measure, for there is nothing here in English academic circles that corresponds to the German savagery. I do hope we may meet in Switzerland shortly, and you can then tell me what Erdmann's greatness consists in. . . .

[142]

To DICKINSON S. MILLER [*1893*]

I have done hardly any reading since the beginning of March. My genius for being frustrated and interrupted, and our unsettled mode of life have played too well into each other's hands. The consequence is that I rather long for settlement, and the resumption of the harness. If I only had working strength not to require these abominably costly vacations! Make the most of these days, my dear Miller. They will never exactly return, and will be looked back to by you hereafter as quite ideal. I am glad you have assimilated the German opportunities so well. Both Hodder and Angell have spoken with admiration of the methodical way in which you have forged ahead. It is a pity you have not had a chance at England, with which land you seem to have so many inward affinities. If you are to come here let me know, and I can give you introductions. Hodgson is in Yorkshire and I've missed him. Myers sails for the Chicago Psychic Congress, Aug. 2nd. Sidgwick may still be had, perhaps, and Bryce, who will give you an order to the Strangers' Gallery. The House of Commons, cradle of all free institutions, is really a wonderful and moving sight, and at bottom here the people are more good-natured on the Irish question than one would think to listen to their strong words. The cheery, active English temperament beats the world, I believe, the Deutschers included. But so cartilaginous and unsentimental as to the *Gemüth!* The girls like boys and the men like horses!

I shall be greatly interested in your article. As for Uphues, I am duly uplifted that such a man should read me, and am ashamed to say that amongst my pile of sins is that of having carried about two of his books with me for three or four years past, always meaning to read, and never actually reading them. I only laid them out again yesterday to take back to Switzerland with me. Such things make me despair. Paulsen's *Einleitung* is the greatest treat I have enjoyed of late. His synthesis is to

[143]

my mind almost lamentably unsatisfactory, but the book makes a station, an *étape*, in the expression of things. Good-bye—my wife comes in, ready to go out to lunch, and thereafter to Haslemere for the night. She sends love, and so do I. Address us when you get to Switzerland to M. Cérésole, as above, "la Chiesaz sur Vevey (Vaud), and believe me ever yours,

Wm. James

To HENRY JAMES

The Salters' Hill-top
[near Chocorua], Sept. 22, 1893

. . . I am up here for a few days with Billy, to close our house for the winter, and get a sniff of the place. The Salters have a noble hill with such an outlook! and a very decent little house and barn. But oh! the difference from Switzerland, the thin grass and ragged waysides, the poverty-stricken land, and sad American sunlight over all—sad because so empty. There is a strange thinness and femininity hovering over all America, so different from the stoutness and masculinity of land and air and everything in Switzerland and England, that the coming back makes one feel strangely sad and hardens one in the resolution never to go away again unless one can go to end one's day. Such a divided soul is very bad. To you, who now have real practical relations and a place in the old world, I should think there was no necessity of ever coming back again. But Europe has been made what it is by men staying in their homes and fighting stubbornly generation after generation for all the beauty, comfort and order that they have got—we must abide and do the same. As England struck me newly and differently last time, so America now—force and directness in the people, but a terrible grimness, more ugliness than I ever realized in things, and a greater weakness in nature's beauty, such as it is. One must pitch one's whole sensibility first in a different key— then gradually the quantum of personal happiness of which one is susceptible fills the cup—but the moment of change of key is lonesome. . . .

We had the great Helmholtz and his wife with us one afternoon, gave them tea and invited some people to meet them; she, a charming woman of the world, brought up by her aunt, Madame Mohl, in Paris; he the most monumental example of benign calm and speechlessness that I ever saw. He is growing old, and somewhat weary, I think, and makes no effort beyond that of smiling and inclining his head to remarks that are made. At least he made no response to remarks of mine; but Royce, Charles Norton, John Fiske, and Dr. Walcott, who surrounded him at a little table where he sat with tea and beer, said that he spoke. Such power of calm is a great possession.

I have been twice to Mrs. Whitman's, once to a lunch and reception to the Bourgets a fortnight ago. Mrs. G——, it would seem, has kept them like caged birds (probably because they wanted it so); Mrs. B. was charming and easy, he ill at ease, refusing to try English unless compelled, and turning to *me* at the table as a drowning man to a "hencoop," as if there were safety in the presence of anyone connected with you. I could do nothing towards inviting them, in the existent state of our ménage; but when, later, they come back for a month in Boston, I shall be glad to bring them into the house for a few days. I feel quite a fellow feeling for him; he seems a very human creature, and it was a real pleasure to me to see a Frenchman of B.'s celebrity *look* as ill at ease as I myself have often *felt* in fashionable society. They are, I believe, in Canada, and have only too much society.

I shan't go to Chicago, for economy's sake—besides I *must*

get to work. But *everyone* says one ought to sell all one has and mortgage one's soul to go there; it is esteemed such a revelation of beauty. People cast away all sin and baseness, burst into tears and grow religious, etc., under the influence!! *Some* people evidently. . . .

The people about home are very pleasant to meet. . . . Yours ever affectionately,

Wm. James

To PRESIDENT ELIOT

Cambridge, March 3, 1895

Dear President,—

I hate to hunt you down with disagreeable college problems, but how is a Supreme Being to hide from his creatures? The problem is this. The Philosophic Department has met to arrange the courses for next year, and my taking charge of psychology means . . . that the important course in "Cosomolgy" or "Philosophy of Nature" . . . must either be dropped for next year or given to some outsider. Now I want to propose to you no less a person than Charles S. Peirce, whose name I don't suppose will make you bound with eagerness at first, but you may think better of it after a short reflection. . . . The better graduates would flock to hear him—his name is one of mysterious greatness for them now—and he would leave a wave of influence, tradition, gossip, etc. that wouldn't die away for many years. *I* should learn a lot from his course. Everyone knows of Peirce's personal uncomfortableness; and if I were President I shouldn't hope for a harmonious wind-up to his connection with the University. But I should take that as part of the disagreeableness of the day's work, and shut my eyes and go ahead, knowing that from the highest intellectual point of view it would be the best thing that could happen for the graduates of the Philosophical Department. It would also advertise us as doing all we could, and making the best of every emergency; and it would be a recognition of C. S. P.'s strength, which I am sure is but justice to the poor fellow. I truly believe that the path of (possibly) least comfort is here the *true* path, so I have no hesitation in urging my opinion. . . . Always truly yours,

Wm. James

To MRS. HENRY WHITMAN
Springfield Centre, N.Y., June 16, 1895
My dear Friend,—

About the 22nd! I will come if you command it; but reflect on my situation ere you do so. Just reviving from the addled and corrupted condition in which the Cambridge year has left me; just at the portals of that Adirondack wilderness for the breath of which I have sighed for years, unable to escape the cares of domesticity and get there; just about to get a little health into me, a little simplification and solidification and purification and sanification—things which will never come again if this one chance be lost; just filled to satiety with all the simpering conventions and vacuous excitements of so-called civilization; hungering for their opposite, the smell of the spruce, the feel of the moss, the sound of the cataract, the bath in its waters, the divine outlook from the cliff or hill-top over the unbroken forest—oh, Madam, Madam! do you know what medicinal things you ask me to give up? Alas!

I aspire downwards, and really *am* nothing, *not becoming* a savage as I would be, and failing to be the civilizee that I really ought to be content with being! But I wish that *you*

[147]

also aspired to the wilderness. There are some nooks and summits in that Adirondack region where one can really "recline on one's divine composure," and, as long as one stays up there, seem for a while to enjoy one's birth-right of freedom and relief from every fever and falsity. Stretched out on such a shelf,—with thee beside me singing in the wilderness,—what babblings might go on, what judgment-day discourse!

Command me to give it up and return, if you will, by telegram addressed "Adirondack Lodge, North Elba, N.Y." In any case I shall return before the end of the month, and later shall be hanging about Cambridge some time in July, giving lectures (for my sins) in the Summer School. I am staying now with a cousin on Otsego Lake, a dear old country-place that has been in their family for a century, and is rich and ample and reposeful. The Kipling visit went off splendidly—he's a regular little brick of a man; but it's strange that with so much sympathy with the insides of every living thing, brute or human, drunk or sober, he should have so little sympathy with those of a Yankee—who also is, in the last analysis, one of God's creatures. I have stopped at Williamstown, at Albany, at Amsterdam, at Utica, at Syracuse, and finally here, each time to visit human beings with whom I had business of some sort or other. The best was Benj. Paul Blood at Amsterdam, a son of the soil, but a man with extraordinary power over the English tongue, of whom I will tell you more some day. I will by the way enclose some clippings from his latest "effort." "Yes, Paul is quite a *correspondent!*" as a citizen remarked to me from whom I inquired the way to his dwelling. Don't you think "correspondent" rather a good generic term for "man of letters," from the point of view of the country-town newspaper reader?...

Now, dear, noble, incredibly perfect Madam, you won't take

ill my reluctance about going to Beverly, even to your abode, so soon. I am a badly mixed critter, and I experience a certain organic need for simplification and solitude that is quite imperious, and so vital as actually to be respectable even by others. So be indulgent to your ever faithful and worshipful,

W. J.

III

1896-1906: YEARS OF LECTURING, ILLNESS, *THE VARIETIES OF RELIGIOUS EXPERIENCE*

JAMES "was not credulous, but *suffered from incredulity*," Ralph Barton Perry says in connection with *The Will to Believe*, published in 1897. This book was dedicated to the philosopher Charles Peirce. Peirce's letter of acknowledgment, quoted by Perry, says, "as to 'belief' and 'making up one's mind,' if they mean anything more than this, that we have a plan of procedure, and that according to that plan we will try a given description of behavior, I am inclined to think they do more harm than good. 'Faith,' and the sense that one will adhere consistently to a given line of conduct, is highly necessary in affairs. But if it means that you are not going to be alert for indications that the moment has come to change your tactics, I think it ruinous in practice."

During the nineteenth century Americans went in hugely for the public lecture, and James hugely supplied them, especially after his work in psychology had made him known to large audiences. Trips to New York and Chicago were nothing to this compulsive traveler, who was also likely to add California and Rome to a spring schedule. In the summer of 1898 he sought to overcome the fatigue of writing, teaching and lecturing, of embarking and disembarking, by a holiday given over to mountain climbing in the Adirondacks. The results of this were sad. His son, Henry James, writes that the "prolonged physical exertion of the two days' climb, aggravated by the fact that he carried a pack all the second day, was too much for a man of his years and sedentary occupations. As the summer wore on, pain or discomfort in the region of his heart became constant. He tried to persuade himself that it was nothing. . . . The fact was that the strain of the two days' climb had caused a valvular lesion that was irreparable."

The next year James went on another trip to the mountains and suffered a further straining of his heart. The whole of the period from 1899-1902 was spent abroad in search of his health, a search that sent him back to some of the same spas and clinics he had visited during his early sufferings. Nevertheless, this late period of "collapse" produced the Gifford lectures, which were delivered in Edinburgh in 1901. These lectures were published in 1902 as *The Varieties of Religious Experience, A Study in Human Nature*—a supremely lively and enduring work.

To HIS CLASS AT RADCLIFFE COLLEGE WHICH HAD SENT A POTTED AZALEA TO HIM AT EASTER

Cambridge, Apr. 6, 1896

Dear Young Ladies,—

I am deeply touched by your remembrance. It is the first time anyone ever treated me so kindly, so you may well believe that the impression on the heart of the lonely sufferer will be even more durable than the impression on your minds of all the teachings of Philosophy 2A. I now perceive one immense omission in my Psychology,—the deepest principle of Human Nature is the *craving to be appreciated,* and I left it out altogether from the book, because I had never had it gratified till now. I fear you have let loose a demon in me, and that all my actions will now be for the sake of such rewards. However, I will try to be faithful to this one unique and beautiful azalea tree, the pride of my life and delight of my existence. Winter and summer will I tend and water it—even with my tears. Mrs. James shall never go near it or touch it. If it dies, I will die too; and if I die, it shall be planted on my grave.

Don't take all this too jocosely, but believe in the extreme pleasure you have caused me, and in the affectionate feelings with which I am and shall always be faithfully your friend,

Wm. James

To HENRY JAMES

Chocorua, June 11, 1896

Dear Heinrich:—

Your long letter of Whitsuntide week in London came yesterday evening, and was read by me aloud to Alice and Harry as we sat at tea in the window to get the last rays of the Sunday's [sun]. You have too much feeling of duty about corresponding with us, and, I imagine, with everyone. I think you have behaved most handsomely of late—and always, and though your letters are the great *fête* of our lives, I won't be "on your mind" for worlds. Your general feeling of unfulfilled obligations is one that runs in the family—I at least am often afflicted by it— but it is "morbid." The horrors of *not* living in America, as you so well put it, are not shared by those who do live here. All that the telegraph imparts are the shocks; the "happy homes," good husbands and fathers, fine weather, honest business men, neat new houses, punctual meetings of engagements, etc., of which the country mainly consists, are never cabled over. Of course, the Saint Louis disaster is dreadful, but it will very likely end by "improving" the city. The really bad thing here is the silly wave that has gone over the public mind—protection humbug, silver, jingoism, etc. It is a case of "mob-psychology." Any country is liable to it if circumstances conspire, and our circumstances have conspired. It is very hard to get them out of the rut. It *may* take another financial crash to get them out— which, of course, will be an expensive method. It is no more foolish and considerably less damnable than the Russophobia of England, which would seem to have been responsible for the Armenian massacres. That to me is the biggest indictment "of our boasted civilization"!! It *requires* England, I say nothing of the other powers, to maintain the Turks at that business. We have let our little place, our tenant arrives the day after tomorrow, and Alice and I and Tweedie have been here a week enjoying it and cleaning house and place. She has worked like a beaver. I had two days spoiled by a psychological experiment with *mescal*, an intoxicant used by some of our Southwestern Indians in their religious ceremonies, a sort of cactus bud, of which the U. S. Government had distributed a supply to certain medical men, including Weir Mitchell who sent me some to try. He had himself been "in fairyland." It gives the most glorious visions of color—every object thought of appears in a jeweled splendor unknown to the natural world. It disturbs the stomach somewhat, but that, according to W. M., was a cheap price, etc. I took one bud three days ago, was violently sick for 24 hours, and had no other symptom whatever except that and the *Katzenjammer* the following day. I will take the visions on trust!

We have had three days of delicious rain—it all soaks into

the sandy soil here and leaves no mud whatever. The little place is the most curious mixture of sadness with delight. The sadness of *things*—things every one of which was done either by our hands or by our planning, old furniture renovated, there isn't an object in the house that isn't associated with past life, old summers, dead people, people who will never come again, etc., and the way it catches you round the heart when you first come and open the house from its long winter sleep is most extraordinary.

I have been reading Bourget's "Idylle Tragique," which he very kindly sent me, and since then have been reading in Tolstoy's "War and Peace," which I never read before, strange to say. I must say that T. rather kills B., for my mind. B.'s moral atmosphere is anyhow so foreign to me, a lewdness so obligatory that it hardly seems as if it were part of a moral *donnée* at all; and then his overlabored descriptions, and excessive explanations. But with it all an earnestness and enthusiasm for getting it said as well as possible, a richness of epithet, and a warmth of heart that makes you like him, in spite of the unmanliness of all the things he writes about. I suppose there is a stratum in France to whom it is all manly and ideal, but he and I are, as Rosina says, a bod combination. . . .

Tolstoy is immense!

I am glad *you* are in a writing vein again, to go still higher up the scale! I have abstained on principle from the "Atlantic" serial, wishing to get it all at once. I am not going abroad; I can't afford it. I have a chance to give $1500 worth of summer lectures here, which won't recur. I have a heavy year of work next year, and shall very likely *need* to go the following summer, which will anyhow be after a more becoming interval than this, so, *somme toute*, it is postponed. If I went I should certainly enjoy seeing you at Rye more than in London, which I confess tempts me little now. I love to *see* it, but staying there doesn't seem to agree with me, and only suggests constraint and money-spending, apart from seeing you. I wish you could see how comfortable our Cambridge house has got at last to be. Alice who is upstairs sewing whilst I write below by the lamp—a great wood fire hissing in the fireplace—sings out her thanks and love to you. . . .

The following excerpts from letters to his wife were written from Chautauqua, where James was lecturing.

To MRS. JAMES

Chautauqua, July 23, 1896

. . . The audience is some 500, in an open-air auditorium where (strange to say) everyone seems to hear well; and it is very good-looking—mostly teachers and women, but they make the best impression of any audience of that sort that I have seen except the Brooklyn one. So here I go again! . . .

July 24, 9:30 P.M.

. . . X—— departed after breakfast—a good inarticulate man, farmer's boy, four years soldier from private to major, business man in various States, great reader, editor of a "Handbook of Facts," full of swelling and bursting *Weltschmerz* and religious melancholy, yet no more flexibility or self-power in his mind than in a boot-jack. Altogether, what with the teachers, him and others whom I've met, I'm put in conceit of college training. It certainly gives glibness and flexibility, if it doesn't give earnestness and depth. I've been meeting minds so earnest and

helpless that it takes them half an hour to get from one idea
to its immediately adjacent next neighbor, and that with infinite
creaking and groaning. And when they've got to the next idea,
they lie down on it with their whole weight and can get no
farther, like a cow on a door-mat, so that you can get neither in
nor out with them. Still, glibness is not all. Weight is something, even cow-weight. Tolstoy feels these things so—I am still
in "Anna Karenina," volume I, a book almost incredible and
supernatural for veracity. I wish we were reading it aloud
together. It has rained at intervals all day. Young Vincent, a
powerful fellow, took me over and into the whole vast college
side of the institution this A.M. I have heard 4½ lectures, including the one I gave myself at 4 o'clock, to about 1200 or more
in the vast open amphitheatre, which seats 6000 and which has
very acoustic properties. I think my voice sufficed. I can't judge
of the effect. Of course I left out all that gossip about my medical degree, etc. But I don't want any more sporadic lecturing—
I must stick to more inward things.

July 26, 12:30 P.M.

. . . 'T is the sabbath and I am just in from the amphitheatre,
where the Rev. —— has been chanting, calling and bellowing
his hour-and-a-quarter-long sermon to 6000 people at least—a
sad audition. The music was bully, a chorus of some 700, splendidly drilled, with the audience to help. I have myself been
asked to lead, or, if not to lead, at least to do something prominent—I declined so quick that I didn't fully gather what it
was—in the exercise which I have marked on the program I
enclose. Young Vincent, whom I take to be a splendid young
fellow, told me it was the characteristically "Chautauquan"
event of the day. I would give anything to have you here. I

didn't write yesterday because there is no mail till tomorrow. I went to four lectures, in whole or in part. All to hundreds of human beings, a large proportion unable to get seats, who transport themselves from one lecture-room to another *en masse*. One was on bread-making, with practical demonstrations. One was *walking*, by a graceful young Delsartian, who showed us a lot. One was on telling stories to children, the psychology and pedagogy of it. The audiences interrupt and ask questions occasionally in spite of their size. There is hardly a pretty woman's face in the lot, and they seem to have little or no humor in their composition. No *epicureanism* of any sort!

Yesterday was a beautiful day, and I sailed an hour and a half down the Lake again to "Celoron," "America's greatest pleasure resort,"—in other words popcorn and peep-show place. A sort of Midway-Pleasance in the wilderness—supported Heaven knows how, so far from any human habitation except the odd little Jamestown from which a tramway leads to it. Good monkeys, bears, foxes, etc. Endless peanuts, popcorn, bananas, and soft drinks; crowds of people, a ferris wheel, a balloon ascension, with a man dropping by a parachute, a theatre, a vast concert hall, and all sorts of peep-shows. I feel as if I were in a foreign land; even as far east as this the accent of everyone is terrific. The "Nation" is no more known than the London "Times." I see no need of going to Europe when such wonders are close by. I breakfasted with a Methodist parson with 32 false teeth, at the X's table, and discoursed of demoniacal possession. The wife said she had my portrait in her bedroom with the words written under it, "I want to bring a balm to human lives"!!!!! Supposed to be a quotation from me!!! After breakfast an extremely interesting lady who has suffered from half-possessional insanity gave me a long account of her case. Life *is* heroic indeed, as Harry wrote. I shall stay through tomorrow, and get to Syracuse on Tuesday....

July 27

... It rained hard last night, and today a part of the time. I took a lesson in roasting, in Delsarte, and I made with my own fair hands a beautiful loaf of graham bread with some rolls, long, flute-like, and delicious. I should have sent them to you by express, only it seemed unnecessary, since I can keep the family in bread easily after my return home. Please tell this, with amplifications, to Peggy and Tweedy....

Buffalo, N.Y., July 29

... The Chautauqua week, or rather six and a half days, has been a real success. I have learned a lot, but I'm glad to get into something less blameless but more admiration-worthy. The flash of a pistol, a dagger, or a devilish eye, anything to break the unlovely level of 10,000 good people—a crime, murder, rape, elopement, anything would do. I don't see how the younger Vincents stand it, because they are people of such spirit....

Syracuse, N.Y., July 31

... Now for Utica and Lake Placid by rail, with East Hill in prospect for tomorrow. You bet I rejoice at the outlook—I long to escape from tepidity. Even an Armenian massacre, whether to be killer or killed, would seem an agreeable change from the blamelessness of Chautauqua as she lies soaking year after year in her lakeside sun and showers. Man wants to be *stretched* to his utmost, if not in one way then in another! ...

To THEODORE FLOURNOY

Lake Geneva, Wisconsin, Aug. 30, 1896

My dear Flournoy,—

You see the electric current of sympathy that binds the world together—I turn towards you, and the place I write from repeats the name of your Lake Leman. I was informed yesterday, however, that the lake here was named after Lake Geneva *in the State of New York!* and *that* Lake only has Leman for its God-mother. Still you see how dependent, whether immediately or remotely, America is on Europe. I was at Niagara some three weeks ago, and bought a photograph as souvenir and addressed it to you after getting back to Cambridge. Possibly Madame Flournoy will deign to accept it. I have thought of you a great deal without writing, for truly, my dear Flournoy, there is hardly a human being with whom I feel as much sympathy of aims and character, or feel as much "at home," as I do with you. It is as if we were of the same stock, and I often mentally turn and make a remark to you, which the pressure of life's occupations prevents from ever finding its way to paper.

I am hoping that you may have figured, or at any rate *been*, at the Munich "Congress"—that apparently stupendous affair. If they keep growing at this rate, the next Paris one will be altogether too heavy. I have heard no details of the meeting as yet. But whether you have been at Munich or not, I trust that you have been having a salubrious and happy vacation so far, and that Mrs. Flournoy and the young people are all well. I will venture to suppose that your illness of last year has left no bad effects whatever behind. I myself have had a rather busy and instructive, though possibly not very hygienic summer, making money (in moderate amounts) by lecturing on psychology to teachers at different "summer schools" in this land.

[160]

There is a great fermentation in "pædagogy" at present in the U.S., and my wares come in for their share of patronage. But although I learn a good deal and become a better American for having all the travel and social experience, it has ended by being too tiresome; and when I give the lectures at Chicago, which I begin tomorrow, I shall have them stenographed and very likely published in a very small volume, and so remove from myself the temptation ever to give them again.

Last year was a year of hard work, and before the end of the term came, I was in a state of bad neurasthenic fatigue, but I got through outwardly all right. I have definitely given up the laboratory, for which I am more and more unfit, and shall probably devote what little ability I may hereafter have to purely "speculative" work. My inability to read troubles me a good deal: I am in arrears of several years with psychological literature, which, to tell the truth, does grow now at a pace too rapid for anyone to follow. I was engaged to review Stout's new books (which I fancy is very good) for "Mind," and after keeping it two months had to back out, from sheer inability to read it, and to ask permission to hand it over to my colleague Royce. Have you seen the colossal Renouvier's two vast volumes on the philosophy of history?—that will be another thing worth reading no doubt, yet very difficult to read. I give a course in Kant for the first time in my life (!) next year, and at present and for many months to come shall have to put most of my reading to the service of that overgrown subject. . . .

Of course you have read Tolstoy's "War and Peace" and "Anna Karenina." I never had that exquisite felicity before this summer, and now I feel as if I knew *perfection* in the representation of human life. Life indeed seems less real than his tale of it. Such infallible veracity! The impression haunts me as nothing literary ever haunted me before.

I imagine you lounging on some steep mountainside, with those demoiselles all grown too tall and beautiful and proud to think otherwise than with disdain of their elderly *commensal* who spoke such difficult French when he took walks with them at Vers-chez-les-Blanc. But I hope that they are happy as they were then. Cannot we all pass some summer near each other again, and can't it next time be in Tyrol rather than in Switzerland, for the purpose of increasing in all of us that "knowledge of the world" which is so desirable? I think it would be a splendid plan. At any rate, wherever you are, take my most affectionate regard for yourself and Madame Flournoy and all of yours, and believe me ever sincerely your friend,

Wm. James

To DICKINSON S. MILLER

Lake Geneva, Wisconsin, Aug. 30, 1896

Dear Miller,—

Your letter from Halle of June 22nd came duly, but treating of things eternal as it did, I thought it called for no reply till I should have caught up with more temporal matters, of which there has been no lack to press on my attention. To tell the truth, regarding you as my most penetrating critic and intimate enemy, I was greatly relieved to find that you had nothing worse to say about "The Will to Believe." You say you are no "rationalist," and yet you speak of the "sharp" distinction between beliefs based on "inner evidence" and beliefs based on "craving." I can find *nothing* sharp (or susceptible of schoolmaster's codification) in the different degrees of "liveliness" in hypotheses concerning the universe, or distinguish *a priori* between legitimate and illegitimate cravings. And when an hypothesis *is* once a live one, one *risks* something in one's practical relations towards truth and error, *whichever* of the three positions (affirmation, doubt, or negation) one may take up towards it. *The individual himself is the only rightful chooser of his risk.* Hence respectful toleration, as the only law that logic can lay down.

You don't say a word against my *logic*, which seems to me to cover your cases entirely in its compartments. I class you as one to whom the religious hypothesis is *von vornherein* so dead, that the risk of error in espousing it now far outweighs for you the chance of truth, so you simply stake your money on the field as against it. If you *say* this, of course I can, as logician, have no quarrel with you, even though my own choice of risk (determined by the irrational impressions, suspicions, cravings, senses of direction in nature, or what not, that make religion for me a more live hypothesis than for you) leads me to an opposite methodical decision.

Of course if any one comes along and says that men at large don't need to have facility of faith in their inner convictions preached to them, [that] they have only too much readiness in that way already, and the one thing needful to preach is that they should hesitate with their convictions, and take their faiths out for an airing into the howling wilderness of nature, I should also agree. But my paper wasn't addressed to mankind at large but to a limited set of studious persons, badly under the ban just now of certain authorities whose simple-minded faith in "naturalism" also is sorely in need of an airing—and an airing, as it seems to me, of the sort I tried to give.

But all this is unimportant; and I still await criticism of my *Auseinandersetzung* of the *logical situation* of man's mind *gegenüber* the Universe, in respect to the risks it runs.

I wish I could have been with you at Munich and heard the deep-lunged Germans roar at each other. I care not for the matters uttered, if I only could hear the voice. I hope you met

[Henry] Sidgwick there. I sent him the American Hallucination-Census results, after considerable toil over them, but S. never acknowledges or answers anything, so I'll have to wait to hear from someone else whether he "got them off." I have had a somewhat unwholesome summer. Much lecturing to teachers and sitting up to talk with strangers. But it is instructive and makes one patriotic, and in six days I shall have finished the Chicago lectures, which begin tomorrow, and get straight to Keene Valley for the rest of September. My conditions just now are materially splendid, as I am the guest of a charming elderly lady, Mrs. Wilmarth, here at her country house, and in town at the finest hotel of the place. The political campaign is a bully one. Everyone outdoing himself in sweet reasonableness and persuasive argument—hardly an undignified note anywhere. It shows the deepening and elevating influence of a big topic of debate. It is difficult to doubt of a people part of whose life such an experience is. But imagine the country being saved by a McKinley! If only Reed had been the candidate! There have been some really splendid speeches and documents. . . .

> Ever thine,
> W. J.

To HENRY W. RANKIN

> *Newport, R.I., Feb. 1, 1897*

Dear Mr. Rankin,—

A pause in lecturing, consequent upon our midyear examinations having begun, has given me a little respite, and I am paying a three-days' visit upon an old friend here, meaning to leave for New York tomorrow where I have a couple of lectures to give. It is an agreeable moment of quiet and enables me to write a letter or two which I have long postponed, and chiefly one to you, who have given me so much without asking anything in return.

One of my lectures in New York is at the Academy of Medicine before the Neurological Society, the subject being "Demoniacal Possession." I shall of course duly advertise the Nevius book. I am not as positive as you are in the belief that the obsessing agency is really demonic individuals. I am perfectly willing to adopt that theory if the facts lend themselves best to it; for who can trace limits to the hierarchies of personal existence in the world? But the lower stages of mere automatism shade off so continuously into the highest supernormal manifestations, through the intermediary ones of imitative hysteria and "suggestibility," that I feel as if no *general theory* as yet would cover all the facts. So that the most I shall plead for before the neurologists is the recognition of demon possession as a regular "morbid-entity" whose commonest homologue today is the "spirit-control" observed in test-mediumship, and which tends to become the more benignant and less alarming, the less pessimistically it is regarded. This last remark seems certainly to be true. Of course I shall not ignore the sporadic cases of old-fashioned malignant possession which still occur today. I am convinced that we stand with all these things at the threshold of a long inquiry, of which the end appears as yet to no one, least of all to myself. And I believe that the best theoretic work yet done in the subject is the beginning made by F. W. H. Myers in his papers in the S. P. R. Proceedings. The first thing is to start the medical profession out of its idiotically *conceited ignorance* of all such matters—matters which have everywhere and at all times played a vital part in human history.

You have written me at different times about conversion, and about miracles, getting as usual no reply, but not because I failed to heed your words, which come from a deep life-experience of your own evidently, and from a deep acquaintance with the experiences of others. In the matter of conversion I am quite willing to believe that a new truth may be supernaturally revealed to a subject when he really *asks*. But I am sure that in many cases of conversion it is less a new truth than a new power gained over life by a truth always known. It is a case of the conflict of two *self-systems* in a personality up to that time heterogeneously divided, but in which, after the conversion-crisis, the higher loves and powers come definitively to gain the upper-hand and expel the forces which up to that time had kept them down in the position of mere grumblers and protesters and agents of remorse and discontent. This broader view will cover an enormous number of cases *psychologically*, and leaves all the *religious importance* to the result which it has on any other theory.

As to true and false miracles, I don't know that I can follow you so well, for in any case the notion of a miracle as a mere attestation of superior power is one that I cannot espouse. A miracle must in any case be an expression of personal purpose, but the demon-purpose of antagonizing God and winning away his adherents has never yet taken hold of my imagination. I prefer an open mind of inquiry, first *about the facts*, in all these matters; and I believe that the S. P. R. methods, if pertinaciously stuck to, will eventually do much to clear things up.— You see that, although religion is the great interest of my life, I am rather hopelessly non-evangelical, and take the whole thing too impersonally.

But my College work is lightening in a way. Psychology is being handed over to others more and more, and I see a chance ahead for reading and study in other directions from those to which my very feeble powers in that line have hitherto been

[166]

confined. I am going to give all the fragments of time I can get, after this year is over, to religious biography and philosophy. Shield's book, Steenstra's, Gratry's, and Harris's, I don't yet know, but can easily get at them.

I hope your health is better in this beautiful winter which we are having. I am very well, and so is all my family. Believe me, with affectionate regards, truly yours,

Wm. James

The following letter refers to the memorial sculpture by St. Gaudens done in honor of Colonel Robert Gould Shaw and his Negro regiment. When the monument was unveiled in Boston, May 31, 1897, James delivered the address he mentions.

To HENRY JAMES

Cambridge, June 5, 1897

Dear H.,—

Alice wrote you (I think) a brief word after the crisis of last Monday. It took it out of me nervously a good deal, for it came at the end of the month of May, when I am always fagged to death; and for a week previous I had almost lost my voice with hoarseness. At nine o'clock the night before I ran in to a laryngologist in Boston, who sprayed and cauterized and otherwise tuned up my throat, giving me pellets to suck all the morning. By a sort of miracle I spoke for three-quarters of an hour without becoming perceptibly hoarse. But it is a curious kind of physical effort to fill a hall as large as Boston Music Hall, unless you are trained to the work. You have to shout and bellow, and you seem to yourself wholly unnatural. The day was an extraordinary occasion for sentiment. The

[167]

streets were thronged with people, and I was toted around for two hours in a barouche at the tail end of the procession. There were seven such carriages in all, and I had the great pleasure of being with St. Gaudens, who is a most charming and modest man. The weather was cool and the skies were weeping, but not enough to cause any serious discomfort. They simply formed a harmonious background to the pathetic sentiment that reigned over the day. It was very peculiar, and people have been speaking about it ever since—the last wave of the war breaking over Boston, everything softened and made poetic and unreal by distance, poor little Robert Shaw erected into a great symbol of deeper things than he ever realized himself,— "the tender grace of a day that is dead,"—etc. We shall never have anything like it again. The monument is really superb, certainly one of the finest things of this century. Read the darkey [Booker T.] Washington's speech, a model of elevation and brevity. The thing that struck me most in the day was the faces of the old 54th soldiers, of whom there were perhaps about thirty or forty present, with such respectable old darkey faces, the heavy animal look entirely absent, and in its place the wrinkled, patient, good old darkey citizen.

As for myself, I will never accept such a job again. It is entirely outside of my legitimate line of business, although my speech seems to have been a great success, if I can judge by the encomiums which are pouring in upon me on every hand. I brought in some mugwumpery at the end, but it was very difficult to manage it. . . . Always affectionately yours,

Wm. James

To MISS ELLEN EMMET (MRS. BLANCHARD RAND)

Bar Harbor, Me., Aug. 11, 1897

Dear Old Bay (and dear Rosina),—

For I have letters from both of you and my heart inclines to both so that I can't write to either without the other—I hope you are enjoying the English coast. A rumor reached me not long since that my brother Henry had given up his trip to the Continent in order to be near to you, and I hope for the sakes of all concerned that it is true. He will find in you both that eager and vivid artistic sense, and that direct swoop at the vital facts of human character from which I am sure he has been weaned for fifteen years at least. And I am sure it will rejuvenate him again. It is more Celtic than English, and when joined with those faculties of soul, conscience, or whatever they be that make England rule the waves, as they are joined in you, Bay, they leave no room for any anxiety about the creature's destiny. But Rosina, who is all senses and intelligence, alarms me by her recital of midnight walks on the Boulevard des Italiens with bohemian artists. . . . You can't live by gaslight and excitement, nor can naked intelligence run a *jeune fille's* life. Affections, pieties, and prejudices must play their part, and only let the intelligence get an occasional peep at things from the midst of their smothering embrace. That again is what makes the British nation so great. Intelligence doesn't flaunt itself there quite naked as in France.

As for the MacMonnies Bacchante,[1] I only saw her faintly looming through the moon-light one night when she was *sub judice*, so can frame no opinion. The place certainly calls for a

[1] For a short while MacMonnies's Bacchante stood in the court of the Boston Public Library.

lightsome capricious figure, but the solemn Boston mind declared that anything but a solemn figure would be desecration. As to her immodesty, opinions got very hot. My knowledge of MacMonnies is confined to one statue, that of Sir Henry Vane, also in our Public Library, an impressionist sketch in bronze (I think), sculpture treated like painting—and I must say I don't admire the result *at all*. But you *know;* and I wish I could see other things of his also. How I wish I could *talk* with Rosina, or rather hear her talk, about Paris, *talk in her French* which I doubt not is by this time admirable. The only book she has vouchsafed news of having read, to me, is the d'Annunzio one, which I have ordered in most choice Italian; but of Lemaître, France, etc., she writes never a word. Nor of V. Hugo. She ought to read "La Légende des Siècles." For the picturesque pure and simple, go there! laid on with a trowel so generous that you really get your glut. But the things in French literature that I have gained most from—the next most to Tolstoy, in the last few years—are the whole cycle of Geo. Sand's life: her "Histoire," her letters, and now lately these revelations of the de Musset episode. The whole thing is beautiful and uplifting—an absolute "liver" harmoniously leading her own life and *neither* obedient nor defiant to what others expected or thought.

We are passing the summer very quietly at Chocorua, with our bare feet on the ground. Children growing up bullily, a pride to the parental heart. . . . Alice and I have just spent a rich week at North Conway, at a beautiful 'place," the Merrimans'. I am now here at a really grand place, the Dorrs'—tell Rosina that I went to a domino party last night but was so afraid that some one of the weird and sinister sisters would speak to me that I came home at 12 o'clock, when it had hardly begun. I am so sensitive! Tell her that a lady from Michigan was recently shown the sights of Cambridge by one of my Radcliffe girls. She took her to the Longfellow house, and as the visitor went into the gate, said, "I will just wait here." To her surprise, the visitor went up to the house, looked in to one window after the other, then rang the bell, and the door closed upon her. She soon emerged, and said that the servant had shown her the house. "I'm so sensitive that at first I thought I would only peep in at the windows. But then I said to myself, 'What's the use of being so sensitive?' So I rang the bell."

Pray be happy this summer. I see nothing more of Rosina's in the papers. How is that sort of thing going on? . . . As for your mother, give her my old-fashioned love. For some unexplained reason, I find it very hard to write to her—probably it is the same reason that makes it hard for her to write to me—so we can sympathize over so strange a mystery. Anyhow, give her my best love, and with plenty for yourself, old Bay, and for Rosina, believe me, yours ever,

Wm. James

To CHARLES PEIRCE

Cambridge, Dec. 22 [*1897*]

Dear Charles,—

...I am sorry you are sticking so to formal logic. I know our graduate school here, and so does Royce, and we both agree that there are only three men who could possibly follow your graphs and relatives. Are not such highly abstract and mathematically conceived things to be read rather than heard; and ought you not, at the cost of originality, remembering that a *lecture* must succeed *as such*, to give a very minimum of formal logic and get on to metaphysic, psychology and cosmogony almost immediately?

There is stuff enough in the first two volumes of the prospectus of your system, to give a short course without infringing on any mathematical symbolism, I am sure—to say nothing of the other volumes. Now be a good boy and think a more popular plan out. I don't want the audience to dwindle to three or four, and I don't see how one can help that on the program you propose. I don't insist on an audience of more than fifteen or sixteen, but you ought certainly to aim at that, and that doesn't condemn you to be wishy-washy. *You* can hardly conceive how little interest exists in the purely formal aspects of logic. Things on that subject ought to be *printed* for the scattered few. You are teeming with ideas, and the lectures need not by any means form a continuous whole. Separate topics of a vitally important character would do perfectly well. There would be sure—you lecturing—to be enough unity involuntarily there. What *I* should like is anti-nominalism, categories, attraction of ideas, hypothesis, tychism and synechism. . . . Write, now, that you accept all these conditions, and pray keep the lectures as unmathematical as in you lies. With the best of hopes, I am yours ever,

Wm. James

To MRS. JAMES

St. Hubert's Inn,
Keene Valley, July 9, 1898

. . . I have had an eventful 24 hours, and my hands are so stiff after it that my fingers can hardly hold the pen. I left, as I informed you by post-card, the Lodge at seven, and five hours of walking brought us to the top of Marcy—I was carrying 18 lbs. of weight in my pack. As usual, I met two Cambridge acquaintances on the mountain top—"Appalachians" from

Beede's. At four, hearing an axe below, I went down (an hour's walk) to Panther Lodge Camp, and there found Charles and Pauline Goldmark, Waldo Adler and another schoolboy, and two Bryn Mawr girls—the girls all dressed in boys' breeches, and cutaneously desecrated in the extreme from seven of them having been camping without a male on Loon Lake to the north of this. My guide had to serve for the party, and quite unexpectedly to me the night turned out one of the most memorable of all my memorable experiences. I was in a wakeful mood before starting, having been awake since three, and I may have slept a little during this night; but I was not aware of sleeping at all. My companions, except Waldo Adler, were all motionless. The guide had got a magnificent provision of fire-wood, the sky swept itself clear of every trace of cloud or vapor, the wind entirely ceased, so that the fire-smoke rose straight up to heaven. The temperature was perfect either inside or outside the cabin, the moon rose and hung above the scene before midnight, leaving only a few of the larger stars visible, and I got into a state of spiritual alertness of the most vital description. The influences of Nature, the wholesomeness of the people round me, especially the good Pauline, the thought of you and the children, dear Harry on the wave, the problem of the Edinburgh lectures, all fermented within me till it became a regular Walpurgis Nacht. I spent a good deal of it in the woods, where the streaming moonlight lit up things in a magical checkered play, and it seemed as if the Gods of all the nature-mythologies were holding an indescribable meeting in my breast with the moral Gods of the inner life. The two kinds of Gods have nothing in common—the Edinburgh lectures made quite a hitch ahead. The intense significance of some sort, of the whole scene, if one could only *tell* the significance; the intense inhuman remoteness of its inner life, and yet the intense *appeal* of

[173]

it; its everlasting freshness and its immemorial antiquity and decay; its utter Americanism, and every sort of patriotic suggestiveness, and you, and my relation to you part and parcel of it all, and beaten up with it, so that memory and sensation all whirled inexplicably together; it was indeed worth coming for, and worth repeating year by year, if repetition could only procure what in its nature I suppose must be all unplanned for and unexpected. It was one of the happiest lonesome nights of my existence, and I understand now what a poet is. He is a person who can feel the immense complexity of influences that I felt, and make some partial tracks in them for verbal statement. In point of fact, I can't find a single word for all that significance, and don't know what it was significant of, so there it remains, a mere boulder of *impression*. Doubtless in more ways than one, though, things in the Edinburgh lectures will be traceable to it.

In the morning at six, I shouldered my undiminished pack and went up Marcy, ahead of the party, who arrived half an hour later, and we got in here at eight [P.M.] after 10½ hours of the solidest walking I ever made, and I, I think, more fatigued than I have been after any walk. We plunged down Marcy, and up Bason Mountain, led by C. Goldmark, who had, with Mr. White, blazed a trail the year before;[1] then down again, away down, and up the Gothics, not counting a third down-and-up over an intermediate spur. It was the steepest sort of work, and, as one looked from the summits, seemed sheer impossible, but the girls kept up splendidly, and were all fresher than I. It was true that they had slept like logs all night, whereas I was "on my nerves." I lost my Norfolk jacket at the last third of the course—high time to say good-bye to that possession—and staggered up to the Putnams to find Hatty Shaw taking

[1] That is, there was here no path to follow, only "blazes" on the trees.

me for a tramp. Not a soul was there, but everything spotless and ready for the arrival today. I got a bath at Bowditch's bathhouse, slept in my old room, and slept soundly and well, and save for the unwashable staining of my hands and a certain stiffness in my thighs, am entirely rested and well. But I don't believe in keeping it up too long, and at the Willey House will lead a comparatively sedentary life, and cultivate sleep, if I can. . . .

W. J.

To WILLIAM M. SALTER

Bad-Nauheim, Sept. 11, 1899

Dear Mackintire,—

The incredible has happened, and Dreyfus, without one may say a single particle of *positive* evidence that he was guilty, has been condemned again. The French Republic, which seemed about to turn the most dangerous corner in her career and enter on the line of political health, laying down the finest set of political precedents in her history to serve as standards for future imitation and habit, has slipped Hell-ward and all the forces of Hell in the country will proceed to fresh excesses of insolence. But I don't believe the game is lost. "Les intellectuels," thanks to the Republic, are now aggressively militant as they never were before, and will grow stronger and stronger; so we may hope. I have sent you the "Figaro" daily; but of course the reports are too long for you to have read through. The most grotesque thing about the whole trial is the pretension of awful holiness, of semi-divinity in the diplomatic documents and waste-paper-basket scraps from the embassies—a farce kept up to the very end—these same documents being, so far as they were anything (and most of them were nothing), mere records of treason, lying, theft, bribery, corruption, and every crime on the part of the diplomatic agents. Either the German and Italian governments will now publish or not publish all the details of their transactions—give the exact documents meant by the *bordereaux* and the exact names of the French traitors. If they do not, there will be only two possible explanations: either Dreyfus's guilt, or the pride of their own sacrosanct etiquette. As it is scarcely conceivable that Deryfus can have been guilty, their silences will be due to the latter cause. (Of course it can't be due to what they owe in honor to Esterhazy and whoever their other allies and servants may have been. E. is safe over the border, and a pension for his services will heal all his wounds. Any other person can quickly be put in similar conditions of happiness.) And they and Esterhazy will then be exactly on a par morally, actively conspiring to have an innocent man bear the burden of their own sins. By their carelessness with the documents they got Dreyfus accused, and now they abandon him, for the sake of their own divine etiquette.

The breath of the nostrils of all these big institutions is crime —that is the long and short of it. We must thank God for America; and hold fast to every advantage of our position. Talk about our corruption! It is a mere fly-speck of superficiality compared with the rooted and permanent forces of corruption that exist in the European states. The only serious permanent force of corruption in America is party spirit. All the other forces are shifting like the clouds, and have no partnerships with any permanently organized ideal. Millionaires and syndicates have their immediate cash to pay, but they have no intrenched prestige to work with, like the church sentiment, the army sentiment, the aristocracy and royalty sentiment, which here can be brought to bear in favor of every kind of individual and collective crime—appealing not only to the immediate pocket of the persons to be corrupted, but to the ideals of their imagination as well. . . . My dear Mack, we "intellectuals" in America must all work to keep our precious birthright of individualism, and freedom from these institutions. *Every* great institution is perforce a means of corruption—whatever good it may also do. Only in the free personal relation is full ideality to be found.—I have vomited all this out upon you in the hope that it may wake a responsive echo. One must do *something* to work off the effect of the Dreyfus sentence.

I rejoice immensely in the purchase [on our behalf] of the two pieces of land [near Chocorua], and pine for the day when I can get back to see them. If all the same to you, I wish that you would buy Burke's in your name, and Mother-in-law Forrest's in her name. But let this be exactly as each of you severally prefers.

We leave here in a couple of days, I imagine. I am better; but I can't tell how much better for a few weeks yet. I hope that you will smite the ungodly next winter. What a glorious gathering together of the forces for the great fight there will be. It seems to me as if the proper tactics were to pound McKinley —put the whole responsibility on him. It is he who by his purely drifting "non-entanglement" policy converted a splendid opportunity into this present necessity of a conquest of extermination. It is he who has warped us from our continuous national habit, which, if we repudiate him, it will not be impossible to resume.

Affectionately thine, Mary's, Aleck's, Dinah's, Augusta's, and everyone's,

W. J.

P.S. Damn it, America doesn't know the meaning of the word corruption compared with Europe! Corruption is so permanently organized here that it isn't thought of as such—it is so transient and shifting in America as to make an outcry whenever it appears.

To MRS. HENRY WHITMAN

Lamb House, Rye, Oct. 5, 1899

Dear Mrs. Whitman,—

You see where at last we have arrived, at the end of the first *étape* of this pilgrimage—the second station of the cross, so to speak—with the Continent over, and England about to begin. The land is bathed in greenish-yellow light and misty drizzle of rain. The little town, with its miniature brick walls and houses and nooks and coves and gardens, makes a curiously vivid and quaint picture, alternately suggesting English, Dutch, and Japanese effects that one has seen in pictures—all exceedingly tiny (so that one wonders how *families* ever could have been reared in most of the houses) and neat and *zierlich* to the last degree. *Refinement* in architecture certainly consists in narrow trim and the absence of heavy mouldings. Modern Germany is incredibly bad from that point of view—much worse, apparently, than America. But the German people are a good safe fact for great powers to be intrusted to—earnest and serious, and pleasant to be with, as we found them, though it was humiliating enough to find how awfully imperfect were one's powers of conversing in their language. French not much better. I remember nothing of this extreme mortification in old times, and am inclined to think that it is due less to loss of ability to speak, than to the fact that, as you grow older, you speak better English, and expect more of yourself in the way of accomplishment. I am sure *you* spoke no such English as now, in the seventies, when

[178]

you came to Cambridge! And how could I, as yet untrained by conversation with you?

Seven mortal weeks did we spend at the *Curort*, Nauheim, for an infirmity of the heart which I contracted, apparently, not much more than a year ago, and which now must be borne, along with the rest of the white man's burden, until additional visits to Nauheim have removed it altogether for ordinary practical purposes. N. was a sweetly pretty spot, but I longed for more activity. A glorious week in Switzerland, solid in its sometimes awful, sometimes beefy beauty; two days in Paris, where I could gladly have stayed the winter out, merely for the fun of the sight of the intelligent and interesting streets; then hither, where H. J. has a real little *bijou* of a house and garden, and seems absolutely adapted to his environment, and very well and contented in the leisure to write and to read which the place affords.

In a few days we go almost certainly to the said H. J.'s apartment, still unlet, in London, where we shall in all probability stay till January, the world forgetting, by the world forgot, or till such later date as shall witness the completion of the awful Gifford job, at which I have not been able to write one line since last January. I long for the definitive settlement and ability to get to work. I am very glad indeed, too, to be in an English atmosphere again. Of course it will conspire better with my writing tasks, and after all it is more congruous with one's nature and one's inner ideals. Still, one loves America above all things, for her youth, her greenness, her plasticity, innocence, good intentions, friends, everything. Je veux que mes cendres reposent sur les bords du Charles, au milieu de ce bon peuple de Harvarr Squerre que j'ai tant aimé. That is what I say, and what Napoleon B. would have said, had his life been enriched by your and my educational and other ex-

[179]

periences—poor man, he knew too little of life, had never even heard of us, whilst we have heard of him!

Seriously speaking, though, I believe that international comparisons are a great waste of time—at any rate, international judgments and passings of sentence are. Every nation has ideals and difficulties and sentiments which are an impenetrable secret to one not of the blood. Let them alone, let each one work out its own salvation on its own lines. They talk of the decadence of France. The hatreds, and the *coups de gueule* of the newspapers there are awful. But I doubt if the better ideals were ever so aggressively strong; and I fancy it is the fruit of the much decried republican régime that they have become so. My brother represents English popular opinion as less cock-a-whoop for war than newspaper accounts would lead one to imagine; but I don't know that he is in a good position for judging. I hope if they do go to war that the Boers will give them fits, and I heartily emit an analogous prayer on behalf of the Philippinos.

I have had pleasant news of Beverly, having had letters both from Fanny Morse and Paulina Smith. I hope that your summer has been a good one, that work has prospered and that Society has been *less énervante* and more nutritious for the higher life of the Soul than it sometimes is. *We* have met but one person of any accomplishments or interest all summer. But I have managed to read a good deal about religion, and religious people, and care less for accomplishments, except where (as in you) they go with a sanctified heart. Abundance of accomplishments, in an unsanctified heart, only make one a more accomplished devil.

Good bye, angelic friend! We both send love and best wishes, both to you and Mr. Whitman, and I am as ever yours affectionately,

W. J.

To GEORGE H. PALMER

Carqueiranne, Apr. 2, 1900

Glorious old Palmer,—

I had come to the point of feeling that my next letter *must* be to you, when in comes your delightful "favor" of the 18th, with all its news, its convincing clipping, and its enclosures from Bakewell and Sheldon. I have had many impulses to write to Bakewell, but they have all aborted—my powers being so small and so much *in Anspruch genommen* by correspondence already under way. I judge him to be well and happy. What think you of his wife? I suppose she is no relation of yours. I shouldn't think any of your three candidates would do for that conventional Bryn Mawr. She stoneth the prophets, and I wish she would get X—and get stung. He made a *deplorable* impression on me many years ago. The only comment *I* heard when I gave my address there lately (the last one in my "Talks") was that A—had hoped for something more technical and psychological! Nevertheless, some good girls seem to come out at Bryn Mawr. I am awfully sorry that Perry is out of place. Unless he gets something good, it seems to me that we ought to get him for a course in Kant. He is certainly the soundest, most normal all-round man of our recent production. Your list for next year interests me muchly. I am glad of Münsterberg's and Santayana's new courses, and hope they'll be good. I'm glad you're back in Ethics and glad that Royce has "Epistemology" —portentous name, and small result, in my opinion, but a substantive *discipline* which ought, *par le temps qui court*, to be treated with due formality. I look forward with eagerness to his new volume.[1] What a colossal feat he has performed in these two years—all thrown in by the way, as it were.

[1] The second volume of *The World and the Individual*. (Gifford Lectures at the University of Aberdeen.)

Certainly Gifford lectures are a good institution for stimulating production. They have stimulated me so far to produce two lectures of wishy-washy generalities. What is that for a "showing" in six months of absolute leisure? The second lecture used me up so that I must be off a good while again.

No! dear Palmer, the best I can possibly hope for at Cambridge after my return is to be able to carry one half-course. So make all calculations accordingly. As for Windelband, how can I ascertain anything except by writing to him? I shall see no one, nor go to any University environment. My impression is that we must go in for budding genius, if we seek a European. If an American, we can get a *sommité!* But who? in either case? Verily there is room at the top. So —— seems to be the only Britisher worth thinking of. I imagine we had better train up our own men. A——, B——, C——, either would no doubt do, especially A—— if his health improves. D—— is our last card, from the point of view of policy, no doubt, but from that of inner organization it seems to me that he may have too many points of coalescence with both Münsterberg and Royce, especially the latter.

The great event in my life recently has been the reading of Santayana's book.[2] Although I absolutely reject the platonism of it, I have literally squealed with delight at the imperturbable perfection with which the position is laid down on page after page; and grunted with delight at such a thickening up of our Harvard atmosphere. If our students now could begin really to understand what Royce means with his voluntaristic-pluralistic monism, what Münsterberg means with his dualistic scientific-ism and platonism, what Santayana means by his pessimistic platonism (I wonder if he and Mg. have had any close mutually encouraging intercourse in this line?), what I mean by my crass

2 *Interpretations of Poetry and Religion.* New York, 1900.

pluralism, what you mean by your ethereal idealism, that these are so many religions, ways of fronting life, and worth fighting for, we should have a genuine philosophic universe at Harvard. The best condition of it would be an open conflict and rivalry of the diverse systems. (Alas! that I should be out of it, just as my chance begins!) The world might ring with the struggle, if we devoted ourselves exclusively to belaboring each other.

I now understand Santayana, the man. I never understood him before. But what a perfection of rottenness in a philosophy! I don't think I ever knew the anti-realistic view to be propounded with so impudently superior an air. It is refreshing to see a representative of moribund Latinity rise up and administer such reproof to us barbarians in the hour of our triumph. I imagine Santayana's *style* to be entirely spontaneous. But it has curious classic echoes. Whole pages of pure Hume in style; others of pure Renan. Nevertheless, how fantastic a philosophy!—as if the "world of values" *were* independent of existence. It is only as *being*, that one thing is better than another. The idea of darkness is as good as that of light, as ideas. There is more value in light's *being*. And the exquisite consolation, when you have ascertained the badness of all fact, in knowing that badness is inferior to goodness, to the end— it only rubs the pessimism in. A man whose egg at breakfast turns out always bad says to himself, "Well, bad and good are not the same, anyhow." That is just the trouble! Moreover, when you come down to the facts, what do your harmonious and integral ideal systems prove to be? in the concrete? Always things burst by the growing content of experience. Dramatic unities; laws of versification; ecclesiastical systems; scholastic doctrines. Bah! Give me Walt Whitman and Browning ten times over, much as the perverse ugliness of the latter at times irritates me, and intensely as I have enjoyed Santayana's attack.

The barbarians are in the line of mental growth, and those who do insist that the ideal and the real are dynamically continuous are those by whom the world is to be saved. But I'm nevertheless delighted that the other view, always existing in the world, should at last have found so splendidly impertinent an expression among ourselves. I have meant to write to Santayana; but on second thoughts, and to save myself, I will just ask you to send him this. It saves him from what might be the nuisance of having to reply, and on my part it has the advantage of being more free-spoken and direct. He is certainly an *extraordinarily distingué* writer. Thank him for existing!

As a contrast, read Jack Chapman's "Practical Agitation." The other pole of thought, and a style all splinters—but a gospel for our rising generation—I hope it will have its effect.

Send me your Noble lectures. I don't see how you could risk it without a MS. If you did fail (which I doubt) you deserved to. Anyhow the printed page makes everything good.

I can no more! Adieu! How is Mrs. Palmer this winter? I hope entirely herself again. You are impartially silent of her and of my wife. The "Transcript" continues to bless us. We move from this hospitable roof to the hotel at Costebelle today. Thence after a fortnight to Geneva, and in May to Nauheim once more, to be reëxamined and sentenced by Schott. Affectionately yours,

W. J.

To MISS FRANCES R. MORSE

Costebelle, Apr. 12, 1900

Dearest Fanny,—

Your letters continue to rain down upon us with a fidelity which makes me sure that, however it may once have been, *now*, on the principle of the immortal Monsieur Perrichon, we must be firmly rooted in your affections. You can never "throw over" anybody for whom you have made such sacrifices. All qualms which I might have in the abstract about the injury we must be inflicting on so busy a Being by making her, through our complaints of poverty, agony, and exile, keep us so much "on her mind" as to tune us up every two or three days by a long letter to which she sacrifices all her duties to the family and state, disappear, moreover, when I consider the character of the letters themselves. They are so easy, the facts are so much the immediate out-bubblings of the moment, and the delicious philosophical reflexions so much like the spontaneous breathings of the soul, that the *effort* is manifestly at the zero-point, and into the complex state of affection which necessarily arises in you for the objects of so much loving care, there enter none of those curious momentary arrows of impatience and vengefulness which might make others say, if they were doing what you do for us, that they wished we were dead or in some way put beyond reach, so that our eternal "appeal" might stop. No, Fanny! we have no repinings and feel no responsibilities towards you, but accept you and your letters as the gifts you are. The infrequency of our answering proves this fact; to which you in turn must furnish the correlative, if the occasion comes. On the day when you temporarily hate us, or don't "feel like" the usual letter, don't let any thought of inconsistency with your past acts worry you about not taking up the pen. Let us go; though it be for weeks and months—I shall know you will come round again. "Neither heat nor frost nor thunder shall ever do away, I ween, the marks of that which once hath been." And to think that you should never have spent a night, and only once taken a meal, in our house! When we get back, we must see each other daily, and may the days of both of us be right long in the State of Massachusetts! Bless her!

I got a letter from J. J. Chapman praising her strongly the other day. And sooth to say the "Transcript" and the "Springfield Republican," the reception of whose "weeklies" has become one of the solaces of my life, do make a first-rate showing for her civilization. One can't just say what "tone" consists in, but these papers hold their own excellently in comparison with the English papers. There is far less alertness of mind in the general make-up of the latter; and the "respectability" of the English editorial columns, though it shows a correcter literary drill, is apt to be due to a remorseless longitude of commonplace conventionality that makes them deadly dull. (The "Spectator" appears to be the only paper with a nervous system, in England—that of a *carnassier* at present!) The English people seem to have positively a passionate hunger for this mass of prosy stupidity, never less than a column and a quarter long. The Continental papers of course are "nowhere." As for our yellow papers—every country has its criminal classes, and with us and in France, they have simply got into journalism as part of their professional evolution, and they must be got out. Mr. Bosanquet somewhere says that so far from the "dark ages" being over, we are just at the beginning of a new dark-age period. He means that ignorance and unculture, which then were merely brutal, are now articulate and possessed of a literary voice, and the fight is transferred from fields and castles and town walls to "organs of publicity"; but it is the same fight, of reason and goodness against stupidity and passions; and it must be fought through to the same kind of success. But it means the reëducating of perhaps twenty more generations; and by that time some altogether new kind of institutional opportunity for the Devil will have been evolved.

April 13th. I had to stop yesterday. . . . Six months ago, I shouldn't have thought it possible that a life deliberately founded on pottering about and dawdling through the day would be endurable or even possible. I have attained such skill that I doubt if my days ever at any time seemed to glide by so fast. But it corrodes one's soul nevertheless. I scribble a little in bed every morning, and have reached page 48 of my third Gifford lecture—though Lecture II, alas! must be rewritten entirely. The conditions don't conduce to an energetic grip of the subject, and I am afraid that what I write is pretty slack and not what it would be if my vital tone were different. The problem I have set myself is a hard one: *first*, to defend (against all the prejudices of my "class") "experience" against "philosophy" as being the real backbone of the world's religious life—I mean prayer, guidance, and all that sort of thing immediately and privately felt, as against high and noble general views of our destiny and the world's meaning; and *second*, to make the hearer or reader believe, what I myself invincibly do believe, that, although all the special manifestations of religion may have been absurd (I mean its creeds and theories), yet the life of it as a whole is mankind's most important function. A task well-nigh impossible, I fear, and in which I shall fail; but to attempt it is *my* religious act.

We got a visit the other day from [a Scottish couple here who have heard that I am to give the Gifford lectures]; and two days ago went to afternoon tea with them at their hotel, next door. *She* enclosed a tract (by herself) in the invitation, and proved to be a [mass] of holy egotism and conceit based on professional invalidism and self-worship. I wish my sister Alice were there to "react" on her with a description! Her husband, apparently weak, and the slave of her. No talk but evangelical talk. It seemed assumed that a Gifford lecturer must be one of Moody's partners, and it gave me rather a foretaste of what the Edinburgh atmosphere may be like. Well, I shall enjoy sticking a knife into its gizzard—if atmospheres have gizzards? Blessed be Boston—probably the freest place on earth, that isn't merely heathen and sensual.

I have been supposing, as one always does, that you "ran in" to the Putnams' every hour or so, and likewise they to No. 12. But your late allusion to the telephone and the rarity of your seeing Jim [Putnam] reminded me of the actual conditions— absurd as they are. (Really you and we are nearer together now at this distance than we have ever been.) Well, let Jim see this letter, if you care to, flattering him by saying that it is more written for him than for you (which it certainly has not been till this moment!), and thanking him for existing in this naughty world. His account of the Copernican revolution (studento-centric) in the Medical School is highly exciting, and I am glad to hear of the excellent little Cannon becoming so prominent a reformer. Speaking of reformers, do you see Jack Chapman's "Political Nursery"? of which the April number has just come. (I have read it and taken my bed-breakfast during the previous page of this letter, though you may not have perceived the fact.) If not, *do* subscribe to it; it is awful fun. He just looks at things, and tells the truth about them—a strange thing even to *try* to do, and he doesn't always succeed. Office 141 Broadway, $1.00 a year.

Fanny, you won't be reading as far as this in this interminable letter, so I stop, though 100 pent-up things are seeking to be said. The weather has still been so cold whenever the sun is withdrawn that we have delayed our departure for Geneva to the 22nd—a week later. We make a short visit to our friends the Flournoys (a couple of days) and then proceed towards Nauheim *via* Heidelberg, where I wish to consult the great Erb about the advisability of more baths in view of my nervous complications, before the great Schott examines me again. I do

wish I could send for Jim for a consultation. Good-bye, dearest
and best of Fannys. I hope your Mother is wholly well again.
Much love to her and to Mary Elliot. It interested me to hear
of Jack E.'s great operation. Yours ever,

W. J.

To HIS DAUGHTER, PEG

Villa Luise,
Bad-Nauheim, May 26, 1900

Darling Peg,—

Your letter came last night and explained sufficiently the
cause of your long silence. You have evidently been in a bad
state of spirits again, and dissatisfied with your environment;
and I judge that you have been still more dissatisfied with the
inner state of trying to consume your own smoke, and grin and
bear it, so as to carry out your mother's behests made after the
time when you scared us so by your inexplicable tragic outcries
in those earlier letters. Well! I believe you have been trying to
do the manly thing under difficult circumstances, but one learns
only gradually to do the *best* thing; and the best thing for you
would be to write at least weekly, if only a post-card, and say
just how things are going. If you are in bad spirits, there is no
harm whatever in communicating that fact, and defining the
character of it, or describing it as exactly as you like. The bad
thing is to pour out the *contents* of one's bad spirits on others
and leave them with it, as it were, on their hands, as if it was for
them to do something about it. That was what you did in your
other letter which alarmed us so, for your shrieks of anguish
were so excessive, and so unexplained by anything you told us
in the way of facts, that we didn't know but what you had suddenly gone crazy. That is the *worst* sort of thing you can do.

[189]

The middle sort of thing is what you do this time—namely, keep silent for more than a fortnight, and when you do write, still write rather mysteriously about your sorrows, not being quite open enough.

Now, my dear little girl, you have come to an age when the inward life develops and when some people (and on the whole those who have most of a destiny) find that all is not a bed of roses. Among other things there will be waves of terrible sadness, which last sometimes for days; and dissatisfaction with one's self, and irritation at others, and anger at circumstances and stony insensibility, etc., etc., which taken together form a melancholy. Now, painful as it is, this is sent to us for an enlightenment. It always passes off, and we learn about life from it, and we ought to learn a great many good things if we react on it rightly. [*From margin.*] (For instance, you learn how good a thing your home is, and your country, and your brothers, and you may learn to be more considerate of other people, who, you now learn, may have their inner weaknesses and sufferings, too.) Many persons take a kind of sickly delight in hugging it; and some sentimental ones may even be proud of it, as showing a fine sorrowful kind of sensibility. Such persons make a regular habit of the luxury of woe. That is the worst possible reaction on it. It is usually a sort of disease, when we get it strong, arising from the organism having generated some poison in the blood; and we mustn't submit to it an hour longer than we can help, but jump at every chance to attend to anything cheerful or comic or take part in anything active that will divert us from our mean, pining inward state of feeling. When it passes off, as I said, we know more than we did before. And we must try to make it last as short a time as possible. The worst of it often is that, while we are in it, we don't *want* to get out of it. We hate it, and yet we prefer staying in it—that is a part of the disease. If we find ourselves like that, we must make ourselves do something different, go with people, speak cheerfully, set ourselves to some hard work, make ourselves sweat, etc.; and that is the good way of reacting that makes of us a valuable character. The disease makes you think of *yourself* all the time; and the way out of it is to keep as busy as we can thinking of *things* and of *other people*—no matter what's the matter with our self.

I have no doubt you are doing as well as you know how, darling little Peg; but we have to learn everything, and I also have no doubt that you'll manage it better and better if you ever have any more of it, and soon it will fade away, simply leaving you with more experience. The great thing for you *now*, I should suppose, would be to enter as friendlily as possible into the interest of the Clarke children. If you like them, or acted as if you liked them, you needn't trouble about the question of whether they like you or not. They probably will, fast enough; and if they don't, it will be their funeral, not yours. But this is a great lecture, so I will stop. The great thing about it is that it is all true.

The baths are threatening to disagree with me again, so I may stop them soon. Will let you know as quick as anything is decided. Good news from home: the Merrimans have taken the Irving Street house for another year, and the Wambaughs (of the Law School) have taken Chocorua, though at a reduced rent. The weather here is almost continuously cold and sunless. Your mother is sleeping, and will doubtless add a word to this when she wakes. Keep a merry heart—"time and the hour run through the roughest day"—and believe me ever your most loving

W. J.

[191]

To JOSIAH ROYCE

Nauheim, Sept. 26, 1900

Beloved Royce,—

Great was my, was *our* pleasure in receiving your long and delightful letter last night. Like the lioness in Æsop's fable, you give birth to one young one only in the year, but that one is a lion. I give birth mainly to guinea-pigs in the shape of postcards; but despite such diversities of epistolary expression, the heart of each of us is in the right place. I need not say, my dear old boy, how touched I am at your expressions of affection, or how it pleases me to hear that you have missed me. I too miss you profoundly. I do not find in the hotel waiters, chambermaids and bath-attendants with whom my lot is chiefly cast, that unique mixture of erudition, originality, profundity and vastness, and human wit and leisureliness, by accustoming me to which during all these years you have spoilt me for inferior kinds of intercourse. You are still the centre of my gaze, the pole of my mental magnet. When I write, 't is with one eye on the page, and one on you. When I compose my Gifford lectures mentally, 't is with the design exclusively of overthrowing your system, and ruining your peace. I lead a parasitic life upon you, for my highest flight of ambitious ideality is to become your conqueror, and go down into history as such, you and I rolled in one another's arms and silent (or rather loquacious still) in one last death-grapple of an embrace. How then, O my dear Royce, can I forget you, or be contented out of your close neighborhood? Different as our minds are, yours has nourished mine, as no other social influence ever has, and in converse with you I have always felt that my life was being lived importantly. Our minds, too, are not different in the *Object* which they envisage. It is the whole paradoxical physico-moral-spiritual Fatness, of

[192]

which most people single out some skinny fragment, which we both cover with our eye. We "aim at him generally"—and most others don't. I don't believe that we shall dwell apart forever, though our formulas may.

Home and Irving Street look very near when seen through these few winter months, and tho' it is still doubtful what I may be able to do in College, for social purposes I shall be available for probably numerous years to come. I haven't got at work yet—only four lectures of the first course written (strange to say)—but I am decidedly better today than I have been for the past ten months, and the matter is all ready in my mind; so that when, a month hence, I get settled down in Rome, I think the rest will go off fairly quickly. The second course I shall have to resign from, and write it out at home as a book. It must seem strange to you that the way from the mind to the pen should be as intraversable as it has been in this case of mine —you in whom it always seems so easily pervious. But Miller will be able to tell you all about my condition, both mental and physical, so I will waste no more words on that to me decidedly musty subject.

I fully understand your great aversion to letters and other off-writing. You have done a perfectly Herculean amount of the most difficult productive work, and I believe you to be much more tired than you probably yourself suppose or know. Both mentally and physically, I imagine that a long vacation, in other scenes, with no sense of duty, would do you a world of good. I don't say the full fifteen months—for I imagine that one summer and one academic half-year would perhaps do the business better—you could preserve the relaxed and desultory condition as long as that probably, whilst later you'd begin to chafe, and *then* you'd better be back in your own library. If *my* continuing aboard is hindering this, my sorrow will be extreme. Of course I must some time come to a definite decision about my own relations to the College, but I am reserving that till the end of 1900, when I shall write to Eliot in full. There is still a therapeutic card to play, of which I will say nothing just now, and I don't want to commit myself before that has been tried.

You say nothing of the second course of Aberdeen lectures, nor do you speak at all of the Dublin course. Strange omissions, like your not sending me your Ingersoll lecture! I assume that the publication of [your] Gifford Volume II will not be very long delayed. I am eager to read them. I can read philosophy now, and have just read the first three *Lieferungen* of K. Fischer's "Hegel." I must say I prefer the original text. Fischer's paraphrases always flatten and dry things out; and he gives no rich sauce of his own to compensate. I have been sorry to hear from Palmer that he also has been very tired. One can't keep going forever! P. has been like an archangel in his letters to me, and I am inexpressibly grateful. Well! everybody has been kinder than I deserve. . . .

To MISS FRANCES R. MORSE

Edinburgh, May 30, 1901

Dearest Fanny,—

. . . Beautiful as the spring is here, the words you so often let drop about American weather make me homesick for that article. It is blasphemous, however, to pine for anything when one is in Edinburgh in May, and takes an open drive every afternoon in the surrounding country by way of a constitutional. The green is of the vividest, splendid trees and acres, and the air itself an *object*, holding watery vapor, tenuous smoke, and ancient sunshine in solution, so as to yield the most exquisite minglings and gradations of silvery brown and blue and pearly gray. As for the city, its vistas are magnificent.

We are *comblés* with civilities, which Harry and Alice are to a certain extent enjoying, though I have to hang back and spend much of the time between my lectures in bed, to rest off the aortic distress which that operation gives. I call it aortic because it feels like that, but I can get no information from the Drs., so I won't swear I'm right. My heart, under the influence of that magical juice, tincture of digitalis,—only 6 drops daily, —is performing *beautifully* and gives no trouble at all. The audiences grow instead of dwindling, and in spite of rain, being about 300 and just crowding the room. They sit as still as death and then applaud magnificently, so I am sure the lectures are a success. Previous Gifford lectures have had audiences beginning with 60 and dwindling to 15. In an hour and a half (I write this in bed) I shall be beginning the fifth lecture, which will, when finished, put me half way through the arduous job. I know you will relish these details, which please pass on to Jim P. I would send you the reports in the "Scotsman," but they distort so much by their sham continuity with vast omission (the reporters get my MS.), that the result is caricature. Edinburgh is *spiritually* much like Boston, only stronger and with more temperament in the people. But we're all growing into much of a sameness everywhere.

I have dined out once—an almost fatal experiment! I was introduced to Lord Somebody: "How often do you lecture?"— "Twice a week."—What do you do between?—play golf?" Another invitation: "Come at 6—the dinner at 7.30—and we can walk or play bowls till dinner so as not to fatigue you"—I having pleaded my delicacy of constitution.

I rejoice in the prospect of Booker W.'s book, and thank your mother heartily. My mouth had been watering for just that volume. Autobiographies take the cake. I mean to read nothing else. Strange to say, I am now for the first time reading Marie Bashkirtseff. It takes hold of me tremenjus. I feel as if I had lived inside of her, and in spite of her hatefulness, esteem and even like her for her incorruptible way of telling the truth. I have not seen Huxley's life yet. It must be delightful, only I can't agree to what seems to be becoming the conventionally accepted view of him, that he possessed the exclusive specialty of living for the truth. A good deal of humbug about that!— at least when it becomes a professional and heroic attitude.

Your base remark about Aguinaldo is clean forgotten, if ever heard. I know you wouldn't harm the poor man, who, unless Malay human nature is weaker than human nature elsewhere, has pretty surely some surprises up his sleeve for us yet. Best love to you all. Your affectionate

Wm. James

To GRACE NORTON

Chocorua, Sept. 12, 1902

My dear Grace,—

. . . Your letter about my book arrived duly and filled me with mixed feelings of interest and sorrow. . . . I don't wonder that the mouldiness and measliness of so many of my saints gave you a revulsion away from other-worldliness to naturalism and humanism. Yours is much the best letter I have received from that point of view, because it is the most gravely expressed and the most profoundly felt. The two points of view, I believe, must work upon each other until they acquire a common content and way of living together, the *material* of the blessed life being thought of in terms of humanity, exclusively, the *inspiration* being felt as a relation to a higher portion of the universe now out of sight. But it will be long ere different persons' formulas will not produce misunderstandings in each other's minds. A real practical difference, so far, is between the healthy-minded (among whom I count you as writer of your letter) and those who seriously despair of straightforward healthy-mindedness as a radical solution. I myself don't see how it can be a *universal* solution, when the world is the seat of so much unhappiness really incurable in ordinary ways, but *cured* (in many individuals) by their religious experience. One can neither ignore the unhappy individuals nor the peculiar form of their relief, as facts of human history; and I, surveying human history objectively, couldn't help seeing *there* its possibly most characteristic manifestation. But I am intensely an individualist, and believe that as a practical problem for the individual, the religion he stands by must be the one which he finds best for *him*, even though there were better individuals, and their religion better for them. Such Stoicism as you stand up for is one of the noblest all-round attitudes yet found out, and as against the insanities of theistic devotion, certainly has an immense part yet to play.

The summer wanes, and I wane too. Possibly 'tis only "need of change," but it is discouraging, in conditions that seem quite paradisiac, to find that the progress of so many weeks gives way to retrogression. I have no doubt that things will move upward again when the term recommences. Thank you again, dear Grace, a thousand times for your good letter, and all the good advice contained in it, and believe me, with loving regards from Alice, your ever affectionate

Wm. James

To HENRY L. HIGGINSON

Cambridge, Mass., Nov. 1, 1902

Dear Henry,—

I am emboldened to the step I am taking by the consciousness that though we are both at least sixty years old and have
known each other from the cradle, I have never but once (or
possibly twice) traded on your well-known lavishness of disposition to swell any "subscription" which I was trying to raise.

Now the doomful hour has struck. The altar is ready, and
I take the victim by the ear. I choose you for a victim because
you still have some undesiccated human feeling about you and
can think in terms of pure charity—for the love of God, without ulterior hopes of returns from the investment.

The subject is a man of fifty who can be recommended to no
other kind of a benefactor. His story is a long one, but it
amounts to this, that Heaven made him with no other power
than that of thinking and writing, and he has proved by this
time a truly pathological inability to keep body and soul together. He is abstemious to an incredible degree, is the most
innocent and harmless of human beings, isn't propagating his
kind, has never had a dime to spend except for vital necessities,
and never has had in his life an hour of what such as *we* call
freedom from care or of "pleasure" in the ordinary exuberant
sense of the term. He is refinement itself mentally and morally;
and his writings have all been printed in first-rate periodicals,
but are too scanty to "pay." There's no excuse for him, I admit.
But God made him; and after kicking and cuffing and prodding
him for twenty years, I have now come to believe that he ought
to be treated in charity pure and simple (even though that be
a vice) and I want to guarantee him $350 a year as a pension
to be paid to the Mills Hotel in Bleecker Street, New York, for

board and lodging and a few cents weekly over and above. I will put in $150. I have secured $100 more. Can I squeeze $50 a year out of you for such a non-public cause? If not, don't reply and forget this letter. If "ja" and you think you really can afford it, and it isn't wicked, let me know, and I will dun you regularly every year for the $50. Yours as ever,

Wm. James

To F. C. S. SCHILLER

Asheville, April 8, 1903

Dear Schiller,—

I believe that I am indebted to you for two good letters, for which this languid scrawl will hardly be a meet reply. Your strictures on my poor syllabus, docked and clipped as it was, were characteristically energetic and definite, but many of them would have proved to have had no application had my hand been more fully shown. That is, I should myself have been on their side. As for the infinite, I don't think we should quarrel about that either. There was something you said about "God" which I thought disclosed a somewhat deeper divergence, but as I have not your letters with me, I had better let that drop.

Has one A. W. Moore of Chicago sent you a paper of his? It tickled me hugely, and I wrote urging him to send it to you and to Sturt. It seems to me a masterly pragmatic production, and it appears now that, under Dewey's inspiration, they have at Chicago a flourishing school of radical empiricism of which I for one have been entirely ignorant, having been led to neglect its utterances by their lack of "terseness," "crispness," "raciness" and other "newspaporial" virtues, though I could discern that Dewey himself was laboring with a big freight, towards the light. They have started from Hegelianism, and they have that temperament (that is, such men as Mead and Lloyd have it strongly) which makes one still suspect that if they do strike Truth eventually, they will mean some mischief to it after all; but still the fact remains that from such opposite poles minds are moving towards a common centre, that old compartments and divisions are breaking down, and that a very inclusive new school may be formed. Once admit that experience is a river which made the channel that now, in part, but only in part, confines it, and it seems to me that all sorts of realities and completenesses are possible in philosophy, hitherto stiffened and cramped by the silly littlenesses of the upper and lower dogmatisms, alternating their petty rationalistic and naturalistic idols of the shop. . . .

Charles Peirce is now giving six public lectures on "pragmatism" at Harvard, which I managed to get up for his benefit, pecuniary and professional. He is a hopeless crank and failure in many ways, but a really extraordinary intellect. I never knew a mind of so many different kinds of spotty intensity or vigor. Miller's health is keeping good, and, although there is a strong basis of old-fashioned rationalism in his mind, which won't give way, I think it is dissolving in spots, and that he will erelong be a full-fledged child of the light.

I am forgetting in all this to notice your review of my "Vagaries" in the *Proceedings*, and that (I now perceive) is what I meant by this second "letter" of yours which I had not acknowledged. It was as usual ultra-generous, and I thank you for it. The energy and literary ease you show fills me more and more with admiration. You ought to get less teaching work, and do more writing. As regards the matter of mysticism, I should like to talk it over with you. I doubt whether you do full justice to its strength. . . . I shall go up to Chocorua on May 1st, and doubt not that I shall recuperate and *on the whole* be as much better next year than this, as I have been this year than last. But lord! how I do want to read as well as write, and with so much left undone, I am getting really anxious lest I be cut off in the bud. Another pathetic Keats case!

I have just composed the first sentence of my forthcoming book—the only one yet written: "Philosophy is a queer thing— at once the most sublime and the most contemptible of human occupations." There is nothing like having made your start! I shouldn't be surprised if the rest were like rolling down hill. I am sure that a book of the systematic sort *can* be written— a philosophy of pure experience, which will immediately prove a centre of crystallization and a new rallying-point of opinion in philosophy. The times are fairly crying aloud for it. I have been extraordinarily pleased at the easy way in which my students this year assimilated the attitude, and reproduced the living pulse of it in their examination and other written work. It is the first time I ever tried to set it forth *ex cathedra.* My success makes me feel very sanguine.

We are about to have a philosophy building, "Emerson Hall," so-called. I learn here by the papers that the subscription is secure, and work will probably commence speedily. I don't care a great deal for it myself, but it will please Palmer egregiously, as well as Münsterberg, whose laboratory is now in very bad quarters. I wrote a review of Myers's book for the *Proceedings* just before leaving home. I was dog tired and it went with difficulty. I wish you had done it. I couldn't go into criticism of detail, so I simply skeletonized the argument, which was very likely a useful service. My opinion of the man is raised by reading the volumes, but not of the solidity of the system. The piles driven into the quicksand are too few for such a structure. But it is essential as a preliminary attempt at methodizing, and will doubtless keep a very honorable place in history. . . . Yours ever fondly,

Wm. James

To CHARLES PEIRCE

Chocorua, June 5, 1903

Dear Charles,—

I return your two lectures under a separate envelope to Milford, but send this to Cambridge, thinking you may possibly still be there. They are wonderful things—I have read the second one twice—but so original, and your categories are so unusual to other minds, that, although I recognize the region of thought and the profundity and reality of the level on which you move, I do not yet assimilate the various theses in the sense of being able to make a use of them for my own purposes. I may get to it later; but at present even first-, second-, and thirdness are outside of my own sphere of practically applying things, and I am not sure even whether I apprehend them as you mean them to be apprehended. I get, throughout your whole business, only the sense of something dazzling and imminent in the way of truth. This is very likely partly due to my mind being so non-mathematical, and to my slight interest in logic; but I am probably typical of a great many of your auditors—of the majority—so my complaint will be theirs. You spoke of publishing these lectures, but not, I hope, *tel quels*. They need too much mediation, by more illustrations, at which you are excellent (non-mathematical ones if possible), and by a good deal of interstitial expansion and comparison with other modes of thought. What I wish myself is that you might *revise these lectures* for your Lowell course, possibly confining yourself to fewer points (such as the uses of the first-, second-, and thirdness distinction, the generality involved in perception, the

[202]

nature of abduction—this last to me tremendously important); make each of them tremendously emphatic, avoid collateral matter, except what is illustrative and comparative, avoid polemic as such (you have very successfully done so), keep the ignoramus in view as your auditor, and I have no doubt you'll be a great success. As things stand, it is only highly skilled technicians and professionals who will sniff the rare perfume of your thought, and *after you are dead*, trace things back to your genius. You ought to gain a bigger audience *when living;* and, if next year you can only score a popular success, it will do much to help your later prospects. I fear that if you make a new course of lectures altogether, they will prove too technical and wonder-arousing and not flagrantly illuminating enough. Whereas, by revising these, you will not only give yourself less trouble, but also do the best possible thing for your audience. You cannot start with too low an idea of their intelligence. Look at me, as one!

Your visit to Cambridge was a refreshing interlude to all of us, I only wish that I had not been in such abominable condition. It was a great pleasure to both myself and my wife to know Mrs. Peirce, to whom pray give our warm regards. Have a good summer, and believe me ever truly yours,

Wm. James

To JOHN DEWEY

Cambridge, Oct. 17, 1903

Dear Dewey,—

I was about to write you in any case this afternoon when your ultra friendly letter came. On returning from the country yesterday, one of the first things that greeted my eyes was your *Logical Studies*, and the to me surprising words that close its Preface. What have I done to merit such a tribute? The Lord, who knoweth all things, knows doubtless about this too, but I accept it rather blindly, and most delightfully, as one of the good things that life sometimes strews in one's way. I feel so the inchoateness of all my publications that it surprises me to hear of anything definite accruing to others from them. I must do better, now that I am "looked up to" so. I thank you from the bottom of my heart! ...

It rejoices me greatly that your School (I mean your philosophic school) at the University of Chicago is, after this long gestation, bringing its fruits to birth in a way that will demonstrate its great unity and vitality, and be a revelation to many people, of American scholarship. I wish now that you would make a collection of your scattered articles, especially on "ethical" subjects. It is only books that tell. They seem to have a penetrating power which the same content in the shape of scattered articles wholly lacks. But the articles prepare buyers for the books. My own book, rather absurdly cackled about before it is hatched, is hardly begun, and with my slow rate of work will take long to finish. A little thing by Harald Höffding called *Philosophische Probleme*, which I have just read ... is quite a *multum in parvo* and puts many things exactly as I should put them. I am sure of a great affinity between your own "monism," since so you call it, and my "pluralism." Ever gratefully and faithfully yours,

Wm. James

To FRANÇOIS PILLON

Cambridge, June 12, 1904

Dear Pillon,—

Once more I get your faithful and indefatigable "Année" and feel almost ashamed of receiving it thus from you, year after year, when I make nothing of a return! So you are 75 years old—I had no idea of it, but thought that you were much younger. I am only(!) 62, and wish that I could expect another 13 years of such activity as you have shown. I fear I cannot. My arteries are senile, and none of my ancestors, so far as I know of them, have lived past 72, many of them dying much earlier. This is my last day in Cambridge; tomorrow I get away into the country, where "the family" already is, for my vacation. I shall take your "Année" with me, and shall be greatly interested in both Dauriac's article and yours. What a mercy it is your eyes, in spite of cataract-operations, are still good for reading. I have had a very bad winter for work—two attacks of influenza, one very long and bad, three of gout, one of erysipelas, etc., etc. I expected to have written at least 400 or 500 pages of my magnum opus,—a general treatise on philosophy which has been slowly maturing in my mind,—but I have written only 32 pages! That tells the whole story. I resigned from my professorship, but they would not accept my resignation, and owing to certain peculiarities in the financial situation of our University just now, I felt myself obliged in honor to remain.

My philosophy is what I call a radical empiricism, a pluralism, a "tychism," which represents order as being gradually won and always in the making. It is theistic, but not *essentially* so. It rejects all doctrines of the Absolute. It is finitist; but it does not attribute to the question of the Infinite the great methodological importance which you and Renouvier attribute to it. I fear that you may find my system too *bottomless* and romantic. I am sure that, be it in the end judged true or false, it is essential to the evolution of clearness in philosophic thought that *someone* should defend a pluralistic empiricism radically. And all that I fear is that, with the impairment of my working powers from which I suffer, the Angel of Death may overtake me before I can get my thoughts on to paper. Life here in the University consists altogether of *interruptions.*

I thought much of you at the time of Renouvier's death, and I wanted to write; but I let that go, with a thousand other things that had to go. What a life! and what touching and memorable last words were those which M. Pratt published in the "Revue de Métaphysique"—memorable, I mean from the mere fact that the old man could dictate them at all. I have left unread his last publications, except for some parts of the "Monadologie" and the "Personalisme." He will remain a great figure in philosophic history; and the sense of his absence must make a great difference to your consciousness and to that of Madame Pillon. My own wife and children are well. . . . Ever affectionately yours,

Wm. James

To HENRY JAMES

Cambridge, June 28, 1904

Dear H,—

I came down from Chocorua yesterday A.M. to go to—
Mrs. Whitman's funeral!
She had lost ground steadily during the winter. The last time I saw her was five weeks ago, when at noon I went up to her studio thinking she might be there. . . . She told me that she was to go on the following day to the Massachusetts General Hospital, for a cure of rest and seclusion. There she died last Friday evening, having improved in her cardiac symptoms, but pneumonia supervening a week ago. It's a great mercy that the end was so unexpectedly quick. What I had feared was a slow deterioration for a year or more to come, with all the nameless misery—peculiarly so in her case—of death by heart disease.

As it was, she may be said to have died standing, a thing she always wished to do. She went to every dinner-party and evening party last winter, had an extension, a sort of ball-room, built to her Mount Vernon house, etc. The funeral was beautiful both in Trinity Church and at the grave in Mt. Auburn. I was one of the eight pall-bearers—the others of whom you would hardly know. The flowers and greenery had been arranged in absolutely Whitmanian style by Mrs. Jack Gardner, Mrs. Henry Parkman, and Sally Fairchild. The scene at the grave was *beautiful*. She had no blood relatives, and all Boston —I mean the few whom we know—had gone out, and seemed swayed by an overpowering emotion which abolished all estrangement and self-consciousness. It was the sort of ending that would please her, could she know of it. An extraordinary and indefinable creature! I used often to feel coldly towards her on account of her way of taking people as a great society "business" proceeding, but now that her agitated life of tip-toe reaching in so many directions, of genuinest amiability, is over, pure tenderness asserts its own. Against that dark background of natural annihilation she seems to have been a pathetic little slender worm, writhing and curving blindly through its little day, expending such intensities of consciousness to terminate in that small grave.

She was a most peculiar person. I wish that you had known her whole life here more intimately, and understood its significance. You might then write a worthy article about her. For me, it is impossible to define her. She leaves a dreadful vacuum in Boston. I have often wondered whether I should survive her —and here it has come in the night, without the sound of a footstep, and the same world is here—but without her as its witness. . . .

[207]

To MRS. JAMES

Amalfi, Mar. 30, 1905

...It is good to get something in full measure, without haggling or stint, and today I have had the picturesque ladled out in buckets full, heaped up and running over. I never realized the beauties of this shore, and forget (in my habit of never noticing proper names till I have been there) whether you have ever told me of the drive from Sorrento to this place. Anyhow, I wish that you could have taken it with me this day. "Thank God for this day!" We came to Sorrento by steamer, and at 10:30 got away in a carriage, lunching at the half-way village of Positano; and proceeding through Amalfi to Ravello, high up on the mountain side, whence back here in time for a 7:15 o'clock dinner. Practically six hours driving through a scenery of which I had never realized the beauty, or rather the interest, from previous descriptions. The lime-stone mountains are as *strong* as anything in Switzerland, though of course much smaller. The road, a *Cornice* affair cut for the most part on the face of cliffs, and crossing little ravines (with beaches) on the side of which nestle hamlets, is positively ferocious in its grandeur, and on the side of it the azure sea, dreaming and blooming like a bed of violets. I didn't look for such Swiss strength, having heard of naught but beauty. It seems as if this were a race such that, when anyone wished to express an emotion of any kind, he went and built a bit of stone-wall and limed it onto the rock, so that now, when they have accumulated, the works of God and man are inextricably mixed, and it is as if mankind had been a kind of immemorial coral insect. Every possible square yard is terraced up, reclaimed and planted, and the human dwellings are the fiercest examples of cliff-building, cave-habitation, staircase and footpath you can imagine. How I do wish that you could have been along today....

Mar. 31, 1905

From half-past four to half-past six I walked alone through the *old* Naples, hilly streets, paved from house to house and swarming with the very poor, vocal with them too (their voices carry so that every child seems to be calling to the whole street, goats, donkeys, chickens, and an occasional cow mixed in), and no light of heaven getting indoors. The street floor composed of cave-like shops, the people doing their work on chairs in the street for the sake of light, and in the black inside, beds and a stove visible among the implements of trade. Such light and shade, and grease and grime, and swarm, and apparent amiability would be hard to match. I have come here too late in life, when the picturesque has lost its serious reality. Time was when hunger for it haunted me like a passion, and such sights would have been the solidest of mental food. I put up then with such inferior substitutional suggestions as Geneva and Paris afforded—but these black old Naples streets are not suggestions, they are the reality itself—full orchestra. I have got such an impression of the essential sociability of this race, especially in the country. A smile will go so far with them— even without the accompanying copper. And the children are so sweet. Tell Aleck to drop his other studies, learn *Italian* (real Italian, not the awful gibberish I try to speak), cultivate his beautiful smile, learn a sentimental song or two, bring a tambourine or banjo, and come down here and fraternize with the common people along the coast—he can go far, and make friends, and be a social success, even if he should go back to a clean hotel of some sort for sleep every night....

[209]

To GEORGE SANTAYANA

Orvieto, May 2, 1905

Dear Santayana,—

I came here yesterday from Rome and have been enjoying the solitude. I stayed at the exquisite Albergo de Russie, and didn't shirk the Congress—in fact they stuck me for a "general" address, to fill the vacuum left by Flournoy and Sully, who had been announced and came not (I spoke *agin* "consciousness," but nobody understood) and I got *fearfully tired*. On the whole it was an agreeable nightmare—agreeable on account of the perfectly charming *gentillezza* of the bloody Dagoes, the way they caress and flatter you—"il piu grand psicologo del mondo," etc., and of the elaborate provisions for general entertainment—nightmare, because of my absurd bodily fatigue. However, these things are "neither here nor there." What I really write to you for is to tell you to send (if not sent already) your "Life of Reason" to the "Revue de Philosophie," or rather to its editor, M. Peillaube, Rue des Revues 160, and to the editor of "Leonardo" (the great little Florentine philosophical journal), Sig. Giovanni Papini, 14 Borgo Albizi, Florence. The most interesting, and in fact genuinely edifying, part of my trip has been meeting this little *cénacle*, who have taken my own writings, *entre autres, au grand sérieux*, but who are carrying on their philosophical mission in anything but a technically serious way, inasmuch as "Leonardo" (of which I have hitherto only known a few odd numbers) is devoted to good and lively literary form. The sight of their belligerent young enthusiasm has given me a queer sense of the gray-plaster temperament of our bald-headed young Ph.D.'s, boring each other at seminaries, writing those direful reports of literature in the "Philosophical Review" and elsewhere, fed on "books of reference," and never confounding "Æsthetik" with "Erkentnisstheorie." Faugh! I shall never deal with them again—on *those* terms! Can't you and I, who in spite of such divergence have yet so much in common in our *Weltanschauung*, start a systematic movement at Harvard against the desiccating and pedantifying process? I have been cracking you up greatly to both Peillaube and Papini, and quoted you twice in my speech, which was in French and will be published in Flournoy's "Archives de Psychologie." I hope you're enjoying the Eastern Empire to the full, and that you had some Grecian "country life." Münsterberg has been called to Koenigsberg and has refused. Better be America's ancestor than Kant's successor! Ostwald, to my great delight, is coming to us next year, not as your replacer, but in exchange with Germany for F. G. Peabody. I go now to Cannes, to meet Strong, back from his operation. Ever truly yours,

Wm. James

To DICKINSON S. MILLER

Cambridge, Nov. 10, 1905

Dear Miller,—

W. R. Warren has just been here and says he has just seen you; the which precipitates me into a letter to you which has long hung fire. I hope that all goes well. You must be in a rather cheerful quarter of the City. Do you go home Sundays, or not? I hope that the work is congenial. How do you like your students as compared with those here? I reckon you get more out of your colleagues than you did here—barring of course *der Einzige*. We are all such old stories to each other that we say nothing. Santayana is the only [one] about whom we had any curiosity, and he has now quenched that. Perry and Holt have some ideas in reserve. . . . The fact is that the classroom exhausts our powers of speech. Royce has never made a syllable of reference to all the stuff I wrote last year—to me, I mean. He may have spoken of it to others, if he has read it, which I doubt. So we live in parellel trenches and hardly show our heads.

Santayana's book[1] is a great one, if the inclusion of opposites is a measure of greatness. I think it will probably be reckoned great by posterity. It has no *rational* foundation, being merely one man's way of viewing things: so much of experience admitted and no more, so much criticism and questioning admitted and no more. He is a paragon of Emersonianism—declare your intuitions, though no other man share them; and the integrity with which he does it is as fine as it is rare. And his naturalism, materialism, Platonism, and atheism form a combination of which the centre of gravity is, I think, very deep. But there is something profoundly alienating in his unsympathetic tone, his "preciousness" and superciliousness. The book is Emerson's first rival and successor, but how different the reader's feeling! The same things in Emerson's mouth would sound entirely different. E. receptive, expansive, as if handling life through a wide funnel with a great indraught; S. as if through a pin-point orifice that emits his cooling spray outward over the universe like a nose-disinfectant from an "atomizer." As he says of Schiller, whose beliefs he so largely reduplicates, "I hate him," so I, even though I should share Santayana's beliefs (and do so in large measure), have to say, "I dislike him!" I fear that the real originality of the book will be lost on nineteen-twentieths of the members of the Philosophical and Psychological Association!! The enemies of Harvard will find lots of blasphemous texts in him to injure us withal. But it is a great

[1] *The Life of Reason.* New York, 1905.

feather in our cap to harbor such an absolutely free expresser of individual convictions. But enough!

"Phil. 9" is going well. I think I *lecture* better than I ever did; in fact I know I do. But this professional evolution goes with an involution of all miscellaneous faculty. I am well, and efficient enough, but purposely going slow so as to keep efficient into the Palo Alto summer, which means that I have written nothing. I am pestered by doubts as to whether to put my resignation through this year, in spite of opposition, or to drag along another year or two. I think it is inertia against energy, energy in my case meaning being my own man absolutely. American philosophers, young and old, seem scratching where the wool is short. Important things are being published; but all of them too technical. The thing will never clear up satisfactorily till someone writes out its resultant in decent English. . . .

IV

1906-1910: LAST YEARS

"IF THERE is anything that God despises more than a man who is constantly making speeches, it is another man who is constantly accepting invitations," James said in a note to a friend, adding that in 1905 he had declined at least 100 invitations to speak. However, early in 1906 we find him in California, at Stanford, and in April he was on hand for the San Francisco earthquake. This same year he gave the Lowell Institute lectures, later published as *Pragmatism*. In 1908, "A Pluralistic Universe" was offered as the Hibbert lectures at Manchester College, Oxford. In the spring of 1910, James again returned to Europe, hoping once more to find the proper treatment for his heart disease. This last trip was marked by misery, fatigue, unsuccessful courses of treatment. At last, accompanied by his brother, Henry, William James came back to his place in Chocorua, New Hampshire. There, on August 26, 1910, he died, at the age of sixty-eight.

To MISS PAULINE GOLDMARK

El Tovar,
Grand Canyon, Arizona, Jan. 3, 1906

Dear Paolina,—

I am breaking my journey by a day here, and it seems a good place from which to date my New Year's greeting to you. But we correspond so rarely that when it comes to the point of tracing actual word with the pen, the last impressions of one's day and the more permanent interest of one's life block the way for each other. I think, however, that a word about the Canyon may fitly take precedence. It certainly is equal to the brag; and, like so many of the more stupendous freaks of nature, seems a first-sight smaller and more manageable than one had supposed. But it grows in immensity as the eye penetrates it more intimately. It is so entirely alone in character, that one has no habits of association with "the likes" of it, and at first it seems a foreign curiosity; but already in this one day I am feeling myself grow nearer, and can well imagine that, with greater intimacy, it might become the passion of one's life—so far as "Nature" goes. The conditions have been unfavorable for intimate communion. Three degrees above zero, and a spring overcoat, prevent that forgetting of "self" which is said to be indispensable to absorption in Beauty. Moreover, I have kept upon the "rim," seeing the Canyon from several points some miles apart. I meant to go down, having but this day; but they couldn't send me or any one today; and I confess that, with my precipice-disliking soul, I was relieved, though it very likely would have proved less uncomfortable than I have been told. (I resolved to go, in order to be worthy of being your correspondent.) As Chas. Lamb says, there is nothing so nice as doing good by stealth and being found out by accident, so I now

[216]

say it is even nicer to make heroic decisions and to be prevented by "circumstances beyond your control" from even trying to execute them. But if ever I get here in summer, I shall go straight down and live there. I'm sure that it is indispensable. But it is vain to waste descriptive words on the wondrous apparition, with its symphonies of architecture and of color. I have just been watching its peaks blush in the setting sun, and slowly lose their fire. Night nestling in the depths. Solemn, solemn! And a unity of design that makes it seem like an individual, an animated being. Good-night, old chasm! . . .

To THEODORE FLOURNOY

Stanford University, Feb. 9, 1906

Dear Flournoy.—

Your post-card of Jan. 22nd arrives and reminds me how little I have communicated with you during the past twelve months. . . .

Let me begin by congratulating Mlle. Alice, but more particularly Mr. Werner, on the engagement which you announce. Surely she is a splendid prize for anyone to capture. I hope that it has been a romantic love-affair, and will remain so to the end. May her paternal and maternal example be the model which their married life will follow! They could find no better model. You do not tell the day of the wedding—probably it is not yet appointed.

Yes! [Richard] Hodgson's death was ultra-sudden. He fell dead while playing a violent game of "hand-ball." He was tremendously athletic and had said to a friend only a week before that he thought he could reasonably count on twenty-five years more of life. None of his work was finished, vast materials amassed, which no one can ever get acquainted with as he had gradually got acquainted; so now good-bye forever to at least two unusually solid and instructive books which he would have soon begun to write on "psychic" subjects. As a *man*, Hodgson was splendid, a real man; as an investigator, it is my private impression that he lately got into a sort of obsession about Mrs. Piper, cared too little for other clues, and continued working with her when all the sides of her mediumship were amply exhibited. I suspect that our American Branch of the S. P. R. will have to dissolve this year, for lack of a competent secretary. Hodgson was our only worker, except Hyslop, and *he* is engaged in founding an "Institute" of his own, which will employ more popular methods. To tell the truth, I'm rather glad of the prospect of the Branch ending, for the Piper-investigation—and nothing else—had begun to bore me to extinction. . . .

To change the subject—you ought to see this extraordinary little University. It was founded only fourteen years ago in the absolute wilderness, by a pair of rich Californians named Stanford, as a memorial to their only child, a son who died at 16. Endowed with I know not how many square miles of land, which some day will come into the market and yield a big income, it has already funds that yield $750,000 yearly, and buildings, of really *beautiful* architecture, that have been paid for out of income, and have cost over $5,000,000. (I mention the cost to let you see that they must be solid.) There are now 1500 students of both sexes, who pay nothing for tuition, and a town of 15,000 inhabitants has grown up a mile away, beyond the gates. The landscape is exquisite and classical, San Francisco only an hour and a quarter away by train; the climate is one of the most perfect in the world, life is absolutely simple, no one being rich, servants almost unattainable (most of the house-work being done by students who come in at odd hours), many of them Japanese, and the professors' wives, I fear, having in great measure to do their own cooking. No social excesses or complications therefore. In fact, nothing but essentials, and *all* the essentials. Fine music, for example, every afternoon, in the Church of the University. There couldn't be imagined a better environment for an intellectual man to teach and work in, for eight or nine months in the year, if he were then free to spend three or four months in the crowded centres of civilization—for the social insipidity is great here, and the historic vacuum and silence appalling, and one ought to be free to change.

Unfortunately the authorities of the University seem not to be gifted with imagination enough to see its proper rôle. Its geographical environment and material basis being unique, they ought to aim at unique quality all through, and get *sommités* to come here to work and teach, by offering large stipends. They might, I think, thus easily build up something very distinguished. Instead of which, they pay small sums to young men who chafe at not being able to travel, and whose wives get worn out with domestic drudgery. The whole thing *might* be Utopian; it *is* only half-Utopian. A characteristic American affair! But the half-success is great enough to make one see the great advantages that come to this country from encouraging public-spirited millionaires to indulge their freaks, however eccentric. In what the Stanfords have already done, there is an assured potentiality of great things of *some* sort for all future time. My coming here is an exception. They have had psychology well represented from the first by Frank Angell and Miss Martin; but no philosophy except for a year at a time. I start a new régime—next year they will have two good professors.

I lecture three times a week to 400 listeners, printing a syllabus daily, and making them read Paulsen's textbook for examinations. I find it hard work, and only pray that I may have strength to run till June without collapsing. The students, though rustic, are very earnest and wholesome.

I am pleased, but also amused, by what you say of Wood-bridge's Journal: "la palme est maintenant à l'Amérique." It is true that a lot of youngsters in that Journal are doing some real thinking, but of all the *bad writing* that the world has seen, I think that our American writing is getting to be the worst. X——'s ideas have unchained formlessness of expression that beats the bad writing of the Hegelian epoch in Germany. I can hardly believe you sincere when you praise the journal as you do. I am so busy teaching that I do no writing and but little reading this year. I have declined to go to Paris next year, and also declined an invitation to Berlin, as "International Exchange" [Professor]. The year after, if asked, I *may* go to Paris—but never to Berlin. We have had Ostwald, a most delightful human *Erscheinung*, as international exchange at Harvard this year. But I don't believe in the system. . . .

To MISS FRANCES R. MORSE

Stanford University, Apr. 22, 1906

Dearest Fanny,—

Three letters from you and nary one from us in all these weeks! Well, I have been heavily burdened, and although disposed to write, have kept postponing; and with Alice—cooking, washing dishes and doing housework, as well as keeping up a large social life—it has been very much the same. All is now over, since the earthquake; I mean that lectures and syllabuses are called off, and no more exams. to be held ("ill-wind," etc.), so one can write. We shall get East again as soon as we can manage it, and tell you face to face. We can now pose as experts on Earthquakes—pardon the egotistic form of talking about the latter, but it makes it more real. The last thing Bakewell said to me, while I was leaving Cambridge, was: "I hope they'll treat you to a little bit of an earthquake while you're there. It's a pity you shouldn't have that local experience." Well, when I lay in bed at about half-past five that morning, wide-awake, and the room began to sway, my first thought was, "Here's Bakewell's earthquake, after all"; and when it went crescendo and reached fortissimo in less than half a minute, and the room was shaken like a rat by a terrier, with the most vicious expression you can possibly imagine, it was to my mind absolutely an *entity* that had been waiting all this time holding back its activity, but at last saying, "Now, *go* it!" and it was impossible not to conceive it as animated by a will, so vicious was the temper displayed—everything *down*, in the room, that could go down, bureaus, etc., etc., and the shaking so rapid and vehement. All the while no fear, only admiration for the way a wooden house could prove its elasticity, and glee over the vividness of the manner in which such an "abstract idea" as "earthquake" could verify itself into sensible reality. In a couple of minutes everybody was in the street, and then we saw, what I hadn't suspected in my room, the extent of the damage. Wooden houses almost all intact, but every chimney down but one or two, and the higher University buildings largely piles of ruins. Gabble and babble, till at last automobiles brought the dreadful news from San Francisco.

I boarded the only train that went to the City, and got out in the evening on the only train that left. I shouldn't have done it, but that our co-habitant here, Miss Martin, became obsessed by the idea that she *must* see what had become of her sister, and I had to stand by her. Was very glad I did; for the spectacle was memorable, of a whole population in the streets with what baggage they could rescue from their houses about to burn, while the flames and the explosions were steadily advancing and making everyone move farther. The fires most beautiful in the effulgent sunshine. Every vacant space was occupied by trunks and furniture and people, and thousands have been sitting by them now for four nights and will have to longer. The fire seems now controlled, but the city is practically wiped out (thank Heaven, as to much of its architecture!). The order has been wonderful, even the criminals struck solemn by the disaster, and the military has done great service.

But you will know all these details by the papers better than I know them now, before this reaches you, and in three weeks we shall be back.

I am very glad that Jim's [Putnam] lectures went off so well. He wrote me himself a good letter—won't you, by the way, send him this one as a partial answer?—and his syllabus was first-rate and the stuff must have been helpful. It is jolly to think of both him and Marian really getting off together to enjoy themselves! But between Vesuvius and San Francisco enjoyment has small elbow-room. Love to your mother, dearest Fanny, to Mary and the men folks, from us both. Your ever affectionate,

W. J.

To HENRY JAMES AND WILLIAM JAMES, JR.

Cambridge, May 9, 1906

Dearest Brother and Son,—

Your cablegram of response was duly received, and we have been also "joyous" in the thought of your being together. I knew, of course, Henry, that you would be solicitous about us in the earthquake, but didn't reckon at all on the extremity of your anguish as evinced by your frequent cablegrams home, and finally by the letter to Harry which arrived a couple of days ago and told how you were unable to settle down to any other occupation, the thought of our mangled forms, hollow eyes, starving bodies, minds insane with fear, haunting you so. We never reckoned on this extremity of anxiety on your part, I say, and so never thought of cabling you direct, as we might well have done from Oakland on the day we left, namely April 27th. I much regret this callousness on our part. For *all* the anguish was yours; and in general this experience only rubs in what I have always known, that in battles, sieges and other great calamities, the pathos and agony is in general solely felt by those at a distance; and although physical pain is suffered most by its immediate victims, those at the *scene of action* have no *sentimental* suffering whatever. Everyone at San Francisco seemed in a good hearty frame of mind; there was work for every moment of the day and a kind of uplift in the sense of a "common lot" that took away the sense of loneliness that (I imagine gives the sharpest edge to the more usual kind of misfortune that may befall a man. But it was a queer sight, on our journey through the City on the 26th (eight days after the disaster), to see the inmates of the houses of the quarter left standing, all cooking their dinners at little brick camp-fires in the middle of the streets, the chimneys being condemned. If such a disaster had to happen, somehow it couldn't have chosen a better place than San Francisco (where everyone knew about camping, and was familiar with the creation of civilizations out of the bare ground), and at five-thirty in the morning, when few fires were lighted and everyone, after a good sleep, was in bed. Later, there would have been great loss of life in the streets, and the more numerous foci of conflagration would have burned the city in one day instead of four, and made things vastly worse.

In general you may be sure that when any disaster befalls our country it will be *you* only who are wringing of hands, and we who are smiling with "interest or laughing with gleeful excitement." I didn't hear one pathetic word uttered at the scene of disaster, though of course the crop of "nervous wrecks" is very likely to come in a month or so.

Although we have been home six days, such has been the stream of broken occupations, people to see, and small urgent jobs to attend to, that I have written no letter till now. Today, one sees more clearly and begins to rest. "Home" looks extraordinarily pleasant, and though damp and chilly, it is the divine budding moment of the year. Not, however, the lustrous light and sky of Stanford University.

I have just read your paper on Boston in the "North American Review." I am glad you threw away the scabbard and made your critical remarks so straight. What you say about "pay" here being the easily won "salve" for privations, in view of which we cease to "mind" them, is as true as it is strikingly pat. *Les intellectuels*, wedged between the millionaires and the handworkers, are the really pinched class here. They feel the frustrations and they can't get the salve. *My* attainment of so much pay in the past few years brings home to me what an all-benumbing salve it is. That whole article is of your best. We long to hear from W., Jr. No word yet. Your ever loving,

W. J.

To JOHN JAY CHAPMAN

Cambridge, May 18, 1906

Dear old Jack C.,—

Having this minute come into the possession of a new typewriter, what can I do better than express my pride in the same by writing to you?

I spent last night at George Dorr's and he read me several letters from you, telling me also of your visit, and of how well you seemed. For years past I have been on the point of writing to you to assure [you] of my continued love and to express my commiseration for your poor wife, who has had so long to bear the brunt of your temper—you see I have been there already and I know how one's irritability is exasperated by conditions of nervous prostration—but now I can write and congratulate you on having recovered, temper and all. (As I write, it bethinks me that in a previous letter I have made identical jokes about your temper which, I fear, will give Mrs. Chapman a very low opinion of my humoristic resources, and in sooth they are small; but we are as God makes us and must not try to be anything else, so pray condone the silliness and let it pass.) The main thing is that you seem practically to have recovered, in spite of everything; and I am heartily glad.

I too am well enough for all practical purposes, but I have to go slow and not try to do too many things in a day. Simplification of life and consciousness I find to be the great thing, but a hard thing to compass when one lives in city conditions. How our dear Sarah Whitman lived in the sort of railroad station she made of her life—I confess it's a mystery to me. If I lived at a place called Barrytown, it would probably go better —don't you ever go back to New York to live!

Alice and I had a jovial time at sweet little Stanford Uni-

versity. It was the simple life in the best sense of the term.
I am glad for once to have been part of the working machine
of California, and a pretty deep part too, as it afterwards turned
out. The earthquake also was a memorable bit of experience,
and altogether we have found it mind-enlarging and are very
glad we ben there. But the whole intermediate West is awful—
a sort of penal doom to have to live there; and in general the
result with me of having lived 65 years in America is to make
me feel as if I had at least bought the right to a certain capriciousness, and were free now to live for the remainder of my
days wherever I prefer and can make my wife and children
consent—it is more likely to be in rural than in urban surroundings, and in the maturer than in the *rawrer* parts of the
world. But the first thing is to get out of the treadmill of teaching, which I hate and shall resign from next year. After that,
I can use my small available store of energy in writing, which
is not only a much more economical way of working it, but
more satisfactory in point of quality, and more lucrative as well.

Now, J. C., when are you going to get at writing again? The
world is hungry for your wares. No one touches certain deep
notes of moral truth as you do, and your humor is *köstlich* and
impayable. You ought to join the band of "pragmatistic" or
"humanistic" philosophers. I almost fear that Barrytown may
not yet have begun to be disturbed by the rumor of their
achievements, the which are of the greatest, and seriously I do
think that the world of thought is on the eve of a renovation no
less important than that contributed by Locke. The leaders of
the new movement are Dewey, Schiller of Oxford, in a sense
Bergson of Paris, a young Florentine named Papini, and last
and least worthy, W. J. H. G. Wells ought to be counted in,
and if I mistake not G. K. Chesterton as well. I hope you know
and love the last-named writer, who seems to me a great teller

of the truth. His systematic preference for contradictions and paradoxical forms of statement seems to me a mannerism somewhat to be regretted in so wealthy a mind; but that is a blemish from which some of our very greatest intellects are not altogether free—the philosopher of Barrytown himself being not wholly exempt. Join us, O Jack, and in the historic and perspective sense your fame will be secure. All future Histories of Philosophy will print your name.

But although my love for you is not exhausted, my typewriting energy is. It communicates stiffness and cramps, both to the body and the mind. Nevertheless I think I have been doing pretty well for a first attempt, don't you? If you return me a good long letter telling me more particularly about the process of your recovery, I will write again, even if I have to take a pen to do it, and in any case I will do it much better than this time.

Believe me, dear old J. C., with hearty affection and delight at your recovery—all these months I have been on the brink of writing to find out how you were—and with very best regards to your wife, whom some day I wish we may be permitted to know better. Yours very truly,

Wm. James

Everyone dead! Hodgson, Shaler, James Peirce this winter—to go no further afield! *Resserrons les rangs!*

To HENRY JAMES AND WILLIAM JAMES, JR.

Cambridge, Feb. 14, 1907

Dear Brother and Son,—

I dare say that you will be together in Paris when you get this, but I address it to Lamb House all the same. You twain are more "blessed" than I, in the way of correspondence this winter, for you give more than you receive, Bill's letters being as remarkable for wit and humor as Henry's are for copiousness, considering that the market value of what he either writes or types is so many shillings a word. When *I* write other things, I find it almost impossible to write letters. I've been at it *stiddy*, however, for three days, since my return from New York, finding, as I did, a great stack of correspondence to attend to. The first impression of New York, if you stay there not more than 36 hours, which has been my limit for twenty years past, is one of repulsion at the clangor, disorder, and permanent earthquake conditions. But this time, installed as I was at the Harvard Club (44th St.) in the centre of the cyclone, I caught the pulse of the machine, took up the rhythm, and vibrated *mit*, and found it simply magnificent. I'm surprised at you, Henry, not having been more enthusiastic, but perhaps that superbly powerful and beautiful subway was not opened when you were there. It is an *entirely* new New York, in soul as well as in body, from the old one, which looks like a village in retrospect. The courage, the heaven-scaling audacity of it all, and the *lightness* withal, as if there was nothing that was not easy, and the great pulses and bounds of progress, so many in directions all simultaneous that the coördination is indefinitely future, give a kind of *drumming background* of life that I never felt before. I'm sure that once *in* that movement, and at home, all other places would seem insipid. I observe that your book,— "The American Scene,"—dear H., is just out. I must get it and devour again the chapters relative to New York. On my last night, I dined with Norman Hapgood, along with men who were successfully and happily in the vibration. H. and his most winning-faced young partner, Collier, Jerome, Peter Dunne, F. M. Colby, and Mark Twain. (The latter, poor man, is only good for monologue, in his old age, or for dialogue at best, but he's a dear little genius all the same.) I got such an impression of easy efficiency in the midst of their bewildering conditions of speed and complexity of adjustment. Jerome, particularly, with the world's eyes on his court-room, in the very crux of the Thaw trial, as if he had nothing serious to do. Balzac ought to come to life again. His Rastignac imagination sketched the possibility of it long ago. I lunched, dined, and sometimes breakfasted, out, every day of my stay, vibrated between 44th St., seldom going lower, and 149th, with Columbia University at 116th as my chief relay station, the magnificent space-devouring Subway roaring me back and forth, lecturing to a thousand daily, and having four separate dinners at the Columbia Faculty Club, where colleagues severally compassed me about, many of them being old students of mine, wagged their tongues at me and made me explain. It was certainly the high tide of my existence, so far as *energizing* and being "recognized" were concerned, but I took it all very "easy" and am hardly a bit tired. Total abstinence from every stimulant whatever is the one condition of living at a rapid pace. I am now going whack at the writing of the rest of the lectures, which will be more original and (I believe) important than my previous works....

To F. C. S. SCHILLER

Cambridge, Apr. 19, 1907

Dear Schiller,—

Two letters and a card from you within ten days is pretty good. I have been in New York for a week, so haven't written as promptly as I should have done.

All right for the Gilbert Murrays! We shall be glad to see them.

Too late for "humanism" in my book—all in type! I dislike "pragmatism," but it seems to have the *international* right of way at present. Let's both go ahead—God will know his own!

When your book first came I lent it to my student Kallen (who was writing a thesis on the subject), thereby losing it for three weeks. Then the grippe, and my own proofs followed, along with much other business, so that I've only read about a quarter of it even now. The essays on Freedom and the Making of Reality seem to be written with my own heart's blood—it's startling that two people should be found to think so exactly alike. A great argument for the truth of what they say, too! I find that my own chapter on Truth printed in the J. of P. already,[1] convinces no one as yet, not even my most *gleichgesinnten* cronies. It will have to be worked in by much future labor, for I *know* that I see all round the subject and they don't, and I think that the theory of truth is the key to all the rest of our positions.

You ask what I am going to "reply" to Bradley. But why need one reply to everything and everybody? B.'s article is constructive rather than polemic, is evidently sincere, softens much of his old outline, is difficult to read, and ought, I think, to be left to its own destiny. How sweetly, by the way, he feels towards me as compared with you! All because you have been too bumptious. I confess I think that your *gaudium certaminis* injures your influence. *We*'ve got a thing big enough to set forth now affirmatively, and I think that readers generally hate *minute* polemics and recriminations. All polemic of ours should, I believe, be either very broad statements of contrast, or fine points treated singly, and as far as possible impersonally. Inborn rationalists and inborn pragmatists will never convert

1 "Pragmatism's Conception of Truth." Included in *Selected Essays and Reviews.*

each other. We shall always look on them as spectral and they on us as trashy—irredeemably both! As far as the rising generation goes, why not simply express ourselves positively, and trust that the truer view quietly will displace the other. Here again "God will know his own." False views don't need much direct refutation—they get superseded, and I feel absolutely certain of the supersessive power of pragmato-humanism, if persuasively enough set forth. . . . The world is wide enough to harbor various ways of thinking, and the present Bradley's units of mental operation are so diverse from ours that the labor of reckoning over from one set of terms to the other doesn't bring reward enough to pay for it. Of course his way of treating "truth" as an entity trying all the while to identify herself with reality, while reality is equally trying to identify herself with the more ideal entity truth, isn't *false*. It's one way, very remote and allegorical, of stating the facts, and it "agrees" with a good deal of reality, but it has so little pragmatic value that its tottering form can be left for time to deal with. The good it does him is small, for it leaves him in this queer, surly, grumbling state about the best that can be done by it for philosophy. His great vice seems to me his perversity in logical activities, his bad reasonings. I vote to go on, from now on, not trying to keep account of the relations of his with our system. He can't be influencing disciples, being himself nowadays so difficult. And once for all, there *will* be minds who *cannot help* regarding our growing universe as *sheer trash*, metaphysically considered. Yours ever,

W. J.

To CLIFFORD W. BEERS

Cambridge, Apr. 21, 1907

Dear Mr. Beers,—

You ask for my opinion as to the advisability and feasibility of a National Society, such as you propose, for the improvement of conditions among the insane.

I have never ceased to believe that such improvement is one of the most "crying" needs of civilization; and the functions of such a Society seem to me to be well drawn up by you. Your plea for its being founded before your book appears is well grounded, you being an author who naturally would like to cast seed upon a ground already prepared for it to germinate practically without delay.

I have to confess to being myself a very impractical man, with no experience whatever in the details, difficulties, etc., of philanthropic or charity organization, so my opinion as to the *feasibility* of your plan is worth nothing, and is undecided. Of course the first consideration is to get your money, the second, your Secretary and Trustees. All that *I* wish to bear witness to is the great need of a National Society such as you describe, or failing that, of a State Society somewhere that might serve as a model in other States.

Nowhere is there massed together as much suffering as in the asylums. Nowhere is there so much sodden routine, and fatalistic insensibility in those who have to treat it. Nowhere is an ideal treatment more costly. The officials in charge grow resigned to the conditions under which they have to labor. They cannot plead their cause as an auxiliary organization can plead it for them. Public opinion is too glad to remain ignorant. As mediator between officials, patients, and the public conscience, a society such as you sketch is absolutely required, and the sooner it gets under way the better. Sincerely yours,

William James

To HENRY JAMES

Salisbury, Conn., May 4, 1907

Dearest H.—

... I've been so overwhelmed with work, and the mountain of the *Unread* has piled up so, that only in these days here have I really been able to settle down to your "American Scene," which in its peculiar way seems to me *supremely great.* You know how opposed your whole "third manner" of execution is to the literary ideals which animate my crude and Orson-like breast, mine being to say a thing in one sentence as straight and explicit as it can be made, and then to drop it forever; yours being to avoid naming it straight, but by dint of breathing and sighing all round and round it, to arouse in the reader who may have had a similar perception already (Heaven help him if he hasn't!) the illusion of a solid object, made (like the "ghost" at the Polytechnic) wholly out of impalpable materials, air, and the prismatic interferences of light, ingeniously focused by mirrors upon empty space. But you *do* it, that's the queerness! And the complication of innuendo and associative reference on the enormous scale to which you give way to it does so *build out* the matter for the reader that the result is to solidify, by the mere bulk of the process, the like perception from which *he* has to start. As air, by dint of its volume, will weigh like a corporeal body; so his own poor little initial perception, swathed in this gigantic envelopment of suggestive atmosphere, grows like a germ into something vastly bigger and more substantial. But it's the rummest method for one to employ systematically as you do nowadays; and you employ it at your peril. In this crowded and hurried reading age, pages that require such close attention remain unread and neglected. You can't skip a word if you are to get the effect, and 19 out of 20 worthy readers grow intolerant. The method seems perverse: "Say it *out*, for God's sake," they cry, "and have done with it." And so I say now, give us *one* thing in your older directer manner, just to show that, in spite of your paradoxical success in this unheard-of method, you *can* still write according to accepted canons. Give us that interlude; and then continue like the "curiosity of literature" which you have become. For gleams and innuendoes and felicitous verbal insinuations you are unapproachable, but the *core* of literature is solid. Give it to us *once* again! The bare perfume of things will not support existence, and the effect of solidity you reach is but perfume and simulacrum.

For God's sake don't *answer* these remarks, which (as Uncle Howard used to say of Father's writings) are but the peristaltic belchings of my own crabbed organism. For one thing, your account of America is largely one of its omissions, silences, vacancies. You work them up like solids, for those readers who already germinally perceive them (to others you are *totally* incomprehensible). I said to myself over and over in reading: "How much greater the triumph, if instead of dwelling thus only upon America's vacuities, he could make positive suggestion of what in 'Europe' or Asia may exist to fill them." That would be nutritious to so many American readers whose souls are only too ready to leap to suggestion, but who are now too inexperienced to know what is meant by the contrast-effect from which alone your book is written. If you could supply the background which is the foil, in terms more full and positive! At present it is supplied only by the abstract geographic term

"Europe." But of course anything of that kind is excessively difficult; and you will probably say that you *are* supplying it all along by your novels. Well, the verve and animal spirits with which you can keep your method going, first on one place then on another, through all those tightly printed pages is something marvelous; and there are pages surely doomed to be immortal, those on the "drummers," *e.g.*, at the beginning of "Florida." They are in the best sense Rabelaisian.

But a truce, a truce! I had no idea, when I sat down, of pouring such a bath of my own subjectivity over you. Forgive! forgive! and don't reply, don't at any rate in the sense of defending yourself, but only in that of attacking *me*, if you feel so minded. I have just finished the proofs of a little book called "Pragmatism" which even you *may* enjoy reading. It is a very "sincere" and, from the point of view of ordinary philosophy-professorial manners, a very unconventional utterance, not particularly original at any one point, yet, in the midst of the literature of the way of thinking which it represents, with just that amount of squeak or shrillness in the voice that enables one book to *tell*, when others don't, to supersede its brethren, and be treated later as "representative." I shouldn't be surprised if ten years hence it should be rated as "epoch-making," for of the definitive triumph of that general way of thinking I can entertain no doubt whatever—I believe it to be something quite like the protestant reformation.

You can't tell how happy I am at having thrown off the nightmare of my "professorship." As a "professor" I always felt myself a sham, with its chief duties of being a walking encyclopedia of erudition. I am now at liberty to be a *reality*, and the comfort is unspeakable—literally unspeakable, to be my own man, after 35 years of being owned by others. I can now live for truth pure and simple, instead of for truth accom-

modated to the most unheard-of requirements set by others. . . .
Your affectionate

W. J.

The book by Bergson referred to in the next letter is
L'Évolution Créatice.

To HENRI BERGSON

Chocorua, June 13, 1907

O my Bergson, you are a magician, and your book is a marvel,
a real wonder in the history of philosophy, making, if I mistake
not, an entirely new era in respect of matter, but unlike the
works of genius of the "transcendentalist" movement (which
are so obscurely and abominably and inaccessibly written), a
pure classic in point of form. You may be amused at the comparison, but in finishing it I found the same after-taste remaining as after finishing "Madame Bovary," such a flavor of
persistent *euphony,* as of a rich river that never foamed or ran
thin, but steadily and firmly proceeded with its banks full to
the brim. Then the aptness of your illustrations, that never
scratch or stand out at right angles, but invariably simplify the
thought and help to pour it along! Oh, indeed you are a magician! And if your next book proves to be as great an advance
on this one as this is on its two predecessors, your name will
surely go down as one of the great creative names in philosophy.

There! have I praised you enough? What every genuine
philosopher (every genuine man, in fact) craves most is *praise*—
although the philosophers generally call it 'recognition'! If you
want still more praise, let me know, and I will send it, for my

[236]

features have been on a broad smile from the first page to the last, at the chain of felicities that never stopped. I feel rejuvenated.

As to the content of it, I am not in a mood at present to make any definite reaction. There is so much that is absolutely new that it will take a long time for your contemporaries to assimilate it, and I imagine that much of the development of detail will have to be performed by younger men whom your ideas will stimulate to coruscate in manners unexpected by yourself. To me at present the vital achievement of the book is that it inflicts an irrecoverable death-wound upon Intellectualism. It can never resuscitate! But it will die hard, for all the inertia of the past is in it, and the spirit of professionalism and pedantry as well as the æsthetic-intellectual delight of dealing with categories logically distinct yet logically connected, will rally for a desperate defense. The *élan vital*, all contentless and vague as you are obliged to leave it, will be an easy substitute to make fun of. But the beast *has* its death-wound now, and the manner in which you have inflicted it (interval *versus* temps d'arrêt, etc.) is masterly in the extreme. I don't know why this latter *rédaction* of your critique of the mathematics of movement has seemed to me so much more telling than the early statement— I suppose it is because of the wider *use* made of the principle in the book. You will be receiving my own little "pragmatism" book simultaneously with this letter. How jejune and inconsiderable it seems in comparison with your great system! But it is so congruent with parts of your system, fits so well into interstices thereof, that you will easily understand why I am so enthusiastic. I feel that at bottom we are fighting the same fight, you a commander, I in the ranks. The position we are rescuing is "Tychism" and a really growing world. But whereas I have hitherto found no better way of defending Tychism than by affirming the spontaneous addition of *discrete* elements of being (or their subtraction), thereby playing the game with intellectualist weapons, you set things straight at a single stroke by your fundamental conception of the continuously creative nature of reality. I think that one of your happiest strokes is your reduction of "finality," as usually taken, to its status alongside of efficient causality, as the twin-daughters of intellectualism. But this vaguer and truer finality restored to its rights will be a difficult thing to give content to. Altogether your reality lurks so in the background, in this book, that I am wondering whether you *couldn't* give it any more development *in concreto* here, or whether you perhaps were holding back developments, already in your possession, for a future volume. They are sure to come to you later anyhow, and to make a new volume; and altogether, the clash of these ideas of yours with the traditional ones will be sure to make sparks fly that will illuminate all sorts of dark places and bring innumerable new considerations into view. But the process may be slow, for the ideas are so revolutionary. Were it not for your style, your book might last 100 years unnoticed; but your way of writing is so absolutely commanding that your theories have to be attended to immediately. I feel very much in the dark still about the relations of the progressive to the regressive movement, and this great precipitate of nature subject to static categories. With a frank pluralism of *beings* endowed with vital impulses you can get oppositions and compromises easily enough, and a stagnant deposit; but after my one reading I don't exactly "catch on" to the way in which the continuum of reality resists itself so as to have to act, etc., etc.

The only part of the work which I felt like positively criticising was the discussion of the idea of nonentity, which seemed to me somewhat overelaborated, and yet didn't leave me with a sense that the last word had been said on the subject. But all these things must be very slowly digested by me. I can see that, when the tide turns in your favor, many previous tendencies in philosophy will start up, crying "This is nothing but what *we* have contended for all along." Schopenhauer's blind will, Hartmann's unconscious, Fichte's aboriginal freedom (re-ëdited at Harvard in the most "unreal" possible way by Münsterberg) will all be claimants for priority. But no matter— all the better if you are in some ancient lines of tendency. Mysticism also must make claims and doubtless just ones. I say nothing more now—this is just my first reaction; but I am so enthusiastic as to have said only two days ago, "I thank heaven that I have lived to this date—that I have witnessed the Russo-Japanese war, and seen Bergson's new book appear—the two great modern turning-points of history and of thought!" Best congratulations and cordialest rgeards!

Wm. James

To DICKINSON S. MILLER

Lincoln, Mass., Aug. 5, 1907

Dear Miller,—

I got your letter about "Pragmatism," etc., some time ago. I hear that you are booked to review it for the "Hibbert Journal." Lay on, Macduff! as hard as you can—I want to have the weak places pointed out. I sent you a week ago a "Journal of Philosophy" with a word more about Truth in it, written *at* you mainly; but I hardly dare hope that I have cleared up my position. A letter from Strong, two days ago, written after receiving a proof of that paper, still thinks that I deny the existence of realities outside of the thinker; and [R. B.] Perry, who seems to me to have written far and away the most important critical remarks on Pragmatism (possibly the *only* important ones), accused Pragmatists (though he doesn't name *me*) of ignoring or denying that the real object plays any part in deciding what ideas are true. I confess that such misunderstandings seem to me hardly credible, and cast a "lurid light" on the mutual understandings of philosophers generally. Apparently it all comes from the *word* Pragmatism—and a most unlucky word it may prove to have been. I am a natural realist. The world *per se* may be likened to a cast of beans on a table. By themselves they spell nothing. An onlooker may group them as he likes. He may simply count them all and map them. He may select groups and name these capriciously, or name them to suit certain extrinsic purposes of his. Whatever he does, so long as he *takes account* of them, his account is neither false nor irrelevant. If neither, why not call it true? It *fits* the beans-*minus*-him, and *expresses* the *total* fact, of beans-*plus*-him. Truth in this total sense is partially ambiguous, then. If he simply counts or maps, he obeys a subjective interest as much as if he traces figures. Let that stand for pure "intellectual" treatment of the beans, while grouping them variously stands for non-intellectual interests. All that Schiller and I contend for is that there is *no* "truth" without *some* interest, and that non-intellectual interests play a part as well as intellectual ones. Whereupon we are accused of denying the beans, or denying being in anyway constrained by them! It's too silly! . . .

To HENRY JAMES

Stonehurst, Intervale, N.H., Oct. 6, 1907

Dearest Brother,—

I write this at the [James] Bryces', who have taken the Merrimans' house for the summer, and whither I came the day before yesterday, after closing our Chocorua house, and seeing Alice leave for home. We had been there a fortnight, trying to get some work done, and having to do most of it with our own hands, or rather with Alice's heroic hands, for mine are worth almost nothing in these degenerate days. It is enough to make your heart break to see the scarcity of "labor," and the whole country tells the same story. Our future at Chocorua is a somewhat problematic one, though I think we shall manage to pass next summer there and get it into better shape for good renting, thereafter, at any cost (not the renting but the shaping). After that what *I* want is a free foot, and the children are now not dependent on a family summer any longer....

I spent the first three weeks of September—warm ones—in my beloved and exquisite Keene Valley, where I was able to do a good deal of uphill walking, with good rather than bad effects, much to my joy. Yesterday I took a three hours walk here, three quarters of an hour of it uphill. I have to go alone, and slowly; but it's none the worse for that and makes one feel like old times. I leave this P.M. for two more days at Chocorua—at the hotel. The fall is late, but the woods are beginning to redden beautifully. With the sun behind them, some maples look like stained-glass windows. But the penury of the human part of this region is depressing, and I begin to have an appetite for Europe again. Alice too! To be at Cambridge with no lecturing and no students to nurse along with their thesis-work is an almost incredibly delightful prospect. I am going to settle down to the composition of another small book, more original and ground-breaking than anything I have yet put forth (!), which I expect to print by the spring; after which I can lie back and write at leisure more routine things for the rest of my days.

The Bryces are wholly unchanged, excellent friends and

hosts, and I like her as much as him. The trouble with him is that his insatiable love of information makes him try to pump *you* all the time instead of letting you pump *him*, and I have let my own tongue wag so, that, when gone, I shall feel like a fool, and remember all kinds of things that I have forgotten to ask him. I have just been reading to Mrs. B., with great gusto on her part and renewed gusto on mine, the first few pages of your chapter on Florida in "The American Scene." *Köstlich* stuff! I had just been reading to myself almost 50 pages of the New England part of the book, and fairly melting with delight over the Chocorua portion. Evidently that book will last, and bear reading over and over again—a few pages at a time, which is the right way for "literature" fitly so called. It all makes me wish that we had you here again, and you will doubtless soon come. I mustn't forget to thank you for the gold pencil-case souvenir. I have had a plated silver one for a year past, now worn through, and experienced what a "comfort" they are. Good-bye, and Heaven bless you. Your loving

W. J.

To HENRY ADAMS

Cambridge, Feb. 9, 1908

Dear Adams:

I have at last "got round" to the reading of your "Education," and wish to express my thanks to you for having written it and endowed me with it. Parts of it I find obscure, but parts of it (as the curate at the Bishop's table said of the egg) are excellent, superlatively so. The boyhood part is really superlative. It and the London part should become classic historic documents. There is a hodge-podge of world-fact, private fact, philosophy, irony, (with the word "education" stirred in too much for my appreciation!) which gives a unique cachet to the thing, and gives a very pleasant *gesammt-eindruck* of H. A.'s *Self*. A great deal of the later diplomatic history is dealt with so much by hint and implication, that to an ignoramus like W. J. it reads obscurely. Above all I should like to understand more precisely just what Hay's significance really was. You speak of the perfection of his work, but it is all esoteric. Isn't it your mission now to write a life of Hay, defining him and his work exactly, to be published perhaps posthumously? No one else will ever be so qualified; and it is evidently an important *moment* in our historical evolution.

I don't follow or share your way of conceiving the historic problem, as the determination of a curve by points. I think that that applies only to what is done and over, in other words it is retrospection projected on the future. But unless the future contains genuine novelties, unless the present is really creative of them, *I don't see the use of time at all*. Space would be a sufficient theatre for these statically determined relations to be arranged in. But halte-là! This is converting epistolation into dialectics.

This gives me a desire to see you again before we die. If I ever go to Washington I will knock at your door.

Believe me, dear H. A., ever truly

Yours,
Wm. James

To MISS PAULINE GOLDMARK

London, June 2, 1908

Dear Pauline—

Don't think that I am going to write you every day, as I did during that memorable time 3 years ago—I probably shan't write again for weeks, but nothing is awake in London, as you

know, until about 9 o'clock, so being awake now at ½ six, I
had better do some good indoor action, and what could be
better than writing a postscript to my letter of Sunday to yourself? Tempora mutantur! even London changes, and approxi-
mates to New York. One of the vulgarizing effects of growing
old is that greatness shrinks and impressiveness becomes as
naught. There was a time when London at the height of the
season, as now, intimidated and overawed my young imagination. The brown air and light, the infinitely numerous equip-
ages, the thousands of glorious swells of both sexes, drest to kill,
the echoes in all the streets of an earlier literature, the generation of Waterloo, and of times before that, the solidity, wealth,
and splendour of it all made every other place seem scrappy,
poor and parvenu in comparison. But apart from one's own
inward changes, London itself is growing scrappy and ameri-
canized. Lots of new screeching buildings, motor cars of every
description making the streets dangerous and chaotic, standards
of dress are polymorphic, Regent and Bond St. shops have a
cheap-jack expression, the women look tired and sharp as they
do in Boston, in short the splendor has utterly departed for
my jaded and blasé vision, and I never want to see the cheap
and vulgar old place again. It has all disintegrated! Last night
I dined with Henry at the Reform Club. In 1881 (I think)
when he first showed it to me, it seemed a palace of grandeur,
last night I saw it as a rather stupidly built and in some respects
shabby little club. It is because one has become small and
shabby one's self, I suppose, that the world thus changes its
face, and the only things that stay sublime are certain of the
inward and abstract standards and ideas, and even they shrink
and totter a good deal. Oxford is not screeching and chaotic,
and altho it seems far lighter in weight than formerly, it has
its own definite form and character and beauty, and appeals to

me far more than London. A jolly world to live in and be a part of, and at bottom entirely democratic. The humanly great there, or what ranks as such, is all self-made, simply *affablé* in the clothes of the past, and one would never suspect in living there, that one was in a country that possessed a "nobility and gentry." The world is getting democratic and socialistic faster and faster, and out of it all a new civilization will emerge. Will it ever simplify and solidify itself again? Or will it get more and more like an infinite pack of firecrackers exploding? How strange that Rome in the midst of it all should feel still like a quiet little provincial place. I wish I could "place" you there in my mind's eye—i.e., imagine when and how you live there. Write and say [erasure]; or don't write! if you don't feel just like it.

I had a humanly delightful 36 hours at Birmingham with the Lodges. He is a *splendid* Olympian kind of fellow, self-made, simple and generous, and the social tone was just like home—a lot of university people, direct and straightforward, and some very fine young female "lecturers." I must say that there is a type of tall, slender, vigorous, cultivated-minded woman in this country that impresses me very much, high-colored, lustrous-eyed, somewhat hard-muscled and deficient in the softness that in other countries becomes puffiness and flabbiness, and on the whole very noble. But what's the use, Pauline, of writing so much? You must throw it into the waste basket. Alice comes in from Harrow today, and we go together to Oxford again for another week of lunches, teas, and dinners, the first three or four days of it at Mrs. Fiske Warren's, of Boston, who has won great admiration by getting a "first" in "Greats"—if you can understand that jargon, i.e., passing an examination equivalent to the hardest they can give men, and triumphing at every point. We have been staying for the last

2 weeks at our dear old friend Louis Dyer's who has just been sent by Osler to the Matlock Hydropathic establishment for a very painful shoulder joint. Good friendly learned patient man, with no gall or bitterness in him, sore tried by his wife's protracted insanity, yet never murmuring, as even now not with his shoulder. Good bye, dear Pauline and God bless you. Drink in the spirit of your dear Italy and grow well and happy there. How much more genial, amiable, and *intricate* a set of human suggestions than those of Greece! How rich a world with such a variety of national types—each so unique and unaccountable. Good bye, good bye. Your,

W. J.

To MISS PAULINE GOLDMARK

Patterdale, England, July 2, 1908

Your letter, beloved Pauline, greeted me on my arrival here three hours ago. . . . How I *do wish* that I could be in Italy alongside of you now, now or any time! You could do me so much good, and your ardor of enjoyment of the country, the towns and the folk would warm up my cold soul. I might even learn to speak Italian by conversing in that tongue with you. But I fear that you'd find me betraying the coldness of my soul by complaining of the heat of my body—a most unworthy attitude to strike. Dear Paolina, never, never think of whether your body is hot or cold; live in the *objective* world, above such miserable considerations. I have been up here eight days, Alice having gone down last Saturday, the 27th, to meet Peggy and Harry at London, after only two days of it. After all the social and other fever of the past six and a half weeks (save for the blessed nine days at Bibury), it looked like the beginning of a real vacation, and it would be such but for the extreme heat, and the accident of one of my recent malignant "colds" beginning. I have been riding about on stage-coaches for five days past, but the hills are so treeless that one gets little shade, and the sun's glare is tremendous. It is a lovely country, however, for pedestrianizing in cooler weather. Mountains and valleys compressed together as in the Adirondacks, great reaches of pink and green hillside and lovely lakes, the higher parts quite fully alpine in character but for the fact that no snow mountains form the distant background. A strong and noble region, well worthy of one's life-long devotion, if one were a Briton. And on the whole, what a magnificent land and race is this Britain! Every thing about them is of better quality than the corresponding thing in the U.S.—with but few exceptions, I imagine. And the equilibrium is so well achieved, and the human tone so cheery, blithe and manly! and the manners so delightfully good. Not one *unwholesome*-looking man or woman does one meet here for 250 that one meets in America. Yet I believe (or suspect) that ours is eventually the bigger destiny, if we can only succeed in living up to it, and thou in 22nd St. and I in Irving St. must do our respective strokes, which after 1000 years will help to have made the glorious collective resultant. Meanwhile, as my brother Henry once wrote, thank God for a world that holds so rich an England, so rare an Italy! Alice is entirely *aufgegangen* in her idealization of it. And truly enough, the gardens, the manners, the manliness are an excuse.

But profound as is my own moral respect and admiration, for a *vacation* give me the Continent! The civilization here is too heavy, too *stodgy*, if one could use so unamiable a word. The very stability and good-nature of all things (of course we are leaving out the slum-life!) rest on the basis of the national stupidity, or rather unintellectuality, on which as on a safe foundation of non-explosible material, the magnificent minds of the élite of the race can coruscate as they will, safely. Not until those weeks at Oxford, and these days at Durham, have I had any sense of what a part the Church plays in the national life. So massive and all-pervasive, so authoritative, and on the whole so decent, in spite of the iniquity and farcicality of the whole thing. Never were incompatibles so happily yoked together. Talk about the genius of Romanism! It's nothing to the genius of Anglicanism, for Catholicism still contains some haggard elements, that ally it with the Palestinian desert, whereas Anglicanism remains obese and round and comfortable and decent with this world's decencies, without an *acute* note in its whole life or history, in spite of the shrill Jewish words on which its ears are fed, and the nitro-glycerine of the Gospels and Epistles which has been injected into its veins. Strange feat to have achieved! Yet the success is great—the whole Church-machine makes for all sorts of graces and decencies, and is not incompatible with a high type of Churchman, high, that is, on the side of moral and worldly virtue. . . .

How I wish you were beside me at this moment! A breeze has arisen on the Lake which is spread out before the "smoking-room" window at which I write, and is very grateful. The lake much resembles Lake George. Your ever grateful and loving

W. J.

To CHARLES ELIOT NORTON

Patterdale, England, July 6, 1908

Dear Charles,—

Going to Coniston Lake the other day and seeing the moving little Ruskin Museum at Coniston (admission a penny) made me think rather vividly of you, and make a resolution to write to you on the earliest opportunity. It was truly moving to see such a collection of R.'s busy handiwork, exquisite and loving, in the way of drawing, sketching, engraving and note-taking, and also such a varied lot of photographs of him, especially in his old age. Glorious old Don Quixote that he was! At Durham, where Alice and I spent three and a half delightful days at the house of F. B. Jevons, Principal of one of the two colleges of which the University is composed, I had a good deal of talk with the very remarkable octogenarian Dean of the Cathedral and Lord of the University, a thorough liberal, or rather radical, in his mind, with a voice like a bell, and an alertness to match, who had been a college friend of Ruskin's and known him intimately all his life, and loved him. He knew not of his correspondence with you, of which I have been happy to be able to order Kent of Harvard Square to send him a copy. His name is Kitchin.

The whole scene at Durham was tremendously impressive (though York Cathedral made the stronger impression on me). It was so unlike Oxford, so much more American in its personnel, in a way, yet nestling in the very bosom of those mediæval stage-properties and ecclesiastical-principality suggestions. Oxford is all spread out in length and breadth, Durham concentrated in depth and thickness. There is a great deal of flummery about Oxford, but I think if I were an Oxonian, in spite of my radicalism generally, I might vote against all change there. It is an absolutely unique fruit of human endeavor, and like the cathedrals, can never to the end of time be reproduced, when the conditions that once made it are changed. Let other places of learning go in for all the improvements! The world can afford to keep her one Oxford unreformed. I know that this is a superficial judgment in both ways, for Oxford does manage to keep pace with the utilitarian spirit, and at the same time preserve lots of her flummery unchanged. On the whole it is a thoroughly *democratic place*, so far as aristocracy in the strict sense goes. But I'm out of it, and doubt whether I want ever to put foot into it again. . . .

England has changed in many respects. The West End of London, which used at this season to be so impressive from its splendor, is now a mixed and mongrel horde of straw hats and cads of every description. Motor-buses of the most brutal sort have replaced the old carriages, Bond and Regent Streets are cheap-jack shows, everything is tumultuous and confused and has run down in quality. I have been "motoring" a good deal through this "Lake District," owing to the kindness of some excellent people in the hotel, dissenters who rejoice in the name of Squance and inhabit the neighborhood of Durham. It is wondrous fine, but especially adapted to trampers, which I no longer am. Altogether England seems to have got itself into a magnificently fine state of civilization, especially in regard to the cheery and wholesome tone of manners of the people, improved as it is getting to be by the greater infusion of the democratic temper. Everything here seems about twice as good as the corresponding thing with us. But I suspect we have the bigger eventual destiny after all; and give us a thousand years and we may catch up in many details. I think of you as still at Cambridge, and I do hope that physical ills are bearing on more gently. Lily, too, I hope is her well self again. You mustn't think of answering this, which is only an ejaculation of friendship—I shall be home almost before you can get an answer over. Love to all your circle, including Theodora, whom I miss greatly. Affectionately yours,

Wm. James

To CHARLES ELIOT NORTON

Cambridge, Oct. 17, 1908

Dear Charles,—

... I was ... grieved at the account ... of all your sufferings and frustration. What a wrong-way-foremost thing senescence seems to be, and how strange the inharmonious share our different organs take in it! Your brain appears to have no appreciable share, and one hardly knows whether to congratulate you or to condole with you, for its functions being so little blunted. I am as convinced as I can be of anything that this experience of ours is only a part of the experience that is, and with which it has something to do; but *what* or *where* the other parts are, I cannot guess. It only enables one to say "behind the veil, behind the veil!" more hopefully, however interrogatively and vaguely, than would otherwise be the case.

I thank you, dear Charles ... for the superb chrysanthemums, which show that however bedridden a man may be, he can still play a part in the graciousnesses of the world. "Toujours le soleil poudroie par quelque trou." ... I'm going to Chocorua in a couple of hours. ... I hope and trust that when I come back I shall be able to come and "hold your hand." Believe, dear Charles, in your present straits, in the deep and warm reverence and affection in which you are held—by no one more profoundly than by yours ever lovingly,

Wm. James

To T. S. PERRY

Cambridge, Jan. 29, 1909

Beloved Thomas, cher maître et confrère,—

Your delightful letter about my Fechner article and about your having become a professional philosopher yourself came to hand duly, four days ago, and filled the heart of self and wife with joy. I always knew you was one, for to be a real philosopher all that is necessary is to *hate* some one else's type of thinking, and if that some one else be a representative of the "classic" type of thought, then one is a pragmatist and owns the fulness of the truth. Fechner is indeed a dear, and I am glad to have introduced, so to speak, his speculation to the English world, although the Revd. Elwood Worcester has done so in a somewhat more limited manner in a recent book of his called "The Living World"—(Worcester of Emmanuel Church, I mean, whom everyone has now begun to fall foul of for trying to reanimate the Church's healing virtue). Another case of newspaper crime! The reporters all got hold of it with their megaphones, and made the nation sick of the sound of its name. Whereas in former ages men strove hard for fame, obscurity is now the one thing to be *striven* for. For *fame*, all one need do is to exist; and the reporter wil do the rest—especially if you give them the address of your fotographer. I hope you're a spelling reformer—I send you the last publication from that quarter. I'm sure that simple spelling will make a page look better, just as a crowd looks better if everyone's clothes fit.

Apropos of pragmatism, a learned Theban named —— has written a circus-performance of which he is the clown, called "Anti-pragmatisme." It has so much verve and good spirit that I feel like patting him on the back, and "sicking him on," but Lord! what a fool! I think I shall leave it unnoticed. I'm tired of reëxplaining what is already explained to satiety. Let *them* say, now, for it is their turn, what the relation called truth consists in, what it is known as!

I have had you on my mind ever since Jan. 1st, when we had our Friday evening Club-dinner, and I was deputed to cable you a happy New Year. The next day I couldn't get to the telegraph office; the day after I said to myself, "I'll save the money, and save him the money, for if he gets a cable, he'll be sure to cable back; so I'll write"; the following day, I forgot to; the next day I postponed the act; so from postponement to postponement, here I am. Forgive, forgive! Most affectionate remarks were made about you at the dinner, which generally doesn't err by wasting words on absentees, even on those gone to eternity. . . .

I have just got off my report on the Hodgson control, which has stuck to my fingers all this time. It is a hedging sort of an affair, and I don't know what the Perry family will think of it. The truth is that the "case" is a particularly poor one for testing Mrs. Piper's claim to bring back spirits. It is *leakier* than any other case, and intrinsically, I think, no stronger than many of her other good cases, certainly weaker than the G. P. case. I am also now engaged in writing a popular article, "the avowals of a psychical researcher," for the "American Magazine," in which I simply state without argument my own convictions, and put myself on record. I think that public opinion is just now taking a step forward in these matters—*vide* the Eusapian boom! and possibly both these *Schriften* of mine will add their influence. Thank you for the Charmes reception and for the earthquake correspondence! I envy you in clean and intelligent Paris, though our winter is treating us very mildly. A lovely sunny day today! Love to all of you! Yours fondly,

W. J.

The "Charmes reception" was a report of the speeches at the French Academy's reception of Francis Charmes. The "Eusapian boom" will have been understood to refer to current discussion of the medium Eusapia Paladino.

To JOHN JAY CHAPMAN

Cambridge, Apr. 30, 1909

Dear Jack C.,—

I'm not expecting you to *read* my book, but only to "give me a thought" when you look at the cover. A certain witness at a poisoning case was asked how the corpse looked. "Pleasant-like and foaming at the mouth," was the reply. A good description of you, describing philosophy, in your letter. All that you say is true, and yet the conspiracy has to be carried on by us professors. Reality has to be *returned to*, after this long circumbendibus, though *Gavroche* has it already. There *are* concepts, anyhow. I am glad you lost the volume. It makes one less in existence and ought to send up the price of the remainder.

Blessed spring! blessed spring! Love to you both from yours,

Wm. James

To THEODORE FLOURNOY

Chocorua, Sept. 28, 1909

Dear Flournoy,—

We had fondly hoped that before now you might both, accepting my half-invitation, half-suggestion, be with us in this uncared-for-nature, so different from Switzerland, and you getting strengthened and refreshed by the change. *Dieu dispose*, indeed! The fact that *is* never entered into our imagination! I give up all hope of you this year, unless it be for Cambridge, where, however, the conditions of repose will be less favorable for you. . . . I am myself going down to Cambridge on the fifth of October for two days of "inauguration" ceremonies of our new president, Lawrence Lowell. . . . There are so many rival universities in our country that advantage has to be taken of such changes to make the newspaper talk, and keep the name of Harvard in the public ear, so the occasion is to be almost as elaborate as a "Jubilee"; but I shall keep as much out of it as is officially possible, and come back to Chocorua on the 8th, to stay as late into October as we can, though probably not later than the 20th, after which the Cambridge winter will begin. It hasn't gone well with my health this summer, and beyond a little reading, I have done no work at all. I have, however, succeeded during the past year in preparing a volume on the "Meaning of Truth"—already printed papers for the most part—which you will receive in a few days after getting this letter, and which I think may help you to set the "pragmatic" account of Knowledge in a clearer light. I will also send you a magazine article on the mediums, which has just appeared, and which may divert you.[1] Eusapia Paladino, I understand, has just signed a contract to come to New York to be at the disposition of Hereward Carrington, an expert in medium's tricks, and author of a book on the same, who, together with Fielding and Bagally, also experts, formed the Committee of the London S. P. R., who saw her at Naples. . . . After Courtier's report on Eusapia, I don't think any "investigation" here will be worth much "scientifically"—the only advantage of her coming may possibly be to get some scientific men to believe that there is really a problem. Two other cases have been reported to me lately, which are worth looking up, and I shall hope to do so.

How much your interests and mine keep step with each other, dear Flournoy. "Functional psychology," and the twilight region that surrounds the clearly lighted centre of experience! Speaking of "functional" psychology, Clark University, of which Stanley Hall is president, had a little international

---

[1] "The Confidences of a Psychical Researcher," reprinted in *Memories and Studies* under the title "Final Impressions of a Psychical Researcher."

congress the other day in honor of the twentieth year of its existence. I went there for one day in order to see what Freud was like, and met also Yung of Zürich, who professed great esteem for you, and made a very pleasant impression. I hope that Freud and his pupils will push their ideas to their utmost limits, so that we may learn what they are. They can't fail to throw light on human nature; but I confess that he made on me personally the impression of a man obsessed with fixed ideas. I can make nothing in my own case with his dream theories, and obviously "symbolism" is a most dangerous method. A newspaper report of the congress said that Freud had condemned the American religious therapy (which has such extensive results) as very "dangerous" because so "unscientific." Bah!

Well, it is pouring rain and so dark that I must close. Alice joins me, dear Flournoy, in sending you our united love, in which all your children have a share. Ever yours,

W. J.

To DICKINSON S. MILLER

Cambridge, Mar. 26, 1910

Dear Miller,—

Your study of me arrives! and I have pantingly turned the pages to find the eulogistic adjectives, and find them in such abundance that my head swims. Glory to God that I have lived to see this day! to have so much said about me, and to be embalmed in literature like the great ones of the past! I didn't know I was so much, was all these things, and yet, as I read, I see that I was (or am?), and shall boldly assert myself when I go abroad.

To speak in all dull soberness, dear Miller, it touches me to the quick that you should have hatched out this elaborate description of me with such patient and loving incubation. I have only spent five minutes over it so far, meaning to take it on the steamer, but I get the impression that it is almost un-exampled in our literature as a piece of profound analysis of an individual mind. I'm sorry you stick so much to my psychological phase, which I care little for, now, and never cared much. This epistemological and metaphysical phase seems to me more original and important, and I haven't lost hopes of converting you entirely yet. Meanwhile, thanks! thanks! [Émile] Boutroux, who is a regular angel, has just left our house. I've written an account of his lectures which the "Nation" will print on the 31st. I should like you to look it over, hasty as it is.

. . . I hope that all these lectures on contemporaries (What a live place Columbia is!) will appear together in a volume. I can't easily believe that any will compare with yours as a thorough piece of interpretative work.

We sail on Tuesday next. My thorax has been going the wrong way badly this winter, and I hope that Nauheim may patch it up.

Strength to your elbow! Affectionately and gratefully yours,

Wm. James

To J. G. PIDDINGTON

Villa Isolde, Bad Nauheim
Germany, May 21, 1910

Dear Piddington,

I had expected to write to you ere now, but it has been practically impossible owing to corporal fatigue and mental occupation "elsewhere." A fierce 10 days in Paris, adapting myself to the unwonted social environment, a blissful solitude

[257]

in the compartment all by myself to Frankfort, a settlement in this fragrant and bird-haunted and innocent little place, with very definite medical examination, and baths begun, have smoothed out the wrinkles of my soul for the time, so that I can return you-wards at last. I am hoping to lure H. J. hither (and my wife with him) ere the month is out. I am in for 6 or 8 weeks of it, so restlessness may rest. Germany impreses me as calm and great. I hope you're not one of the war-phobists, for *I* enjoy the mere sense of the German civilization about me and don't wish my friends across the Channel to harbor such suspicions of it.

I never wrote a word about the Piper[1] appeal, for I hoped still to see you until the last days at Rye. I fear, from the contents of a letter from T. S. Perry, which I enclose to you confidentially, to show how the wind blows (*please destroy it forthwith!*), that the American harvest is not likely to be big. A dozen years ago I said to Hodgson that we were morally incurring a pecuniary responsibility for her old age, which I personally was unwilling to share, so none of my family saw her for about 8 years, and we have only seen her ½ a dozen times since R. H.'s death. I have steadily foreseen this appeal and have told Dow long since that I would give only the nominal sum of $100.00, having far more pressing charity claims to satisfy. Those whom Mrs. P. sustained spiritually may well feel differently; but from Perry's to her, it would appear that many of them *don't,* and that the divided character of your proposal (which I interpreted as tactfully devised to capture various suffrages) is interpreted the other way about, by the Hodgsonites as frustrating what they want, and by the Piperites as leaving the P.'s unguaranteed. A nasty business! The worst

[1] The famous Boston medium, Mrs. Piper.

complaint seems to be that the English Society never did justice to Hodgson, and isn't properly making it up now. I hate to make conjectural accusations, but it looks as if the real inwardness (subconscious?) of the discontent were nothing more than the ordinary avarice or stinginess "of commerce," calling itself by other names. Of course Mrs. P. awakens but little pathetic sentiment, and her daughters ought now to be falling to work for themselves, nevertheless the debt of honour (in a certain sense) is there. I am curious to see how much will "forth come." Your surmise about Stanley Hall having killed the controls is rather startling. Inconvenient, if true; but "psychically" just as precious as any other fact, and more so than most. I wish that Hall could be induced to publish or at any rate to communicate to you the dialog [*sic*] at his last sitting. He told me it was "unprintable." No wonder; for when he revealed to the R. H. control how he had been fooling him to the top of his bent, said control countered by accusing Hall of having murdered his wife—this at least is what the control afterward imparted to Dow. [Hall's first wife, it is supposed, was not very happy with him, and was found dead in bed one morning, along with her daughter, with the gas turned on. It gave rise to disagreeable rumors.]

I have been too preoccupied with other things, and too pudding-headed to have read Mrs. Verrall's case more than once. My anti-philological mind keeps no details, and finds great difficulty in weaving them into a collective view. I must read the stuff over and over before I get a distinct impression of what it all may mean.

Believe me, dear Piddington, with best remembrances to Mrs. P., and the demoiselle, yours affectionately,

Wm. James

To FRANCOIS PILLON

Bad-Nauheim, May 25, 1910

My dear Pillon,—

I have been here a week, taking the baths for my unfortunate cardiac complications, and shall probably stay six weeks longer. I passed through Paris, where I spent a week, partly with my friend the philosopher Strong, partly at the Fondation Thiers with the Boutrouxs, who had been our guests in America when he lectured a few months ago at Harvard. Every day I said: "I will get to the Pillons this afternoon"; but every day I found it impossible to attempt your four flights of stairs, and finally had to run away from the Boutrouxs' to save my life from the fatigue and pectoral pain which resulted from my seeing so many people. I have a dilatation of the aorta, which causes anginoid pain of a bad kind whenever I make any exertion, muscular, intellectual, or social, and I should not have thought at all of going through Paris were it not that I wished to consult a certain Dr. Moutier there, who is strong on arteries, but who told me that he could do nothing for my case. I hope that these baths may arrest the disagreeable tendency to *pejoration* from which I have suffered in the past year. This is why I didn't come to see the dear Pillons; a loss for which I felt, and shall always feel, deep regret.

The sight of the new "Année Philosophique" at Boutroux's showed me how valiant and solid you still are for literary work. I read a number of the book reviews, but none of the articles, which seemed uncommonly varied and interesting. Your short notice of Schinz's really *bouffon* book showed me to my regret that even you have not yet caught the true inwardness of my notion of Truth. You speak as if I allowed no *valeur de connaissance proprement dite*, which is a quite false accusation.

When an idea "works" successfully among *all the other ideas* which relate to the object of which it is our mental substitute, associating and comparing itself with them harmoniously, the workings are wholly inside of the intellectual world, and the idea's value purely intellectual, for the time, at least. This is my doctrine and Schiller's, but it seems very hard to express it so as to get it understood!

I hope that, in spite of the devouring years, dear Madame Pillon's state of health may be less deplorable than it has been so long. In particular I wish that the neuritis may have ceased. I wish! I wish! but what's the use of wshing, against the universal law that "youth's a stuff will not endure," and that we must simply make the best of it? Boutroux gave some beautiful lectures at Harvard, and is the gentlest and most lovable of characters. Believe me, dear Pillon, and dear Madame Pillon, your ever affectionate old friend,

Wm. James

To HENRY P. BOWDITCH

Bad-Nauheim, June 4, 1910

Dearest Heinrich,—

The envelope in which this letter goes was addrest in Cambridge, Mass., and expected to go towards you with a letter in it, long before now. But better late than never, so here goes! I came over, as you may remember, for the double purpose of seeing my brother Henry, who had been having a sort of nervous breakdown, and of getting my heart, if possible, tuned up by foreign experts. I stayed upwards of a month with Henry, and then came hither *über* Paris, where I stayed ten days. I have been here two and a half weeks, taking the baths, and enjoying the feeling of the strong, calm, successful, new German civilization all about me. Germany is *great*, and no mistake! But what a contrast, in the well-set-up, well-groomed, smart-looking German man of today, and his rather clumsily drest, dingy, and unworldly-looking father of forty years ago! But something of the old *Gemüthlichkeit* remains, the friendly manners, and the disposition to talk with you and take you seriously and to respect the serious side of whatever comes along. But I can write you more interestingly of physiology than I can of sociology. . . . The baths may or may not arrest for a while the downward tendency which has been so marked in the past year —but at any rate it is a comfort to know that my sufferings have a respectable organic basis, and are not, as so many of my friends tell me, due to pure "nervousness." Dear Henry, you see that you are not the only pebble on the beach, or toad in the puddle, of senile degeneration! I admit that the form of your tragedy beats that of most of us; but youth's a stuff that won't endure, in any one, and to have had it, as you and I have had it, is a good deal gained anyhow, while to see the daylight still under *any* conditions is perhaps also better than nothing, and meanwhile the good months are sure to bring the final relief after which, "when you and I behind the veil are passed, Oh, but the long, long time the world shall last!" etc., etc. Rather gloomy moralizing, this, to end an affectionate family letter with; but the circumstances seem to justify it, and I know that you won't take it amiss.

Alice is staying with Henry, but they will both be here in a fortnight or less. I find it pretty lonely all by myself, and the German language doesn't run as trippingly off the tongue as it did forty years ago. Passage back is taken for August 12th. . . .

Well, I must stop! Pray give my love to Selma, the faithful one. Also to Fanny, Harold, and Friedel. With Harold's engagement you are more and more of a patriarch. Heaven keep you, dear Henry.

Believe me, ever your affectionately sympathetic old friend,

Wm. James

The letters which follow concern Henry Adams's "Letter to American Teachers," originally printed for private circulation, but later published, with a preface by Mr. Brooks Adams, under the title: "The Degradation of Democratic Dogma."

To HENRY ADAMS

Bad-Nauheim, June 17, 1910

Dear Henry Adams,—

I have been so "slim" since seeing you, and the baths here have so weakened my brain, that I have been unable to do any reading except trash, and have only just got round to finishing your "letter," which I had but half-read when I was with you at Paris. To tell the truth, it doesn't impress me at all, save by its wit and erudition; and I ask you whether an old man soon about to meet his Maker can hope to save himself from the consequences of his life by pointing to the wit and learning he has shown in treating a tragic subject. No, sir, you can't do it, can't impress God in that way. So far as our scientific conceptions go, it may be admitted that your Creator (and mine) started the universe with a certain amount of "energy" latent in it, and decreed that everything that should happen thereafter should be a result of parts of that energy falling to lower levels; raising other parts higher, to be sure, in so doing, but never in equivalent amount, owing to the constant radiation of unrecoverable warmth incidental to the process. It is customary for gentlemen to pretend to believe one another, and until some one hits upon a newer revolutionary concept (which may be tomorrow) all physicists must play the game by holding religiously to the above doctrine. It involves of course the ultimate cessation of all perceptible happening, and the end of human history. With this general conception as *surrounding* everything you say in your "letter," no one can find any fault—in the present stage of scientific conventions and fashions. But I protest against your interpretation of some of the specifications of the great statistical drift downwards of the original high-level energy. If, instead of criticizing what you seem to me to say, I express my own interpretation dogmatically, and leave you to make the comparison, it will doubtless conduce to brevity and economize recrimination.

To begin with, the *amount* of cosmic energy it costs to buy a certain distribution of fact which humanly we regard as precious, seems to me to be an altogether secondary matter as regards the question of history and progress. Certain arrangements of matter *on the same energy-level* are, from the point of view of man's appreciation, superior, while others are inferior. Physically a dinosaur's brain may show as much intensity of energy-exchange as a man's, but it can do infinitely fewer things, because as a force of detent it can only unlock the dinosaur's muscles, while the man's brain, by unlocking far feebler muscles, indirectly can by their means issue proclamations, write books, describe Chartres Cathedral, etc., and guide the energies of the shrinking sun into channels which never would have been entered otherwise—in short, *make* history. Therefore the man's brain and muscles are, from the point of view of the historian, the more important place of energy-exchange, small as this may be when measured in absolute physical units.

The "second law" is wholly irrelevant to "history"—save that it sets a terminus—for history is the course of things before that terminus, and all that the second law says is that, whatever the history, it must invest itself between that initial maximum and that terminal minimum of difference in energy-level. As the great irrigation-reservoir empties itself, the whole question for us is that of the distribution of its effects, of *which* rills to guide it into; and the size of the rills has nothing to do with their significance. Human cerebration is the most important rill we know of, and both the "capacity" and the "intensity" factor thereof may be treated as infinitesimal. Yet the filling of such rills would be cheaply bought by the waste of whole sums spent in getting a little of the down-flowing torrent to enter them. Just so of human institutions—their value has in strict theory nothing whatever to do with their energy-budget—being wholly a question of the form the energy flows through. Though the *ultimate* state of the universe may be its vital and psychical extinction, there is nothing in physics to interfere with the hypothesis that the penultimate state might be the millennium—in other words a state in which a minimum of difference of energy-level might have its exchanges so skillfully *canalisés* that a maximum of happy and virtuous consciousness would be the only result. In short, the last expiring pulsation of the universe's life might be, "I am so happy and perfect that I can stand it no longer." You don't believe this and I don't say I do. But I can find nothing in "Energetik" to conflict with its possibility. You seem to me not to discriminate, but to treat quantity and distribution of energy as if they formed one question.

There! that's pretty good for a brain after 18 Nauheim baths —so I won't write another line, nor ask you to reply to me. In case you can't help doing so, however, I will gratify you now by saying that I probably won't jaw back.—It was pleasant at Paris to hear your identically unchanged and "undegraded" voice after so many years of loss of solar energy. Yours ever truly,

Wm. James

[Post-card]

Nauheim, June 19, 1910

P.S. Another illustration of my meaning: The clock of the universe is running down, and by so doing makes the hands move. The energy absorbed by the hands and the *mechanical* work they do is the same day after day, no matter how far the weights have descended from the position they were originally wound up to. The *history* which the hands perpetrate has nothing to do with the *quantity* of this work, but follows the *significance* of the figures which they cover on the dial. If they move from O to XII, there is "progress," if from XII to O, there is "decay," etc. etc.

W. J.

[Post-card]

To HENRY ADAMS

Constance, June 26, [1910]

Yours of tne 20th, just arriving, pleases me by its docility of spirit and passive subjection to philosophic opinion. Never, never pretend to an opinion of your own! that way lies every annoyance and madness! You tempt me to offer you another illustration—that of the *hydraulic ram* (thrown back to me in an exam. as a "hydraulic goat" by an insufficiently intelligent student). Let this arrangement of metal, placed in the course of a brook, symbolize the machine of human life. It works, clap, clap, clap, day and night, so long as the brook runs *at all*, and no matter how full the brook (which symbolizes the descending cosmic energy) may be, it works always to the same effect, of raising so many kilogrammeters of water. What the *value* of this work as history may be, depends on the uses to which the water is put in the house which the ram serves.

W. J.

To THEODORE FLOURNOY

Geneva, July 9, 1910

Dearest Flournoy,—

Your two letters, of yesterday, and of July 4th sent to Nauheim, came this morning. I am sorry that the Nauheim one was not written earlier, since you had the trouble of writing it at all. I thank you for all the considerateness you show—you understand entirely my situation. My dyspnœa gets worse at an accelerated rate, and all I care for now is to get home—doing *nothing* on the way. It is partly a spasmodic phenomenon I am sure, for the aeration of my tissues, judging by the color of my lips, seems to be sufficient. I will leave Geneva now without seeing you again—better not come, unless just to shake hands with my wife! Through all these years I have wished I might live nearer to you and see more of you and exchange more ideas, for we seem two men particularly well *faits pour nous comprendre*. Particularly, now, as my own intellectual housekeeping has seemed on the point of working out some good results, would it have been good to work out the less unworthy parts of it in your company. But that is impossible!—I doubt if I ever do any more writing of a serious sort; and as I am able to look upon my life rather lightly, can truly say that "I don't care"—don't care in the least pathetically or tragically, at any rate.—I hope that Ragacz will be a success, or at any rate a wholesome way of passing the month, and that little by little you will reach your new equilibrium. Those dear daughters, at any rate, are something to live for—to show them Italy should be rejuvenating. I can write no more, my very dear old friend, but only ask you to think of me as ever lovingly yours,

W. J.

INDEX